BILL HARE was born in Edinburgh in 1944 and studied at the University of Edinburgh and the Courtauld Institute, University of London in the 1970s. Since then he has taught art history at the University of Edinburgh, Edinburgh College of Art and the Open University. In 1985 he was appointed Exhibition Organiser at the Talbot Rice Gallery, working with many Scottish artists. Since 1995 he has concentrated on teaching and freelance curating, with his main focus on Scottish art since 1945. He has curated a number of important exhibitions both in Scotland and abroad, and has published books and catalogues on a range of different aspects of historical and modern Scottish art. He is currently an Honorary Fellow in Scottish art history at the University of Edinburgh.

Facing the Nation

The Portraiture of Alexander Moffat

BILL HARE

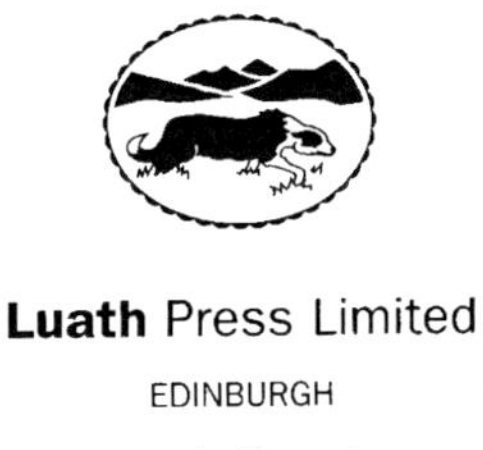

Luath Press Limited

EDINBURGH

www.luath.co.uk

Hardback edition 2018
Paperback edition 2024

ISBN: 978-1-80425-167-6

The artist and the publisher thank the Royal Scottish Academy
(Gillies Bequest) for their financial support towards the
publication of this book.

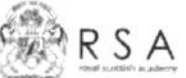

The paper used in this book is recyclable. It is made
from low chlorine pulps produced in a low energy,
low emission manner from renewable forests.

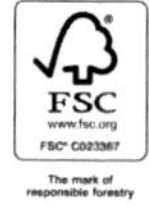

Printed and bound by
Robertson Printers, Forfar

Typeset in 11 point Sabon by Main Point Books, Edinburgh.

Contents

Foreword

THE PORTRAITS OF Alexander Moffat (universally known as Sandy) are now a familiar part of the Scottish cultural landscape – indeed they stand as unique markers of those decades of great creative endeavour in literature, painting and music that are such a visible feature of present day Scotland. In their number, variety of approaches to the task of contemporary portraiture and all the insights they provide, there is nothing quite like them.

When I first became aware of Sandy's work he was classified as a 'Scottish realist', the title of a Scottish Arts Council exhibition in 1968 where the common attribute of the work of the young painters involved was a dedication to a kind of figuration that was opposed to the prevailing fashion of abstraction. One of the most striking paintings in the exhibition was Sandy's portrait of his young wife Susan. Although the paint was worked edgily in an expressionist manner and the colour had a certain rawness, I was struck by the underlying memories of tradition and how, and probably unconsciously, it seemed in some ways a reworking of Velázquez's great portrait of Pope Innocent X. It seemed to suggest a new future for portraiture, away from the moribund tradition that had come to infect boardrooms and universities after the Second World War. So taken was I with this manifestation of a new modernity, that I borrowed the purchase price from my mother-in-law.

Around the same time I had joined the staff of that repository of images of bygone Scots, the Scottish National Portrait Gallery and in time conceived the notion of an exhibition of Sandy's portraits that would make it clear that the 'great tradition' had not ended – and that, in essence, there was no fixed way of conjuring up a human being on canvas or panel. Such a thing had not been attempted before by the Gallery and there was a fear, difficult to believe today, that the members of the art establishment – that is, the Royal Scottish Academy – would be upset by this focus on a young, untried individual. To cross this Rubicon, the exhibition, which eventually happened in 1973, had to be dressed as a kind of investigation of the problems of contemporary portraiture – hence the title, *A View of the Portrait*. But the tide was turning, not only here but more widely, and Sandy's work was a significant part of this change.

The 40-odd portraits included in the exhibition were mainly of Sandy's friends, rather then the celebrities of former times who filled the Portrait Gallery's walls, but among them was an image of Norman MacCaig, by that time well-established as a truly major English language poet. So startlingly expressive was it that it was clearly ripe for joining those other images that told the story of the Scottish literary tradition – Burns, Scott, Stevenson, Barrie. But there was a barrier. The Gallery was still restricted by the Victorian prohibition on acquiring portraits of living subjects. In a belief that the barrier would in time have to give way, the portrait of MacCaig, without the fanfare it deserved and with a certain sleight of hand, was purchased and quietly consigned to storage to await more enlightened times.

That change duly came in 1982 and the Gallery started a process of commissioning portraits of remarkable Scots. Such had been the impact of Sandy's exhibition ten years earlier that he was given one of the earliest of these commissions which resulted in the full-length portrait of Muriel Spark. It is no secret that the sitter had misgivings about her

likeness (that bugbear all who attempt portraits have to contend with).
But for those who knew her and her work there is no doubt that in its
harmony of blue, red and black and its subtle, probing look at the inner
woman, it is one of the great portraits of our time.

I am not going to attempt to trace Sandy's subsequent trajectory
which is done in detail in Bill Hare's texts that follow. In a recent group
portrait of subjects from the Scottish musical world, *Scotland's Voices*,
that echoes his much earlier group of Scottish poets, the now famous
Poets' Pub, Sandy still explores, as he has now done for many years, the
fascinating terrain which hints at a new Scotland.

Duncan Thomson
December 2017

Personal, Particular, Public
The Portraits of Alexander Moffat

Bill Hare

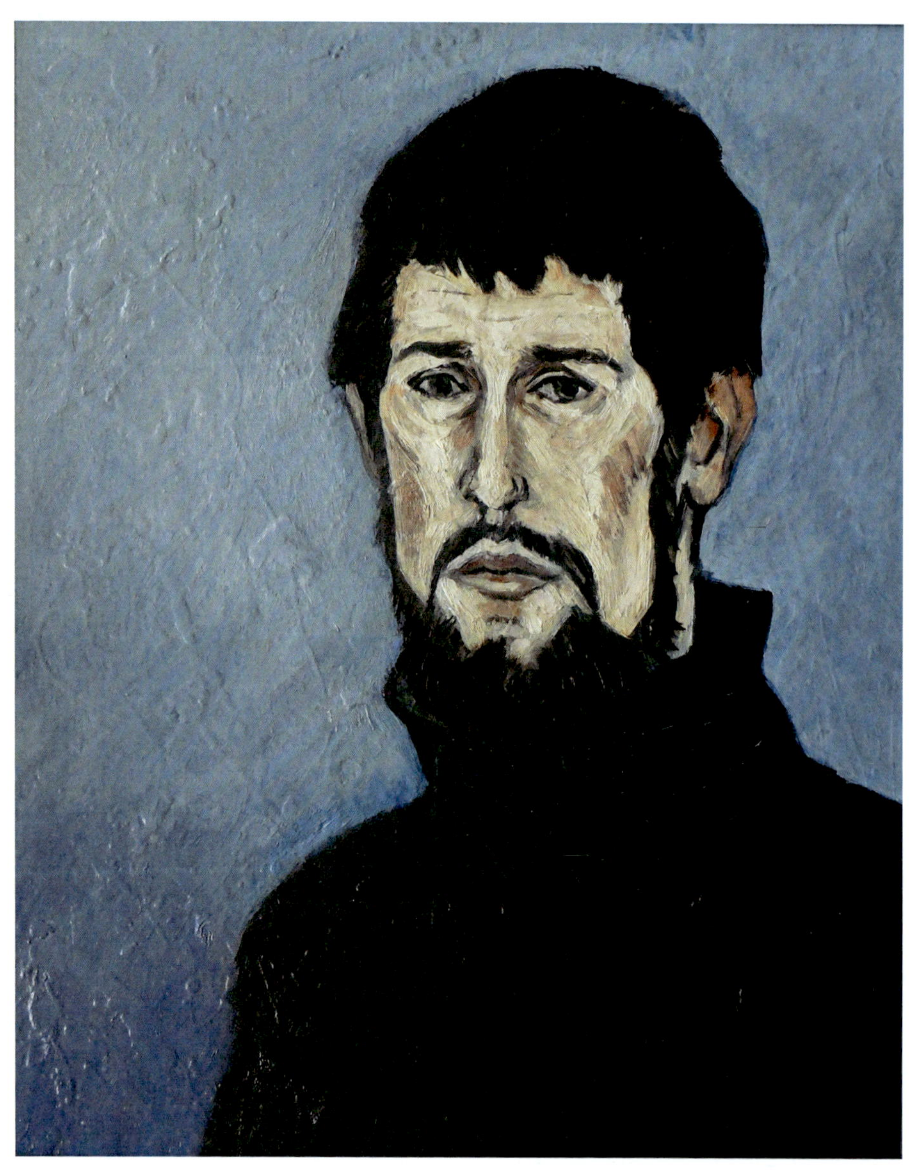

1   *Self-Portrait* 1963 oil on board 55 x 44.5 cm

THE DEMISE OF portraiture has been a long and protracted process. It was first announced in 1839 by the leading French academic painter of the day, Paul Delaroche, who on seeing the early daguerreotype photographs, solemnly declared, 'From today painting is dead.' Certainly this new, cheap and efficient recorder of the human subject proved to be a serious threat to the lucrative commercial trade of professional portrait painting. Portraiture, of course, still continued to be practised over the subsequent decades, but in 1967 another dire pronouncement was made by John Berger in his essay 'The Changing View of Man in the Portrait', which ominously opens with 'It seems to me unlikely that any important portraits will ever be painted again.' It appeared that, like most of the portrait subjects of the past, portraiture itself would also soon become an illustrious corpse.

Around the same time as Berger was driving yet another nail into the coffin of portraiture, a young Edinburgh College of Art student, Alexander (Sandy) Moffat, was setting out on an artistic career in which, contrary to Berger's prognosis, he would distinguish himself as the most important Scottish portrait painter since David Wilkie in the first half of the 19th century. Before we begin to examine Moffat's achievements in the art of portraiture, we must first analyse why this particular artistic genre was seen to be in such a moribund condition when Berger passed his death sentence upon it.

In his essay, Berger rolls out the usual suspect – photography – as the main reason 'why the painted portrait has become outdated'. He points out that photography is 'more accurate, quicker and far cheaper'. For Berger, the photographer has 'taken the place of the portrait painter'. On the other hand, he was prepared to concede that painting could be more 'tensely unified' (a distinguishing aim and characteristic of Moffat's portraits), compared with the more 'arbitrary' nature of the camera. Berger identifies the second main cause of portrait painting's inevitable decline as being the radical changes to social identity and status in modern society. He writes:

> Increasingly for over a century fewer and fewer people in capitalist society have been able to believe in the social value of the social roles offered… We can no longer accept that the identity of a man can be adequately established by preserving and fixing what he looks like from a single viewpoint in one place.

The hostile critic was even dismissive of the 'intimate' portraits of celebrated modern artists' friends, families and models, by painters like Degas, Cézanne, Van Gogh, where 'the social role of the sitter is reduced to *that of being painted*' (Berger's italics). Although Moffat, in his dialogue with me, indicates some sympathy for Berger's opinions, his own views on the contemporary state of portraiture, and his long and committed career as a portrait painter, challenge the terminally negative outlook that Berger expressed on the condition of portraiture in the modern world.

Before we begin to examine in detail the career of Alexander Moffat as a portrait painter, we should briefly look at his work in relationship to the history of portraiture, particularly within a Scottish cultural context. Before the 18th century, Scotland – as was also the case with its much more advantageously situated neighbour, England – had, on the whole, to attract foreign painters from the Continent to carry out the role of portraying the great and the good in the appropriate European courtly manner. A radical change took place in the practice and purpose

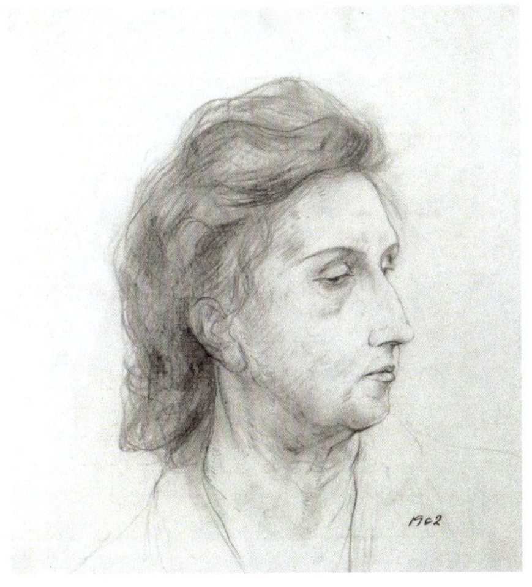

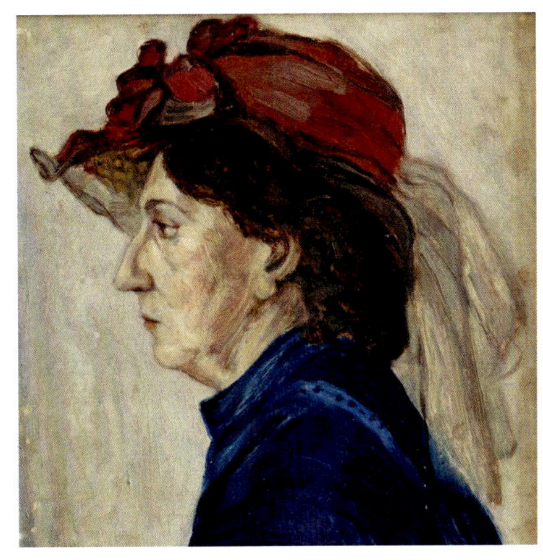

2   *Edinburgh College of Art model* 1962 pencil on paper
24 x 22.5 cm

3   *Edinburgh College of Art model (head study)* 1962 oil on board
30 x 30.5 cm

of portraiture during the period of the Enlightenment when Scottish
artists began to aspire to, and then take over that role, and bring about
a truly 'golden age' in the art of portrait painting. During this most
dynamic era, Scottish portraiture made great advances, producing some
of its most illustrious artists, such as Allan Ramsay, Henry Raeburn
and David Wilkie. The causes and reasons for this celebrated flowering
of achievement in portrait painting are not just artistic, but are wide-
ranging and complex, involving many aspects of the socioeconomic
and cultural changes taking place in Scottish society during the
transformation of Britain into a modern progressive state.

From an art historical point of view, both Duncan Macmillan in
much of his writings on Scottish art of the Enlightenment period, and
Edgar Wind, particularly in his essay 'Hume and the Heroic Portrait'
(1986), make a convincing case for a special and particular link between

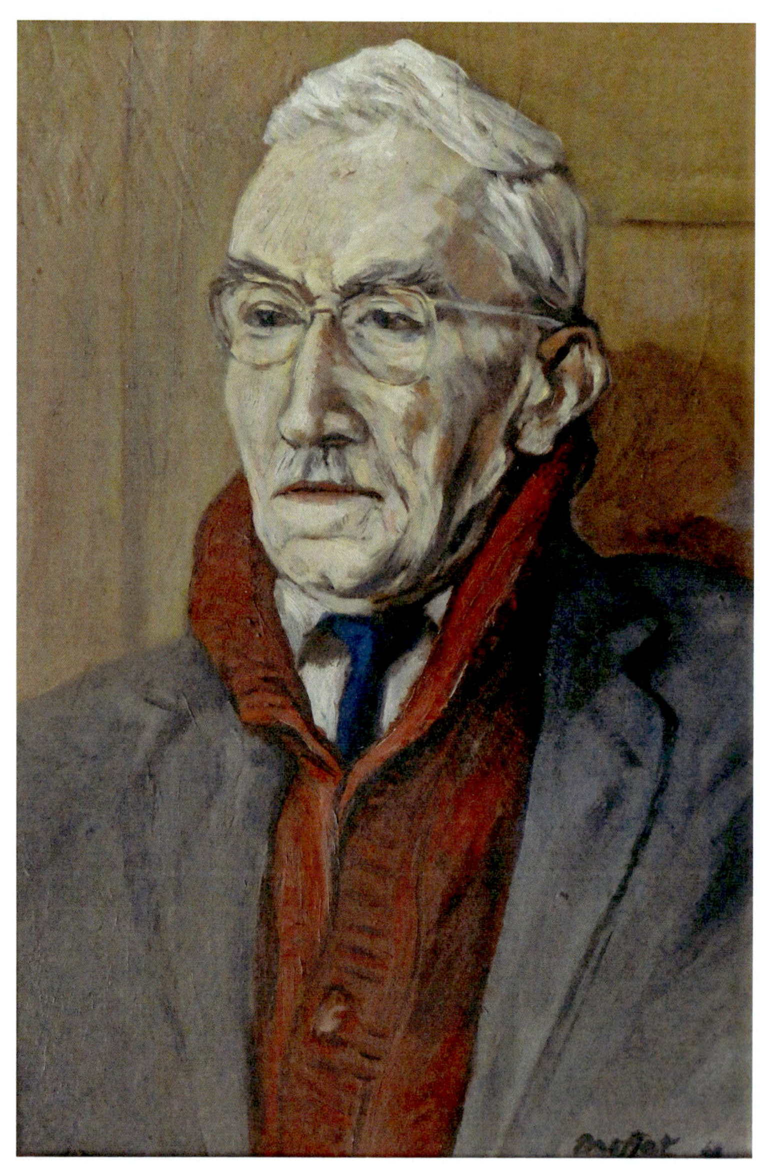

4   *My Grandfather* 1962 oil on board 48.5 x 33.5 cm

the interaction of philosophy and the art of Scottish portraiture in that era. Scottish Enlightenment philosophy in general, and that of David Hume in particular, was fundamentally humanist in its outlook. It is therefore not surprising that the artistic genres dealing with the examination of human nature – the biography, the personal journal, the confessional and the portrait, which intently focused on the human subject and experience – should flourish in such an atmosphere of philosophical and cultural humanist debate. Hume, with his concern for the commonality of human experience, was antipathetic to the heroic, both in life and art, and had little time for the theatricality of the grand style of courtly portrait painting as promoted and practised by the renowned English academic portraitist, Sir Joshua Reynolds, for example. Hume, with his sceptical down-to-earth outlook, preferred to look on a portrait as a 'social situation', as Wind puts it – a view that also comes over very strongly in my dialogue with Moffat, who also sees himself 'as a human-centred figurative painter'. Wind goes on to say that 'there is a correspondence between the objectives of the painter and of the philosopher, the one aiming at the representation of the individual man, the other looking into the nature of Man' in order to produce 'an argument in paint'. This also echoes Moffat's belief that 'good artists don't express themselves, but ideas' which are both aesthetic and moral. Another place where Hume's aesthetic philosophy coincides with Moffat's attitudes and practice as a portrait painter is in the area of expressive style. In his essay 'Of Simplicity and Refinement in Writing', Hume argues that an artist – be it a writer or a painter – requires to refine his mode of expression in accord with the example of his illustrious artistic predecessors; but at the same time, this needs to

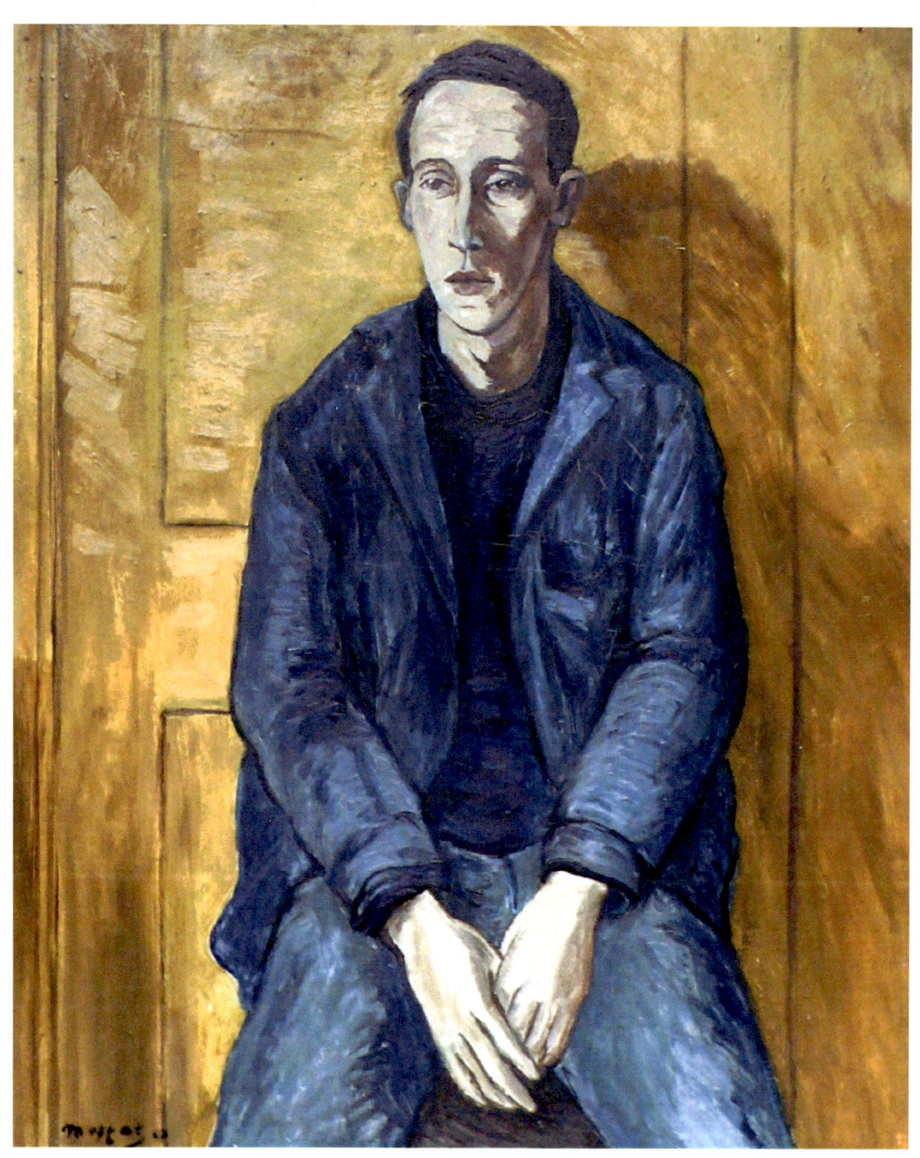

5   *Ken Harrold (The Young Workman)* 1963 oil on board 81 x 61 cm (private collection)

be presented with clarity and simplicity. This is very much in tune with Moffat's approach to his portraits, something that the 18th century would have termed the 'natural' style.

After the great achievements of Scottish portraiture during the period of the Enlightenment there was a rapid decline in the status and practice of the genre. During the Victorian era, Scottish society became increasingly drawn into the social order of the wider British state and its modernising and imperial project, resulting in the gradual loss of a distinctive Scottish identity and cultural outlook. This led to a pronounced duality in the Scottish persona, which in psychological terms has been famously portrayed in the gothic horror novels of James Hogg and Robert Louis Stevenson. As the poet Edwin Muir was later to show, this duality between feeling and reason was also played out in much broader terms throughout Scottish society as a whole – involving artistic taste and critical preference. On the one hand, the backward looking nostalgic Scottish art lover, under the influence of the romantic writings of Sir Walter Scott and later kailyard novelists, opted either for an escapist retreat into a fantasy historical world of tartan-clad heroics and tragedy; or a thatched cottage idyll of couthy rural village life. In contrast, the other faction were the forward looking progressive Scots who preferred to look at life and art with a hard-nosed materialist outlook, based on rational empirical observation. Under such contradictory pressures, Scottish Victorian artists tended to oscillate between the sentimental picturesque and the superficial realistic in their approach to portraiture.

By the time Modernism came to be seen as the future of progressive Scottish art in the later 19th century, the status of portraiture had so declined that it was no longer regarded as a viable contributor to the ambitions of any serious modern artist. This attitude has prevailed throughout most of the 20th century, and as Moffat wrote for *Picture of Ourselves*, an exhibition that he curated for the Scottish Arts Council in 1982, 'Until recently, there was a tendency by the majority of artists and critics to regard portraiture with suspicion, if not with downright contempt.' With the exceptions of the personal exploratory possibilities of self-portraiture and the informal exercise of portraying a friend or family member, critical hostility to portrait painting as a serious art form was so firmly entrenched and prevalent that it was the critical norm when Alexander Moffat turned his attention to the genre. As he has observed, 'In the 1960s when I made my first portraits, portraiture was critically suspect, regarded as a deeply flawed genre.' Thus, not surprisingly, he had to look wider afield for inspiring examples of modern portraiture.

In our dialogue Moffat relates that it was an Oskar Kokoschka exhibition at the Tate Gallery, seen while visiting London in 1962, that inspired him to consider turning his attention to portraiture as a serious means to advance his ambition to become a 'human-centred figurative painter': 'Kokoschka's humanism struck a cord and his youthful portraits... were the works that first convinced me that painting portraits was consistent with my desire to be a modern artist.'

It was, however, not the exaggerated pictorial histrionics of Kokoschka's mystical Expressionism that informed Moffat's early journey into modern portrait painting. He opted for a much more restrained approach. This can be seen in his *Self-Portrait* (1963, ill. 1) from the following year, when he and John Bellany mounted their first

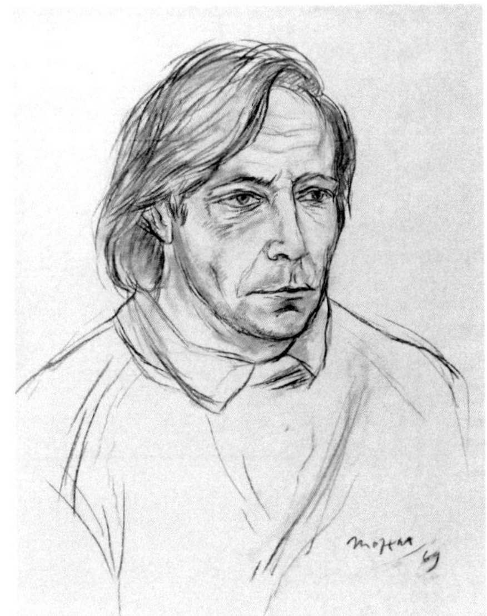 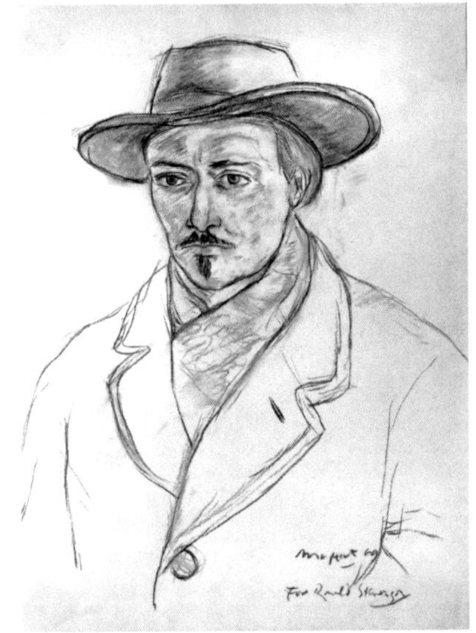

6   *Robert Callender* 1969 charcoal on paper 57 x 45.5 cm   7   *Ronald Stevenson* 1969 charcoal on paper
58 x 42.5 cm

Scottish Realism outdoor exhibition at Castle Terrace during the 1963
Edinburgh International Festival. Moffat's painting is clearly based on
Picasso's *Self-Portrait* of 1900, painted just after the young Spaniard
had arrived in Paris. There is one clear difference: in Picasso's painting,
the figure is three-quarter length, whereas Moffat opts for a head-and-
shoulders format – giving more focus and concentration on the facial
features in accord with his belief that 'everything was really there in the
face'. At this early stage of their respective artistic careers, Picasso and
Moffat give articulated expression to their rather tragic facial features,
in both cases the faces already beginning to take on a modernist mask-
like quality. In these two self-portraits there is a further important
connecting bond between Moffat and Picasso. While Moffat's painting

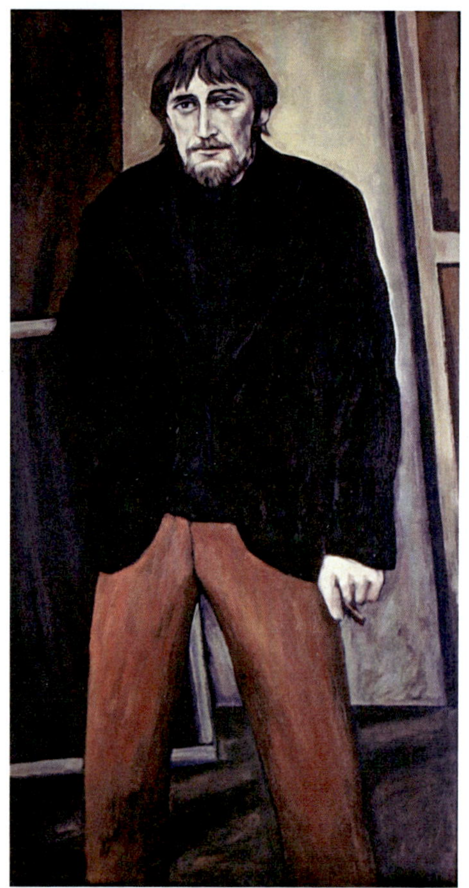

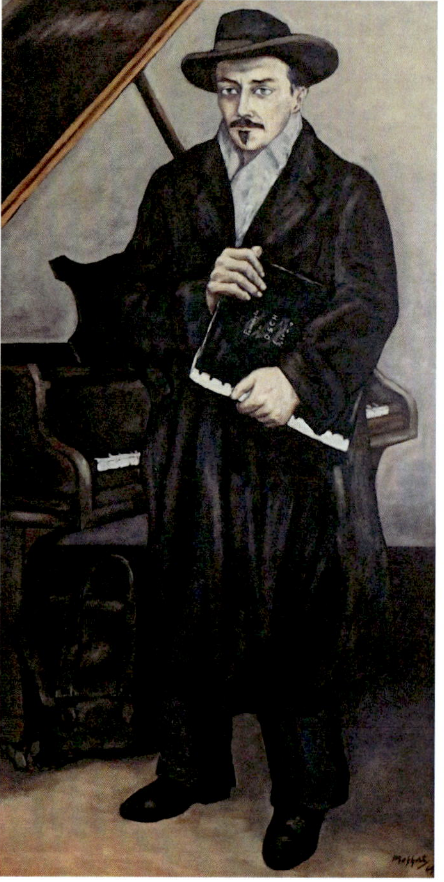

8   *John Bellany* 1968 oil on board 160 x 84 cm
(private collection)

9   *Ronald Stevenson* 1969 oil on board 174 x 91.5 cm

is a homage to the Spanish master of modern art, Picasso's portrait is his
own homage to self-portraits by Van Gogh and, particularly, Cézanne.
Thus, as with Picasso, Moffat's artistic development would also be
deeply informed by the great artists of the past, 'driven by the same
imperatives', in order to seek out 'what Modernism can do and cannot

22

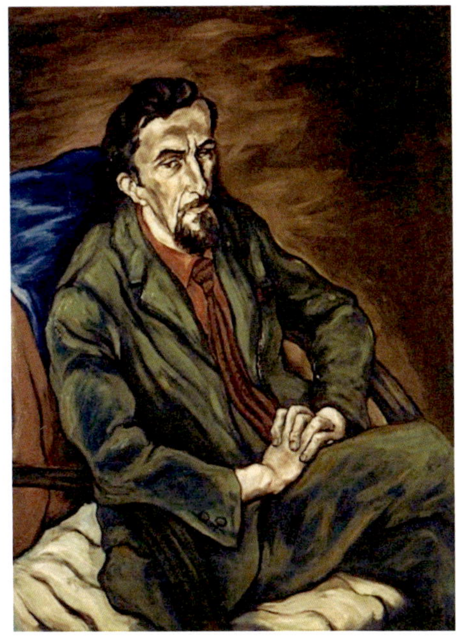

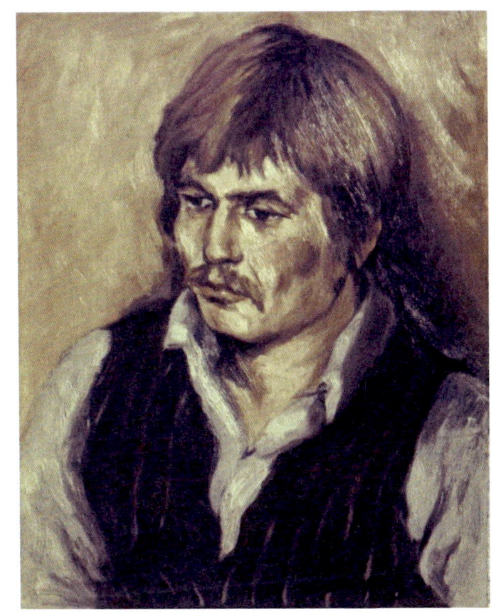

11 *Tam White* 1967 oil on board 40.5 x 30.5 cm
(private collection)

10 *Archie Hind* 1968 oil on board 122 x 91.5 cm
(Scottish National Portrait Gallery)

do in comparison with the great painters of the past'.

Like the young Picasso, who experimented with a range of inherited
early modern styles of painting, Moffat also used his initial practice
in portraiture to experiment stylistically with a range of different
approaches – informed by the example of such modern masters as
Cézanne, Van Gogh, Soutine, Beckmann, Dix and, of course, Picasso.
In the same year that he produced his *Self-Portrait*, he began a group of
paintings of friends and acquaintances which in 1973 would result in
A View of the Portrait, his first major portrait exhibition at the Scottish
National Portrait Gallery. Many of these early portraits are consciously
painted in a manner that recalls the work of one of the modern masters

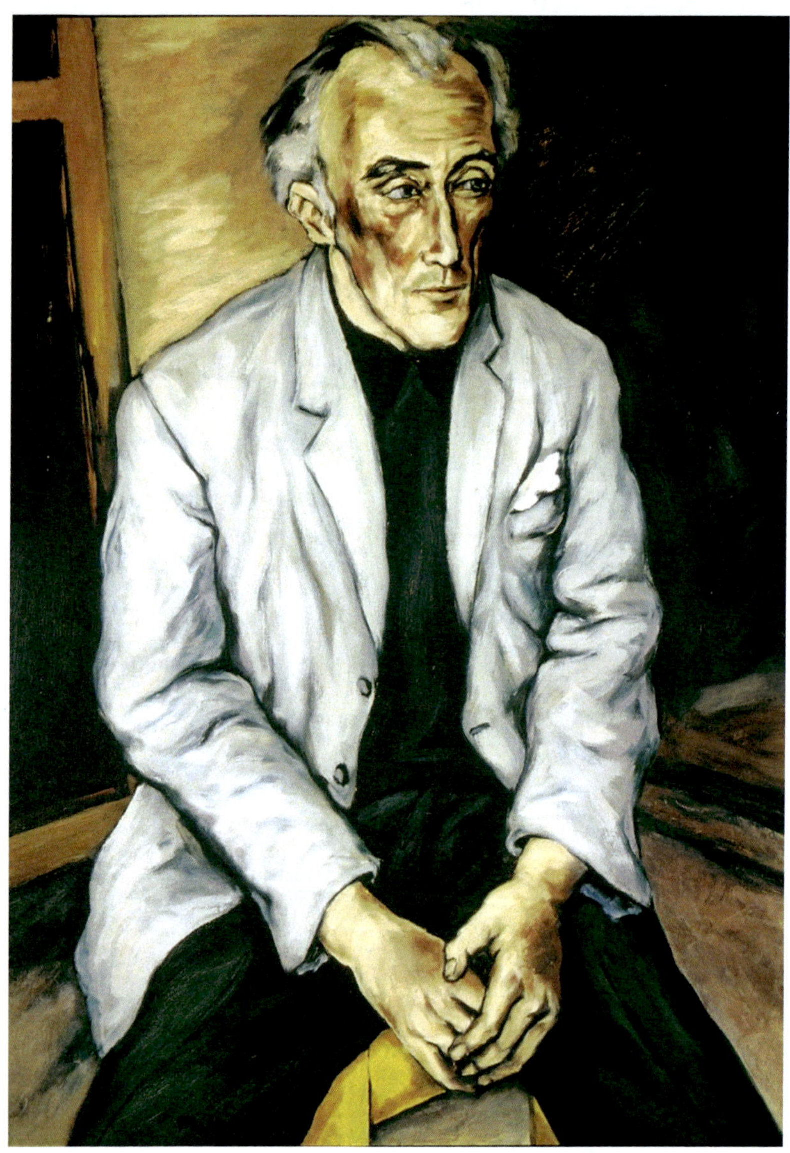

12   *Norman MacCaig* 1968 oil on board 122 x 91.5 cm (Scottish National Portrait Gallery)

greatly admired by Moffat. By doing this Moffat was clearly indicating that his portraits were not merely about capturing a passing likeness, but were also aspiring to be works of modern painting. To reinforce this, Moffat boldly declared in an interview for the exhibition catalogue: 'I paint people the way I want – which is not necessarily what they want – if they don't like it, too bad.' Although he does go on to say, 'I think it is essential that the sitter's personality is not submerged by the artist's vision. One must find a balance.'

This search to find the right 'balance' between the artist's own creative interpretation of his subject and the more conventional expectations of his sitter, as well as those of the wider viewing public, is at the heart of the challenging dilemma of modern portraiture. For it is with portraiture that we experience the troubled interface between the independent aims of modern art and the cultural demands of modern social life. With portraiture, that interface is for most people still based on the accurate depiction of individual likeness and a clear indication of social status. Modern artists have continually devised different strategies to undermine these entrenched expectations. For instance, following Cézanne's example, both Matisse and Picasso often gave their sitters blank, mask-like faces instead of animated features; by contrast, many German Expressionist painters used extreme distortion in their portraits, verging on grotesque caricature. These modernist pictorial assaults on mimetic realism and idealised decorum are justified by modern artists in their pursuit of a much 'deeper truth' about the individual character and social attitude of their sitters than is possible by mere superficial likeness – as embodied, for example, by the photographic snapshot. As Moffat admits, 'The encounter with the sitter is the starting point but

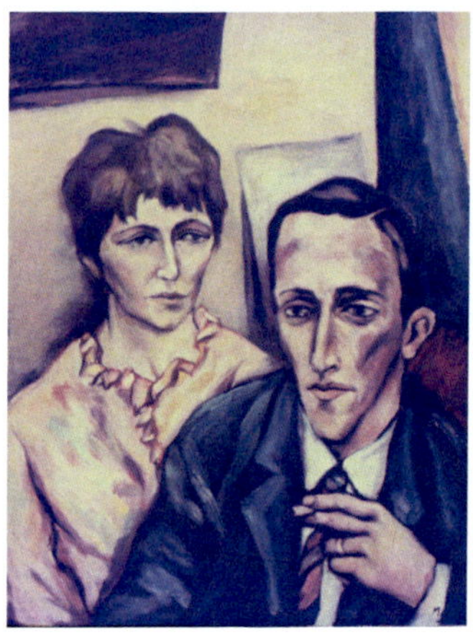

13 *Ken and Fiona Harrold* 1968 oil on board
81 x 61 cm (private collection)

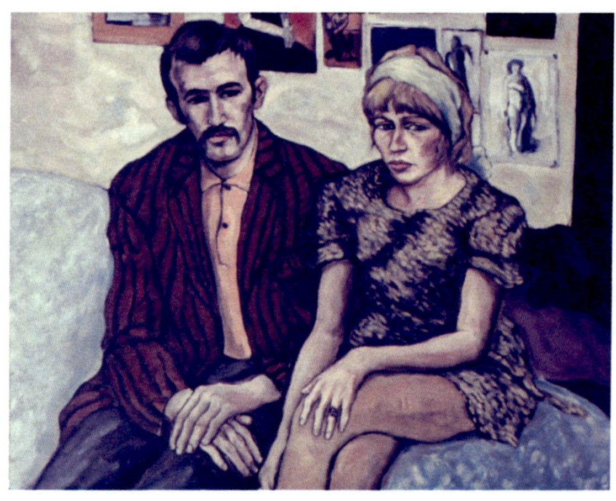

14 *Ian and Patsy Croal* 1968 oil on board 91.5 x 117 cm
(private collection)

there are other ideas that quickly come into play. Painting a portrait is a subjective business linked to stylistic and aesthetic concerns with likeness at the mercy of those conflicting elements.'

Right from the outset, and firmly believing that 'a portrait is an affirmation of an individual human being', Moffat began seriously to paint portraits while a student at Edinburgh College of Art from 1960 to 1964. He selected his sitters by asking willing volunteers, firstly from his family – see his prodigious portrait of his grandfather (1962, ill. 4) – then from his circle of friends. This gave him not only an opportunity to put his egalitarian beliefs into practice – 'all people are equal' – but also allowed him to experiment with the influences which he was keen to draw on from the modern portraitists he admired. This can be seen in his portrait of a young electrician, *Ken Harrold (The Young Workman)* (1963, ill. 5), which the artist now regards as 'a key work, a first step

26

on the road to making a convincing modern portrait'. Remarkably, even at such an early stage of his career, Moffat demonstrates many of the distinctive stylistic features which would become the hallmark of the best work of his later career. With great assurance he reduces the colour scheme to two contrasting areas: the dark blue figure against a golden yellow backdrop allows the painter to almost eliminate the usual pictorial convention of illusionistic depth and focus concentration solely on the figure/ground relationship of the painting. The reduction in the illusion of depth permits the figure to dominate the pictorial composition, and thus grants a much more powerful presence to the sitter. The pale light that illuminates the young sitter's face gives him an intense fixed expression of deep internal meditation – or perhaps just vacant boredom. This creates within the portrait a marked contrasting duality between the almost tactile physical presence of the sitter and the elusive intangible nature of his mental absorption.

This duality between objective and subjective concerns has been a powerful dialectic which has motored the long history of portraiture in Western art. For instance, the reason portraiture was regarded as one of the lower genres – having much less artistic status than the universally acclaimed history painting – was that it was seen as being mainly involved with the mimetic pictorial reproduction of an observed subject – the sitter, whereas history painting involved not only knowledge and understanding of great human actions from sacred and classic sources, but also required creative imagination to turn these actions into absorbing uplifting visual images. Furthermore, history painting dealt in timeless concepts at the highest level of human thought and endeavour, while portraiture merely recorded the appearance and social status of historical individuals at a particular moment in their transitory lives. Little wonder then that the ambitious portrait painter Sir Joshua Reynolds, sought, through his writings as well as his art, to elevate the practice and status of portraiture by incorporating the trappings and ethos of history painting into his work. He influentially argued that 'portraiture may be improved by borrowing from the Grand' – shifting the approach to portrait painting away from the individual and particular towards what Reynolds termed the 'General Idea.'

An alternative strategy employed to raise the cultural reputation and critical discussion surrounding portraiture focused on philosophical – and later, psychological – dimensions. This is much more relevant to the attitude and practice of Moffat, who always wants 'the painting process to go beyond what might be referred to as mere surface appearance'. In this context, portraiture should not be regarded as just dealing with passing appearances and superficial likenesses, but should penetrate to much deeper inner truths about the nature of the human mind and personality. Thus, the great portraitists – old or modern masters – did not merely observe and record the individual likeness of their sitters, but through close and sustained analysis of their facial features, emotional expressions, body language and social posture, produced a visual biography of their subject that revealed the inner nature, as well as the outer appearance, of their fundamental character. This belief that portraiture has the potential to tell us profound truths – not only about other people but by empathic association, about ourselves as well – has sustained its cultural and social value since the mythical Corinth Maid gave birth to portraiture by drawing the outline of her departing lover's silhouetted profile on the wall of her candle-lit room.

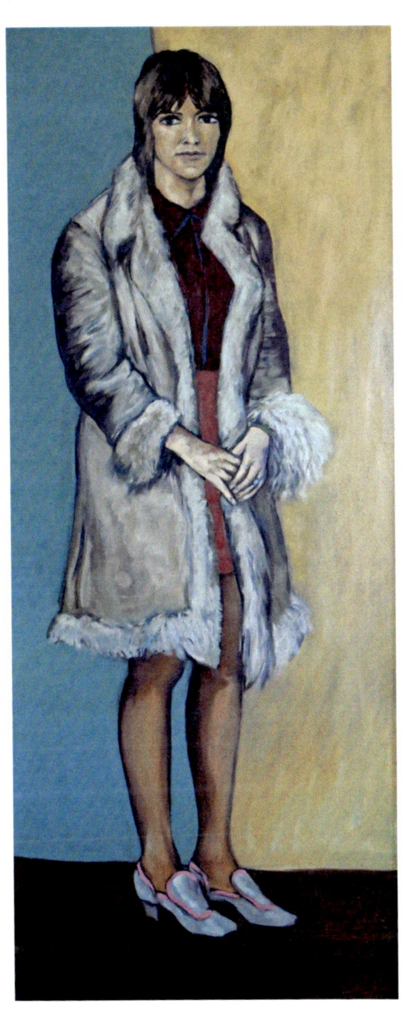

15   *Claire Murray* 1969 oil on board 183 x 76 cm

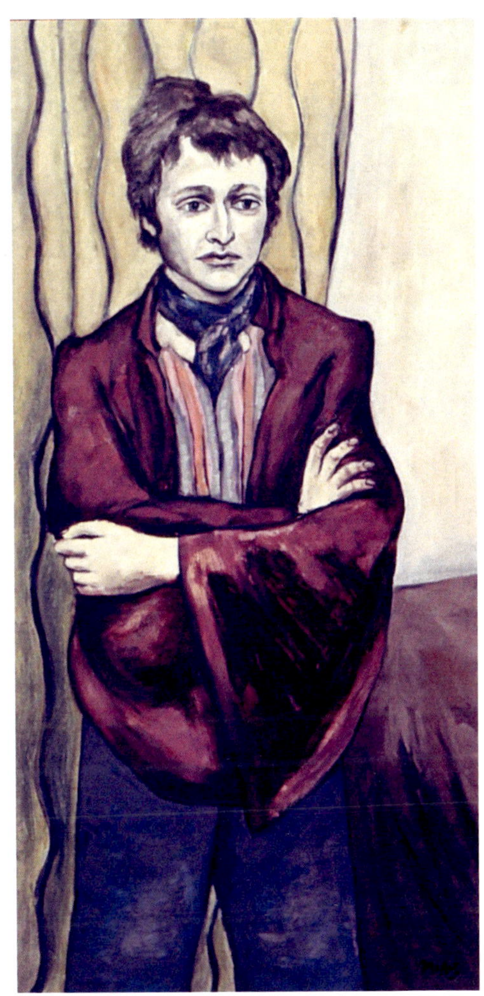

16   *Joseph Bonnar* 1968 oil on board 122 x 61 cm
(private collection)

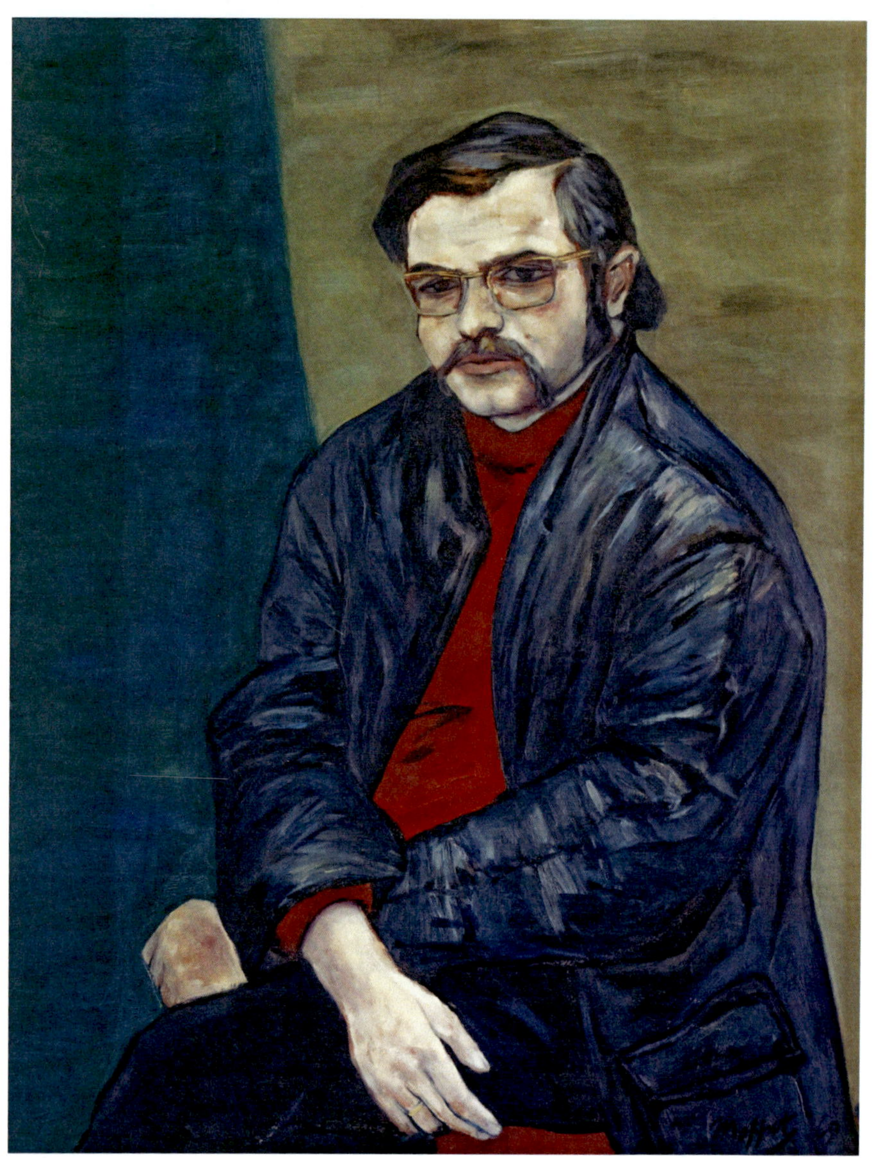

17   *Harro Rösing* 1969 oil on board 107 x 84 cm (private collection)

Alexander Moffat did not bow to the negative and dismissive attitude towards portraiture as something expendable to the mimetic power of photography when he began his artistic career, but bravely and defiantly put portrait painting at the heart of his art. The period of the mid-'60s was one of artistic trial and error, as he set out to find his own distinctive approach to the challenges of modern portraiture. A portrait of Tam White, an Edinburgh Blues singer (1967, ill. 11) – a few years later than the *Ken Harrold* – is competently painted, but not notably modernist in its stylistic features. In this particular work, Moffat seems to be too reliant on the studio techniques learned in student days at a conventional art academy. In 1968 he produced a much more convincingly modern portrait in *Norman MacCaig* (ill. 12). Moffat and his great friend John Bellany had become acquainted with the renowned Scottish poet through their frequent visits to the literary pubs of Rose Street – Edinburgh's bohemia. In this portrait, MacCaig strikes a very similar, high-stool, seated pose to that of the *Ken Harrold* portrait, the head pressing against the top of the picture and the bottom frame cutting off the figure just above the knee. There is, however, a marked difference in the compositional presentation of the sitters in these two works: while Harrold is firmly set frontally to the viewer, Moffat has turned MacCaig off at a slightly oblique angle, with strong receding lines in the background. While the sense of spatial depth is greatly reduced in the earlier portrait, the figure of MacCaig is thus given ample surrounding room to allow the viewer to feel the physical bulk of the poet in the round. The high pictorial viewpoint recalls something of Degas's portrait of Diego Martelli (1879), which Moffat would know from the National Gallery of Scotland's collection. Yet, while Degas's sitter is set back and surrounded by his domestic studio clutter, the figure of MacCaig dominates the whole of Moffat's pictorial composition, with nothing to distract from his physical and intellectual, commanding presence. With a strong use of line, the artist graphically captures the gaunt appearance of the poet's bony physique. In contrast to the unfocused look in the *Ken Harrold* portrait, MacCaig, with his intense attention, sharply looks off into the distance, with the direction of his gaze reinforced by the angle of the floor below. In this portrait Moffat demonstrates a masterly use of dynamic pictorial composition which not only convincingly depicts the physical appearance of the sitter, but also seems to convey the inner life of the poet's powerfully focused imagination.

The dominant subjects of Moffat's portraits in the '60s were the artist's male friends, most of his female subjects being their wives and partners. During this early period Moffat also painted a few psychologically intriguing double portraits of his married male and female sitters which offered more difficult compositional challenges for the painter. For instance Moffat painted Ken Harrold with his wife Fiona in 1968 (ill. 13). In this dual portrait the two figures are tightly tied together, with the wife placed behind her cigarette-smoking husband, creating a claustrophobic tension; there is little sense of communication between the couple, who both stare beyond the picture space in different directions. The sharp angular treatment of the figures heightens the psychological tension in a manner that recalls similar portrait subjects by German Expressionist Max Beckmann. Moffat applied very different compositional arrangement in his painting of friends, Graham and Eileen Martin (1970, ill. 28). Using a horizontal format this time, there is much more space surrounding the figures, who

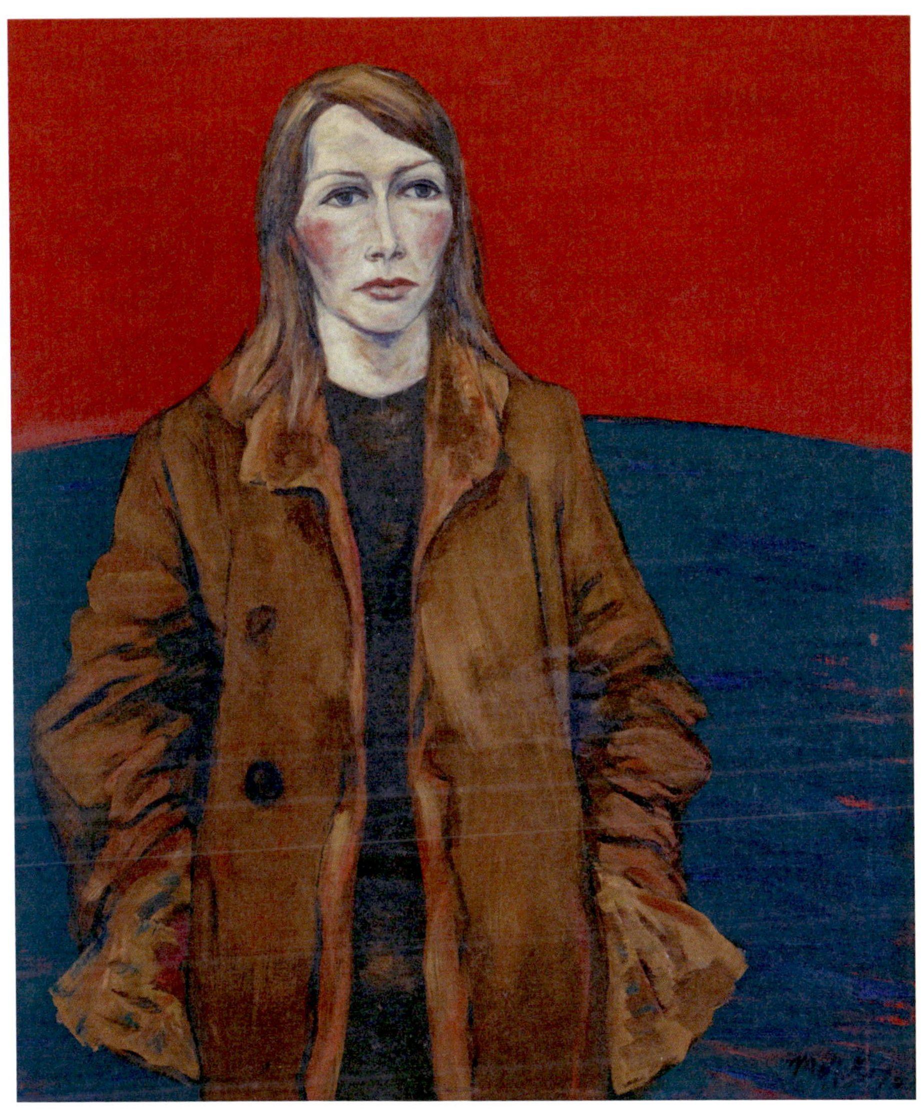

18   *Anna Rösing* 1969 oil on board 107 x 91.5 cm (private collection)

are sitting side by side on a couch, viewed from a slightly elevated point. As in the portrait of the Harrold couple, there is again a marked lack of communication; the husband, with the ubiquitous cigarette in hand, appears quite animated compared with his wife who sits passively with her hands crossed over her knees. Eileen's tight-fitting monochrome dress and long black hair enclose her against the agitated stripes which not only pattern her husband's shirt and trousers, but also flow over the couch they are awkwardly sharing. With the Martins' portrait it is not Beckmann who comes to mind, but rather that obsessive chronicler of psychosexual tensions – Edvard Munch.

The two people closest to Moffat were the writer Alan Bold and his artistic soulmate, John Bellany, both of whom he called upon, on more than one occasion, as subjects for his portraits. He painted a striking portrait of John Bellany in 1968 (ill. 8). By that time Bellany had moved to London, but regularly returned to Edinburgh, and this portrait was painted in Moffat's studio with other canvases stacked against the wall behind Bellany. As with all of Moffat's portraits the figure of the painter fills most of the pictorial space, but is not depicted in the conventional pose of brushes in hand, inspecting a work in progress on his easel: Bellany stands four-square and looks defiantly – almost threateningly – out at the viewer, with a cigar in hand in true Max Beckmann fashion. While the figure and the studio background are rendered in the broad simplified manner of the German modern master, Bellany's head and facial features are much more articulated. This may be because for Moffat 'likeness is important… there's no point in denying that simple fact'. He recalls that he was dissatisfied with how he had handled the painting of Bellany's head at the portrait sitting, and chose to repaint his

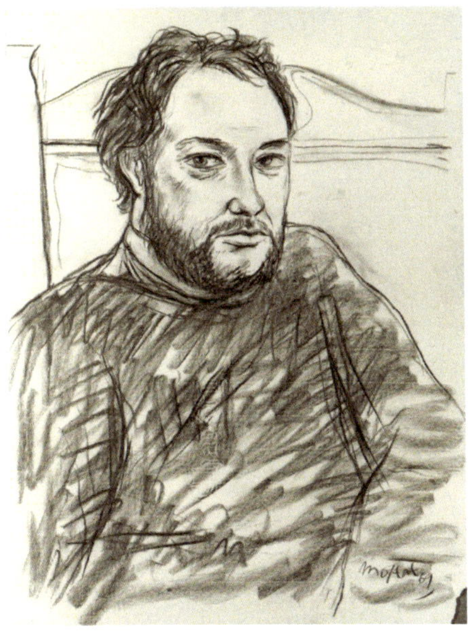

19 *Alan Bold* 1969 charcoal on paper 49 x 46 cm

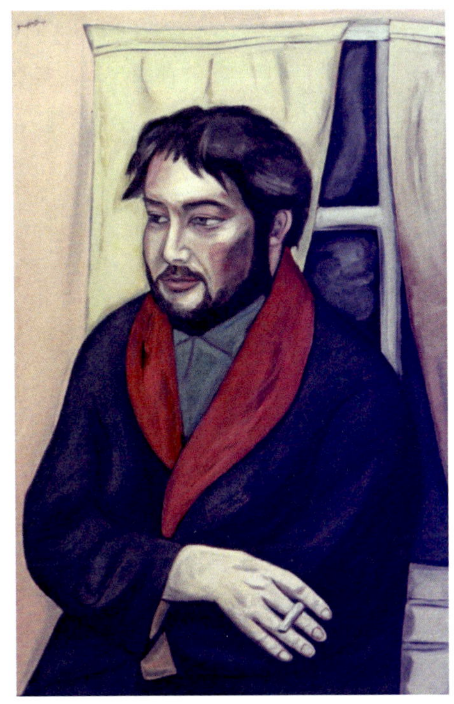

20 *Alan Bold* 1971 oil on board 91.5 x 61 cm
(private collection)

features from photographs and preliminary drawings.

Moffat states in an interview for the catalogue of *A View of the Portrait* exhibition (1973), which included the John Bellany painting: 'I always make a drawing, or drawings, of the sitter before starting the painting – usually head drawings... During the drawing period most of my ideas for the portrait emerge.' He then goes on to tell us that 'I always compose the portrait by drawing in charcoal on the canvas... I work in this way because I do not want my portrait to become too formalised. A portrait must have a "living" quality.' Moffat then

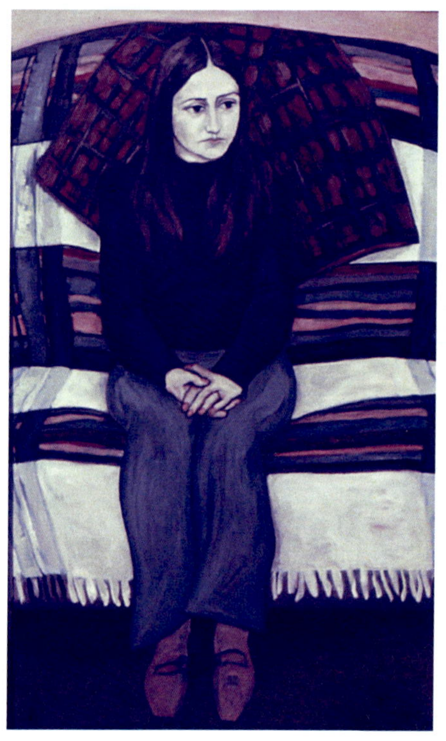

21 *Alice Bold* 1969 oil on board 122 x 76 cm
(private collection)

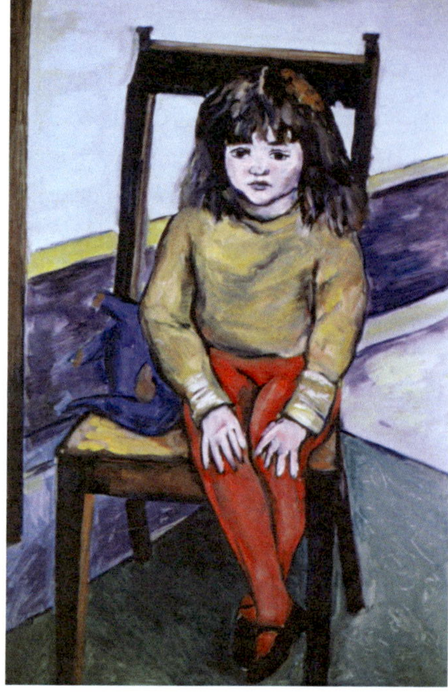

22 *Valentina Bold* 1968 oil on board 91.5 x 61 cm
(private collection)

explains that 'it usually only requires three sittings of one hour each to almost complete the painting… but with certain paintings exactly the opposite happens and three-quarters of the painting is done with the sitter absent.' All this first-hand information from the artist clearly demonstrates the complex procedure that goes into the making of his portraits. This involves a range of strategies and approaches, from the selection and courting of the subject, the close studying of that subject by detailed observation through drawing, and the seeking out of an appropriate image by experimenting with compositional improvisation.

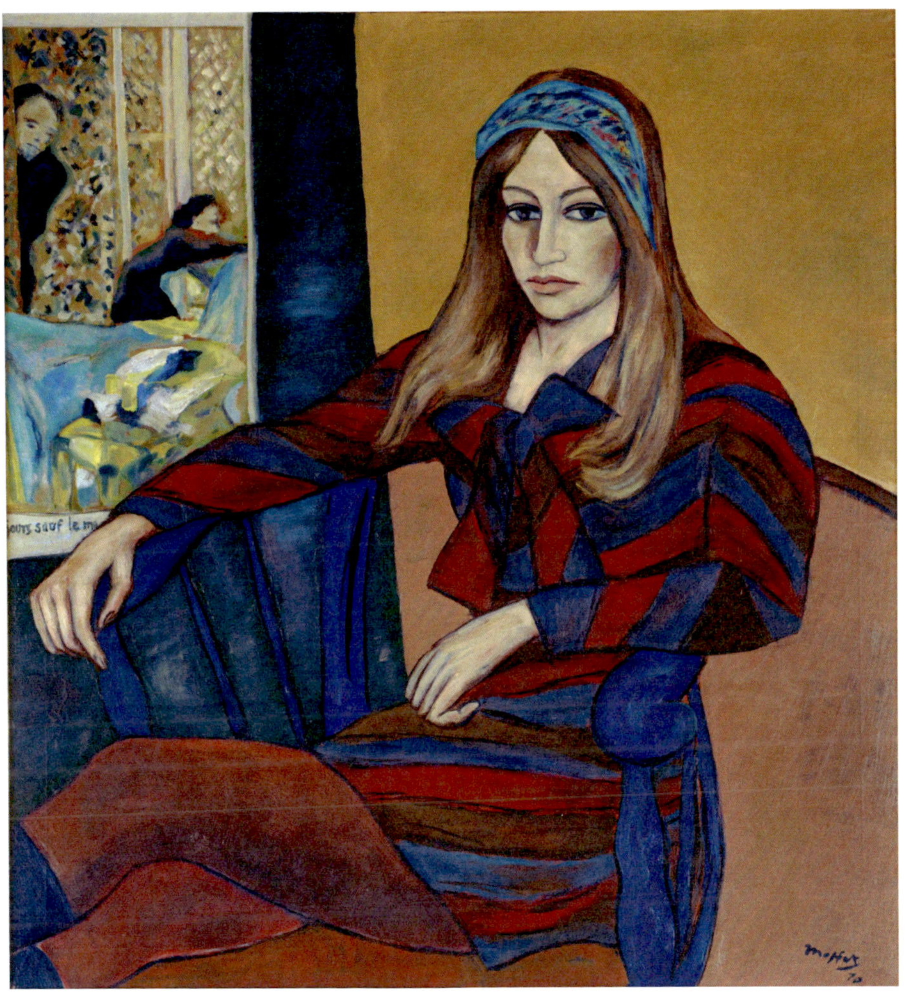

23   *Susan Moffat* 1970 oil on canvas 91.5 x 86.5 cm (private collection)

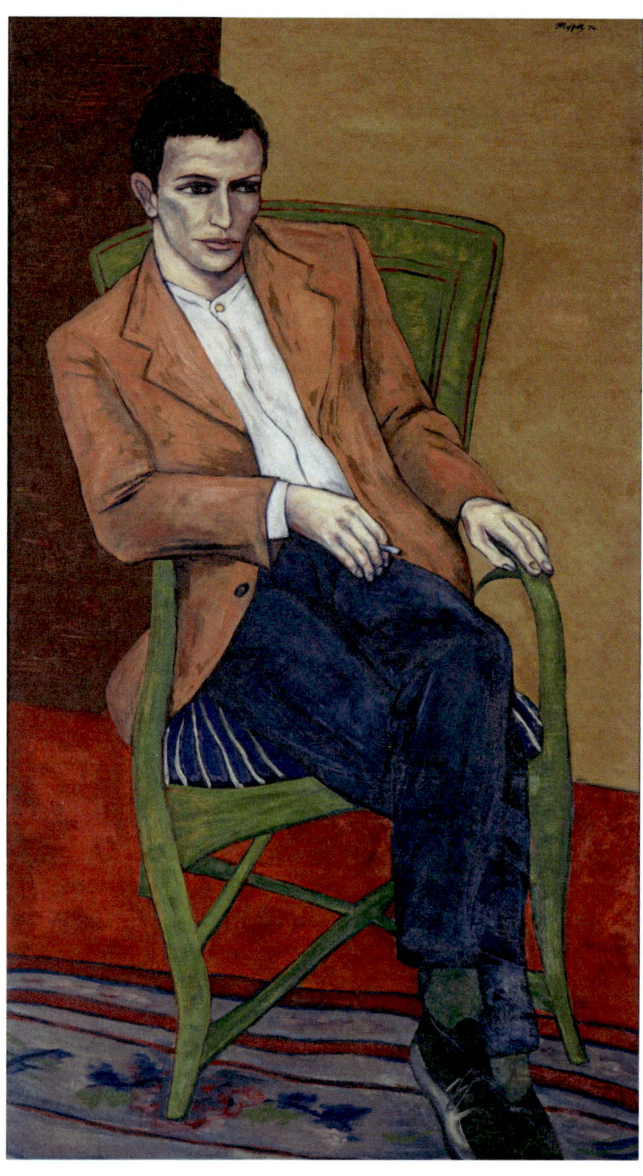

24 *Iain Patterson* 1970 oil on board 137 x 76 cm (private collection)

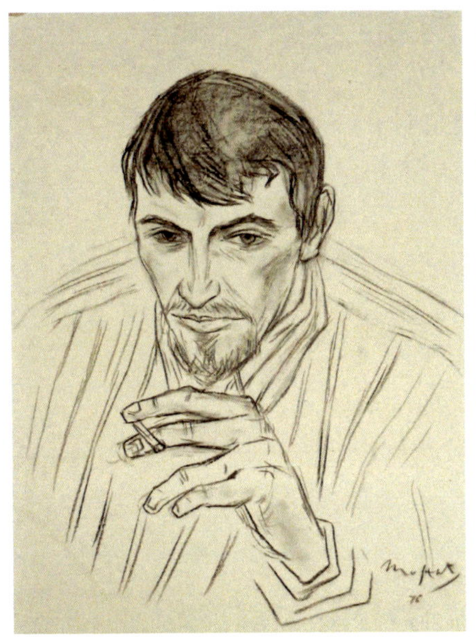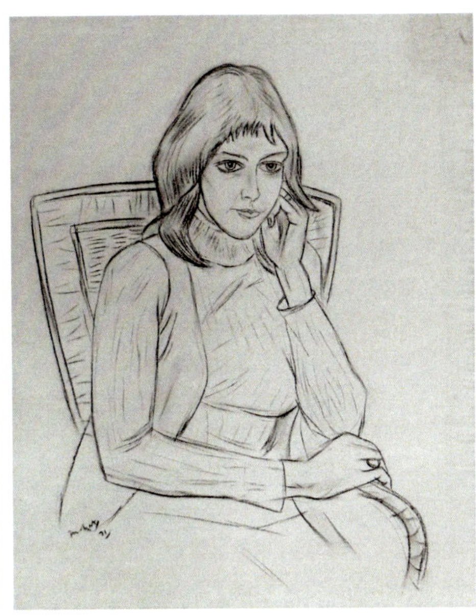

25 *Graham Martin* 1970 charcoal on paper 51 x 38 cm   26 *Margot Duffy* 1971 charcoal on paper 64 x 51 cm

This is followed by the challenge of trying to depict and express the individuality of the sitter's appearance, character and appropriate setting, and finally, by the ultimate requirement of placing the painting within a meaningful relationship to the history of portraiture.

Throughout the '60s Moffat's portrait painting was little known outside his circle of friends and acquaintances in the Edinburgh art world. A few of his portraits were shown – and even purchased – from the open-air exhibitions that he and John Bellany staged at Castle Terrace and The Mound (1963–65). Then, in 1970, Moffat had a solo exhibition at the New 57 Gallery, where he had become chairperson, and in the following year, he was part of the *Scottish Realism* exhibition, curated by his friend Alan Bold at the Scottish Arts Council Gallery in

Charlotte Square. More specifically related to his portraiture career, BBC Scotland broadcast in 1971 a *Scope* film by W Gordon Smith of Moffat painting a portrait of a writer friend, Alan Jackson. This portrait would become part of Moffat's first major portrait exhibition, mounted at the Scottish National Portrait Gallery in 1973. Curated by Duncan Thomson, *A View of the Portrait* was the first time a living portrait painter had been presented in this manner. For the first time Moffat's art as portrait painter had been brought together as a unified body of work, where it could be seen by the general public and critically assessed. The exhibition proved a success and Moffat's artistic reputation was greatly enhanced by a much wider appreciation of his art and his dedication to portrait painting.

We may ask, however, what were the reasons this exhibition proved such an attraction both to the general public and the art critics? Surely most of the portrait subjects on display would have been pictures of total strangers to most of the people who went to see the show. This common feature of the general public's experience of portrait exhibitions appears to demonstrate – as it does throughout the long history of portraiture – that individual recognition and identification of the sitter plays a much smaller part in the appreciation of portraits than most people think. As in everyday life, we do not have to know who another person is to feel some kind of psychological relationship, or even bond, with them. As Aristotle observed, humans are 'relational creatures' and the whole fabric of human society depends on that empathic trait and inclination. This profoundly unifying relationship in human affairs usually begins by looking at other people and assessing them by their facial expressions and body language. That instinctive feature of human

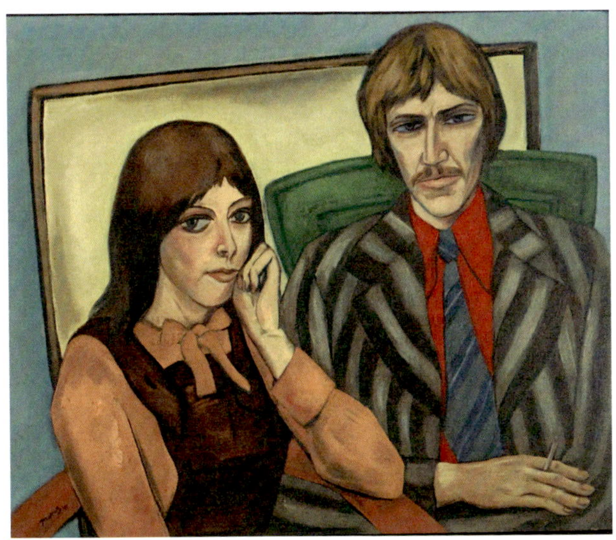

27   *Ken and Margo Duffy* 1971 oil on canvas 61 x 74 cm (private collection)

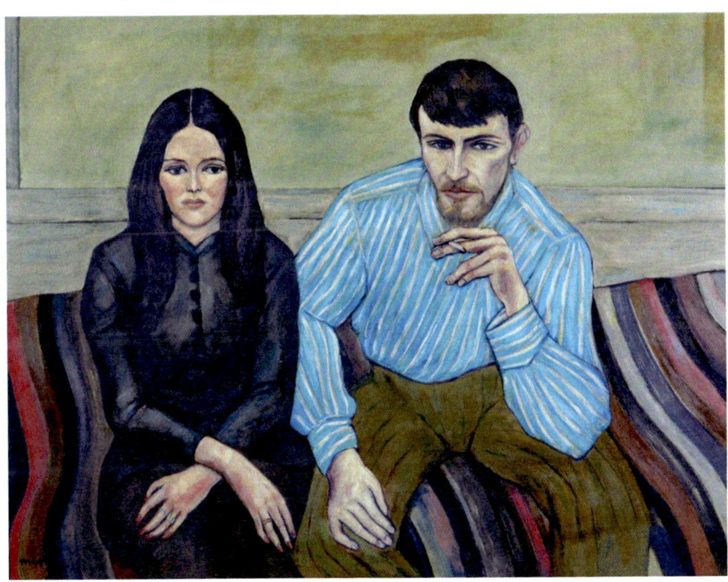

28   *Graham and Eileen Martin* 1970 oil on board 91.5 x 122 cm (private collection)

behaviour then becomes formalised and codified in portraiture, which turns a natural act into a cultural object. In terms of the formalised language of portraiture, the semiotics involved is a three-way ritual between the artist (author), the viewer (reader) and the sitter (the text).

So how does the viewer 'read' the text of the portrait as presented by the artist? This introduces the concept which Professor EH Gombrich termed, in his hugely influential *Art and Illusion*, the 'beholder's share'. On the one hand, the artist, depending on the specifics of the interpretive approach, may give a highly detailed and informative rendering of the sitter's appearance; or, through extreme expressionist distortion of facial features and bodily pose, prefer to focus on the sitter's emotional state of mind. In each case the 'beholder's share' is minimal, as the artist has left little interpretive space for the viewer to formulate their own opinion of, and attitude towards, the subject. On the other hand – and surely this applies to Moffat's approach to portraiture – the artist pares the visual information down to what is deemed necessary and subsequently encourages the viewer to project imaginatively their own instinctive reactions and critical judgements onto the portrait image the artist presents to them. This 'pared down' approach was famously demonstrated by Picasso's reduction of Gertrude Stein's (1905) facial features to a blank mask, as Matisse also did in his portrait *Madame Matisse* (1905). Similarly, Moffat employs such strategies as enigmatic faces, blank stares and unresolved interpersonal relationships. This is one of the intriguing attractions of his portraits, which draw and absorb the viewer into the fascinating mystery of other people's lives.

An attraction for the more art historically knowledgeable visitors to *A View of the Portrait* must have been Moffat's obvious familiarity with

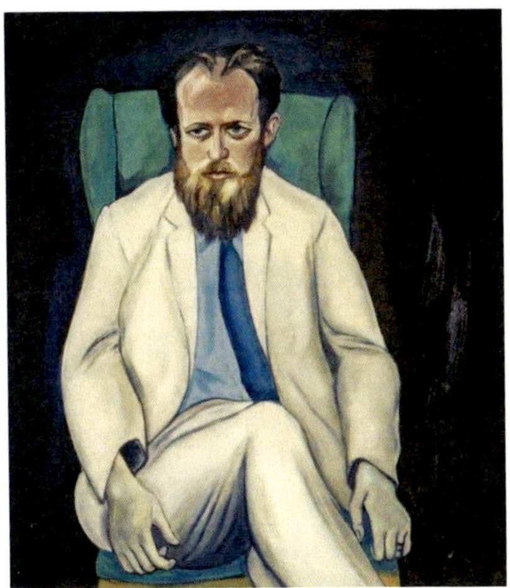

29 *David Morrison* 1971 oil on canvas 85 x 76 cm
(Scottish National Portrait Gallery)

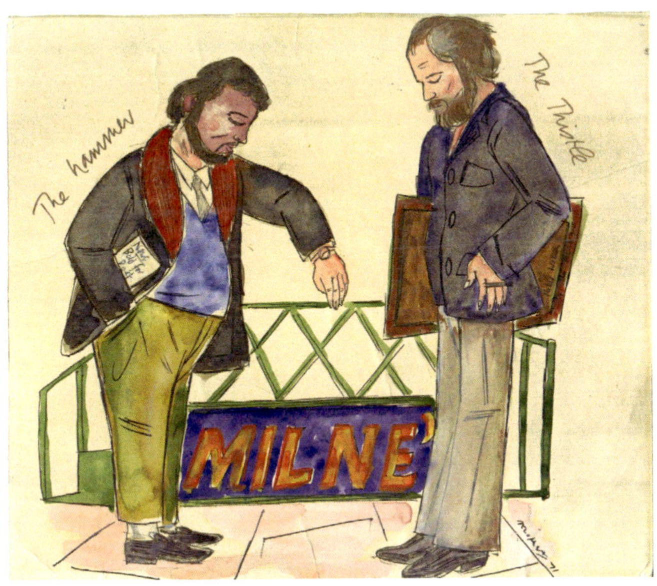

30 *Alan Bold and David Morrison outside Milne's Bar (The Hammer and the Thistle)* 1971
ink and watercolour on paper 21 x 29 cm (Edinburgh Libraries)

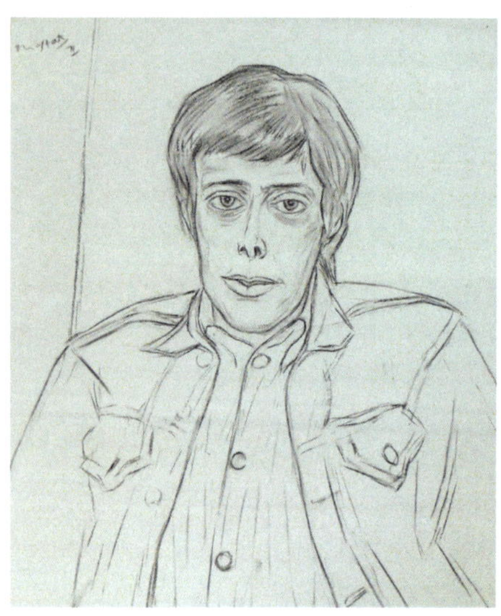

31 *Pete Morgan* 1971 charcoal on paper 51 x 44 cm

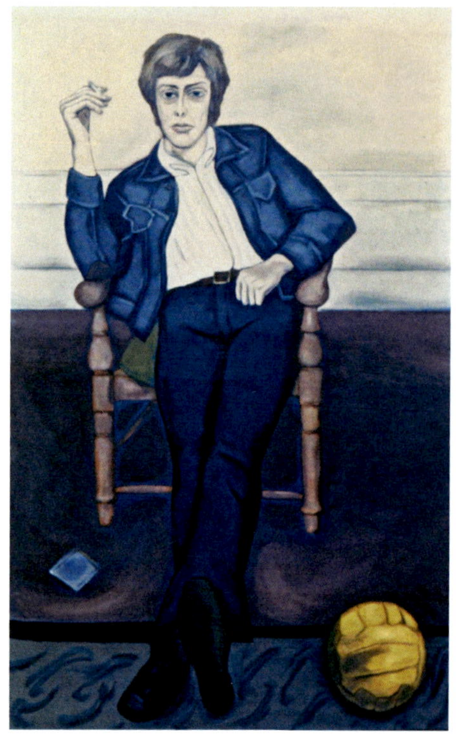

32 *Pete Morgan* 1971 oil on canvas 144.75 x 91.5cm
(private collection)

the inherited language of portrait painting, especially from that of the
modern era. Throughout the exhibition Moffat's paintings demonstrated
that a Scottish artist not only was aware of the great tradition of
European portraiture, but could equally enter into meaningful and
rewarding dialogue with it. His portraits were not the usual Scottish
cringing *hommages* or flattering pastiches of the School of Paris *belle
peinture*, but a genuine creative response to inspiring examples. This
informed referencing from a range of artistic sources further added to

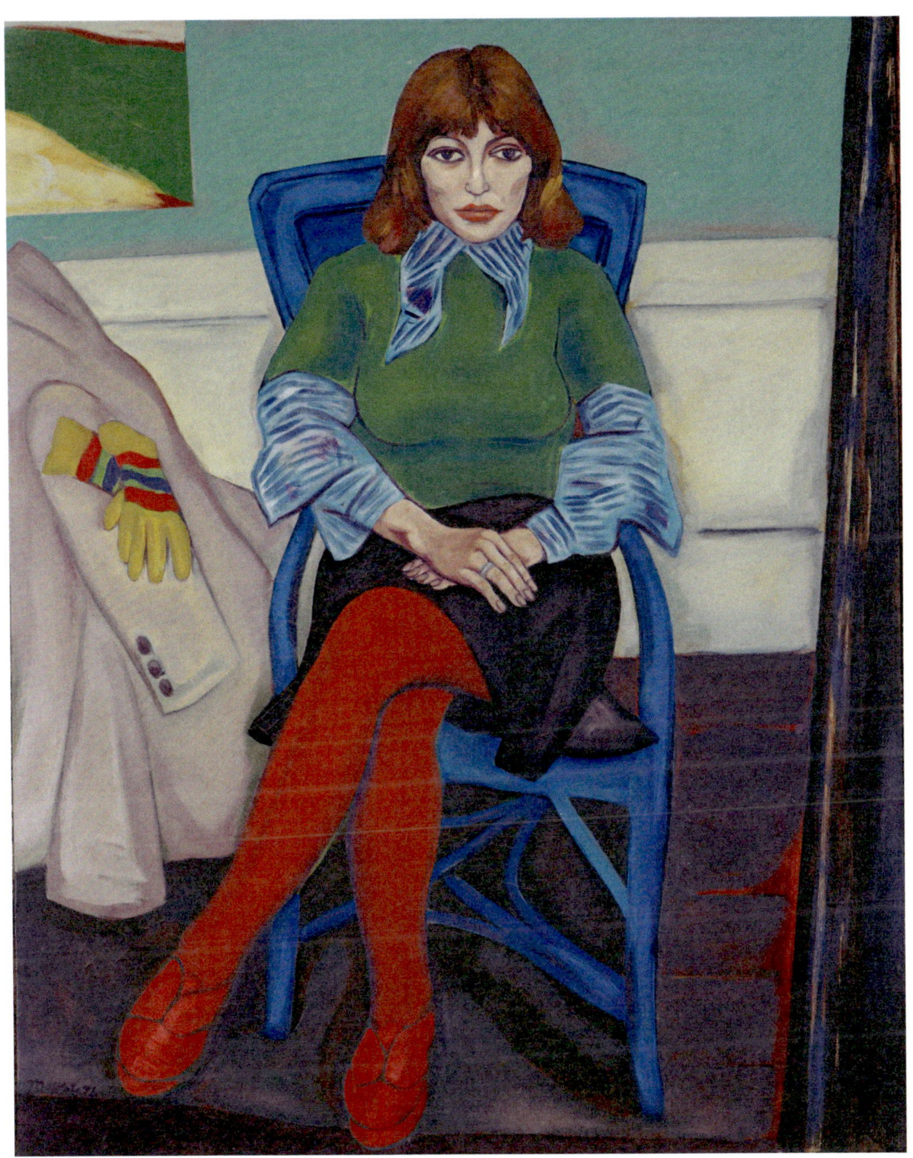

33   *Helen Grant* 1972 oil on canvas 106.5 x 85 cm (private collection)

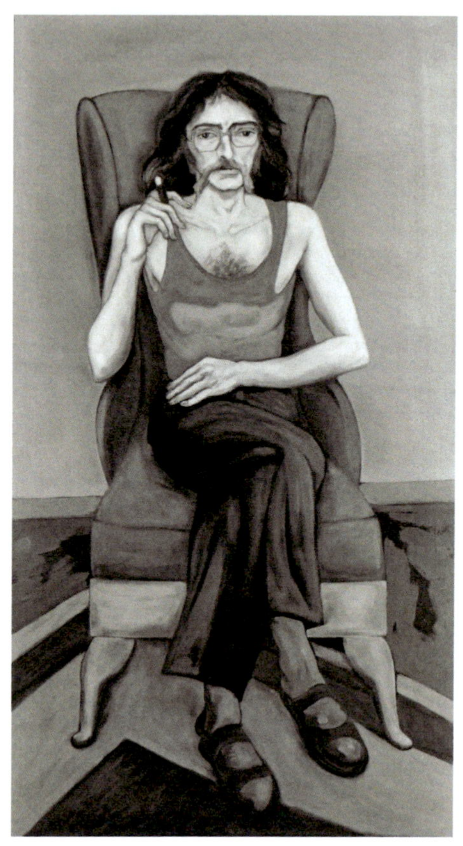

34 *Alan Jackson* 1971 oil on canvas 137 x 76 cm
(private collection)

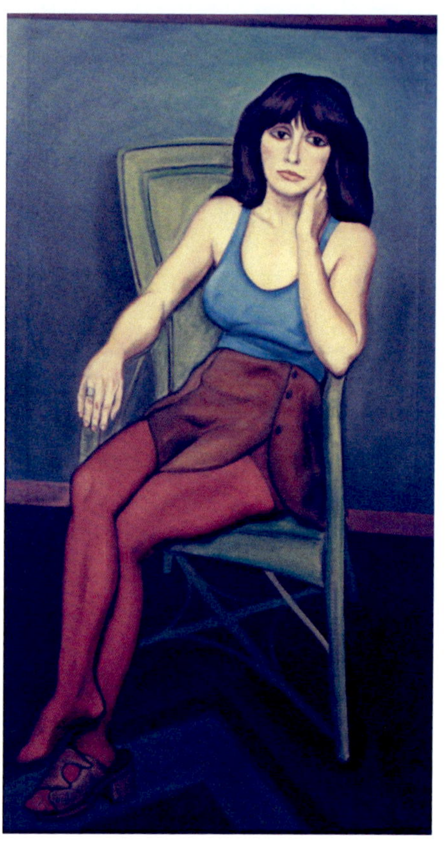

35 *Margaret Jackson* 1971 oil on canvas 137 x 75 cm
(private collection)

the richly appreciated achievement of Moffat's early portraits.

One of the more tangible results of his first major exhibition in
a national public gallery was that Moffat received his first portrait
commission. This came from the University of Edinburgh for an official
portrait of Principal and Vice-Chancellor Sir Michael Swann, on
Swann's retirement in 1974 (ill. 39). Edinburgh University had been the

major patron of one of Scotland's most outstanding portrait painters, Sir Henry Raeburn. As with Raeburn's portraits of the University's Enlightenment literati, Moffat's depiction of Swann dispenses with the conventional pompous trappings of institutional portrait painting and focuses on the figure and personality of the sitter, who is simply dressed in his everyday dark lounge suit. He is placed comfortably crossed-legged in an ordinary office chair, holding his unlit pipe in his lap. There is a strongly egalitarian mood to this straightforward and unpretentious portrait in the way the artist has paid as much attention to the rendering of the sitter's highly polished black shoes as he has to the Principal's balding head. The painting is still very striking, especially through the strategy of playing off the vivid green of the sitter's chair against the rich red of the carpet on which it stands. This new experience of being commissioned to paint a stranger went well for Moffat. Both artist and sitter had agreed as to the format of the portrait, bearing out Moffat's observation that 'all portraits are in a sense collaborations'. The *Michael Swann* commission proved to be useful learning experience when he later took on the much larger and more demanding commission of the *Seven Poets* in 1978.

The *Scotsman* art critic Edward Gage observed of Moffat's paintings in *A View of the Portrait* that 'the overall impression was one of smouldering emotion set in realist drabness'. Although Moffat's basic approach and attitude to portraiture would not fundamentally change during the '70s, the shift in his drawing and painting technique would come to challenge Gage's rather gloomy assessment of his early portraits. As Moffat reflected in an interview with fellow painter Timothy Hyman, for the *Seven Poets* catalogue in 1981, 'The drabness has gone now and

I have distanced myself from the overt emotion of my earlier pictures.'
He still retained the expressionist focus on 'the human condition', but
was now more concerned to express 'ideas' than subjective emotion. In
that interview he goes on to say, 'I have no wish to make any sensational
show of temperament in my work'. Rather than making an immediate
dramatic emotional impact he now wanted the viewer 'to contemplate
my paintings; to come back again and again'. This shift in emphasis and
purpose indicated a move away from the earlier expressionist bias of his
painting to one with a more classical disposition. In the same interview
Moffat admits that, much as he admires Munch, he also greatly admires
Raphael, 'who is an overwhelmingly rational and intellectual artist'.
Then he adds, 'And I love Poussin.' The challenge now for Moffat was
to 'reinvent a genuine contemporary classicism'.

To fulfil this self-appointed task, Moffat could have revisited the
'neo-classical' period of Picasso; instead he chose to turn to an earlier
modern master who also set out to reconcile Modernism with the
classical tradition – Edgar Degas. This is seen most clearly in the change
in Moffat's drawings. He now began to use soft pastel, a medium that
Degas excelled in, and introduced a much more conspicuous graphic
outline to his rendering of the figure. A fine example of his pastel work
can be seen in *Ian Hamilton Finlay* (1975, ill. 42). In this drawing,
Moffat has distilled the appearance and presence of the sitter down to
the absolute pictorial essentials. The sensuous colours are contained
within the sinuous outlines, creating an overall highly decorative
arrangement. Yet despite the abstracted pictorial composition, the
main focus of attention is still on the sitter's facial features, which are
expressive of the poet's inner creative power as he relaxes before taking

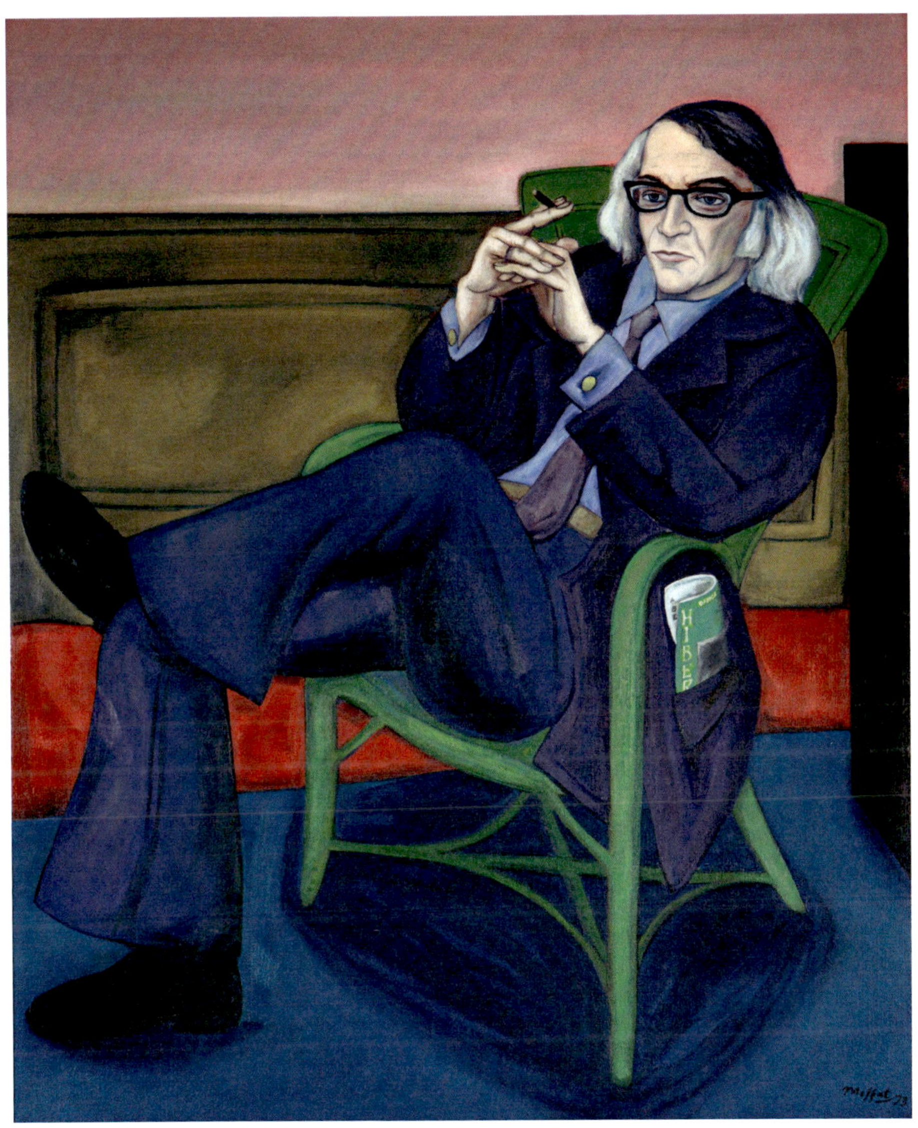

36   *W Gordon Smith* 1973 oil on canvas 112 x 91.5 cm (private collection)

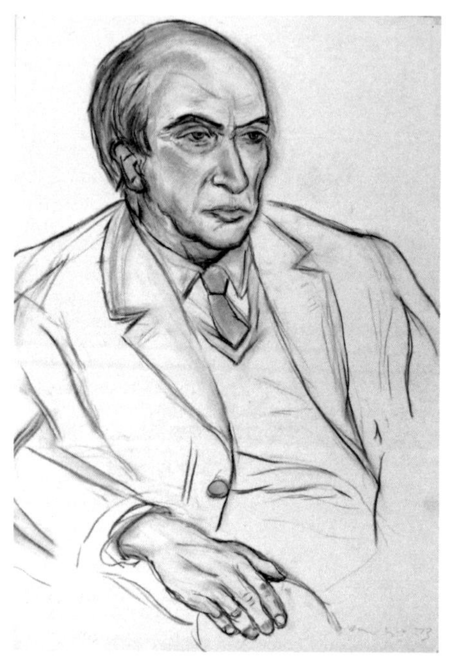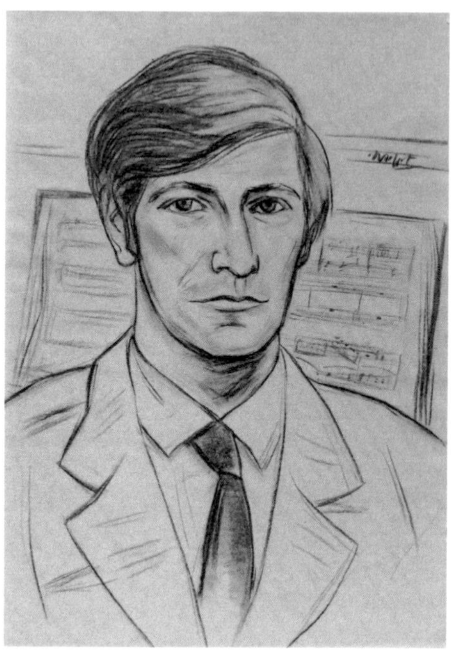

37 *Alan Bush* 1973 charcoal on paper 57 x 40 cm   38 *John Moffat* 1973 charcoal on paper 52 x 39 cm

up yet another artistic and polemic struggle.

These beautiful pastel drawings, because of their lyrical outline and rich colouring, have a strong sensuous appeal that seems particularly appropriate for female subjects. This resulted in women becoming more prominent and numerous in their own right amongst Moffat's sitters. A fine example of this kind of pastel drawing portrait is *Lynda Myles* (1976, ill. 44). Myles at that time was the youngest, and first, female Director of the Edinburgh Film Festival, before she went on to become a successful independent film producer. As usual, the presentation of the sitter is very straightforward, with the subject looking directly at the viewer, and sitting crossed-legged on an almost hidden blue chair in a very spartan studio interior. The only prop is a large brown board on the right-hand side of the composition, which acts as an indicator of spatial depth. The sitter wears an open-neck white blouse under a neat green dress suit which complements her calf-length brown boots – the only jewellery that she sports is a bright yellow watch strap. The artist captures the alert and determined expression of a strong and focused personality at the same time as conveying her engaging demeanour and commenting on the discreet taste of her appearance.

This shift in stylistic treatment and technical practice in Moffat's approach to portraiture raises interesting issues concerning the manner in which emotional content is conveyed by the portraits he painted after the mid-'70s – compared to his earlier work. From his numerous statements during his career, and, of course, the evidence of the paintings themselves, Moffat has always been deeply concerned to bring out the 'inner character' of his sitters. In our dialogue, Moffat reprimands 'influential English critics' for 'carefully avoiding the emotional side' of Cézanne's work, and goes on to say that 'for the artists I admire, mystery, passion and soul come first...' With his early portraits, that desire to infuse his pictures with a powerful emotional dimension is clearly evident through his expressive style and painterly technique. By the mid-'70s, through the effect the use of soft pastel drawing had on his portrait painting, the earlier lexicon of Expressionism, with its youthful anxious and agitated introspection, had given way to a more considered, serene approach, in which decorative colour harmonies and compositional balance were given high priority. This does not mean that Moffat was any less concerned to convey emotional expression in the later portraits – as he says 'painting is a subjective business'. That is a

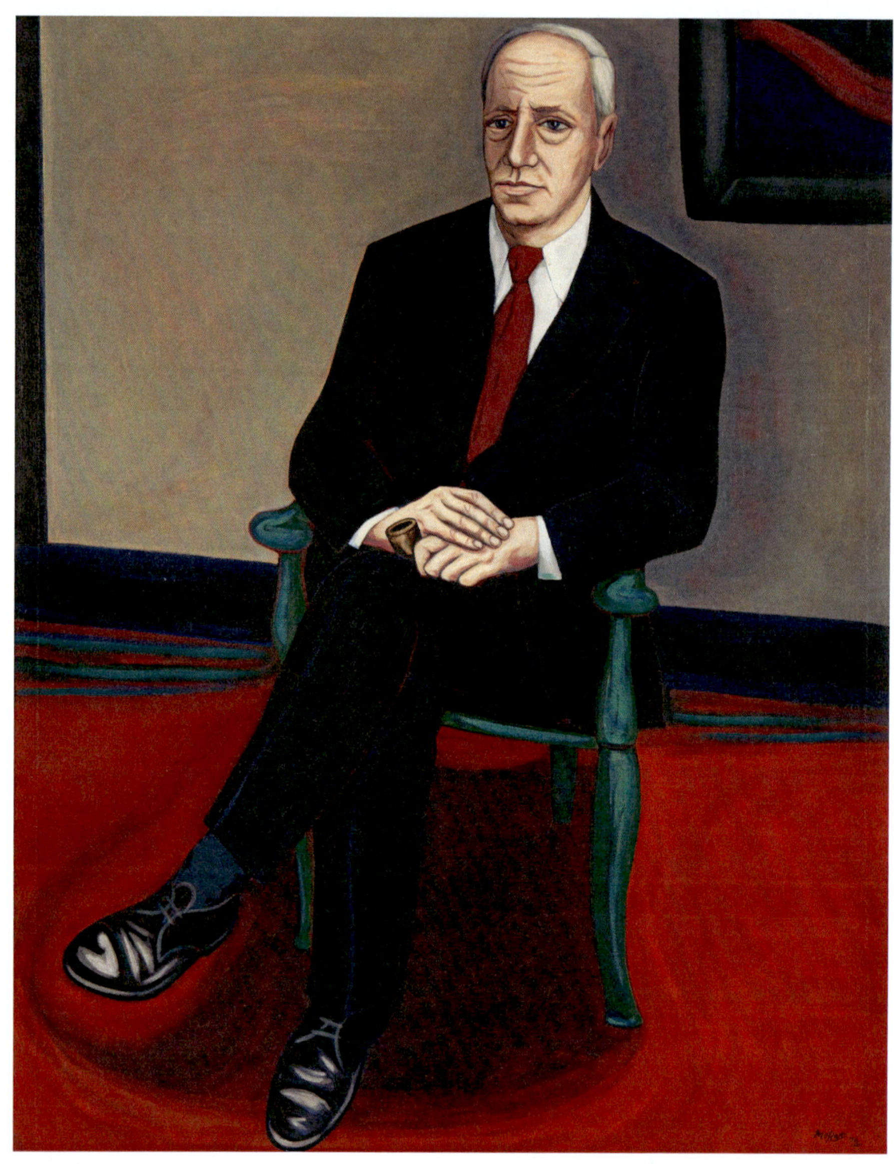

39 *Sir Michael Swann* 1974 acrylic on canvas 152 x 122 cm (University of Edinburgh)

constant throughout all his art. In his later portraits, however, emotion
– to quote the great French master of expressive painting, Henri Matisse
– 'does not reside in passions glowing in a human face, or manifested in
violent movement. The entire arrangement of the picture is expressive,
the place occupied by the figures, the empty spaces around them, the
proportions, everything has its share.' Thus in portraits such as *Lynda
Myles* or *Ian Hamilton Finlay* it is the whole of the pictorial composition
and the colour relationships that impacts on, and affects the response
of the viewers. The overall mood that the entire picture creates is then
projected back by the viewer onto the human subject of the painting
through the power of emotional empathy. The picture as a complete
compositional entity then stimulates a feeling of receptive sociability and
amenability which encourages in the viewer a sense of imagined access
into the company of the sitter, with whom we now feel some kind of
personal relationship and social bond.

To exemplify the crucial importance of this concept of emotional
projection – the way the 'beholder' responds emotionally to a portrait
– we might turn to a famous example to be found in another medium –
cinema. In an experimental film, the Soviet director Kuleshov took a still
photograph of the deadpan face of one of his actors, Mosjoukine. He
then put together a montage film in which he placed the repeated image
of Mosjoukine's expressionless face between other images of various
things – such as a crying child, a dead bird, a bowl of fruit or an idyllic
landscape. He then projected the montage on to a large screen for an
audience to watch. After the showing of his film Kuleshov interviewed
members of his audience and found that they were convinced that
Mosjoukine's facial expression had changed responsively through the

intercutting of the various images. What had really occurred was that with every juxtaposition of face and image, the audience read a different narrative scenario and projected *their* emotional response onto the *imagined* expressive reaction of the actor. This clearly demonstrates that the context of presentation in a work of art is just as powerful an emotional stimulant as the actual subject content of the work.

As with any sensitive portrait painter, Moffat will vary his approach in accord with the personality of his sitter. This can be seen in some of Moffat's more ambitious works of the '70s – such as the double portrait *Susie Raeburn* (1977, ills 54 & 55) – where there is a good deal of over-the-top theatrical posturing on the part of the sitter in order to express her extrovert personality. It is all good, light-hearted fun, allowing Susie to dress up to delight and entertain her audience, as though she had just stepped out of a Seurat circus painting.

Ever since Moffat witnessed Hugh MacDiarmid and Alexander Trocchi fighting over the literary soul of modern Scotland at the Edinburgh Writers Conference in 1962, he has been drawn to the importance of writing and writers as inspiring mentors and important guardians of Scottish contemporary culture. As a young man he regularly frequented the Rose Street pubs with fellow students and admirers Alan Bold and John Bellany. There they were likely to come across their literary heroes. These early contacts eventually led to the beginnings of an important sub-group of portraits within his oeuvre of literary figures, which resulted in some of Moffat's most celebrated paintings.

During the '60s Moffat had painted in an ad hoc manner a number of writers, including Alan Bold, Alan Jackson, Pete Morgan, Archie

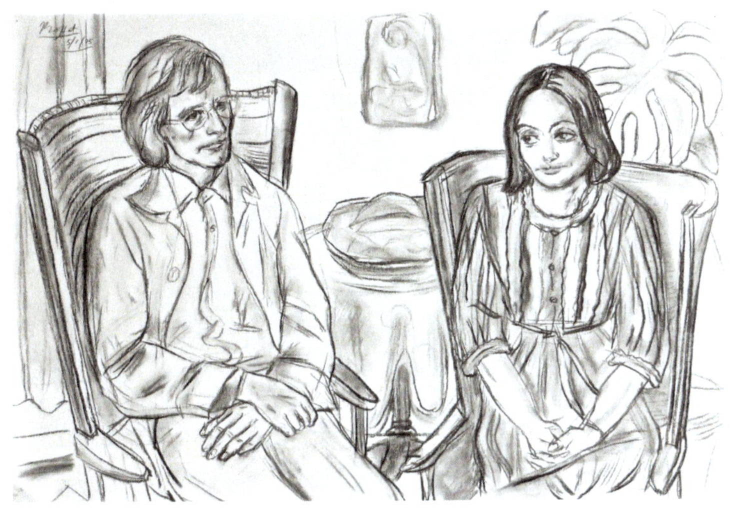

40 *Vincent and Camille Butler* 1975 charcoal on paper 38 x 56 cm

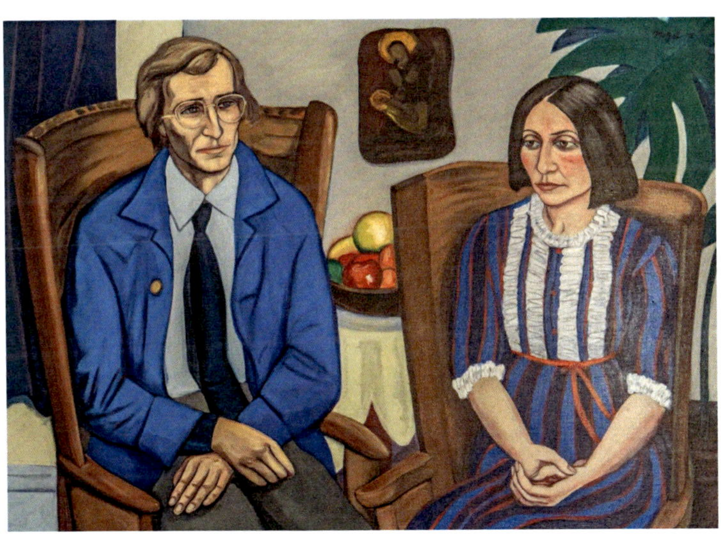

41 *Vincent and Camille Butler* 1975 acrylic on canvas 86 x 122 cm (private collection)

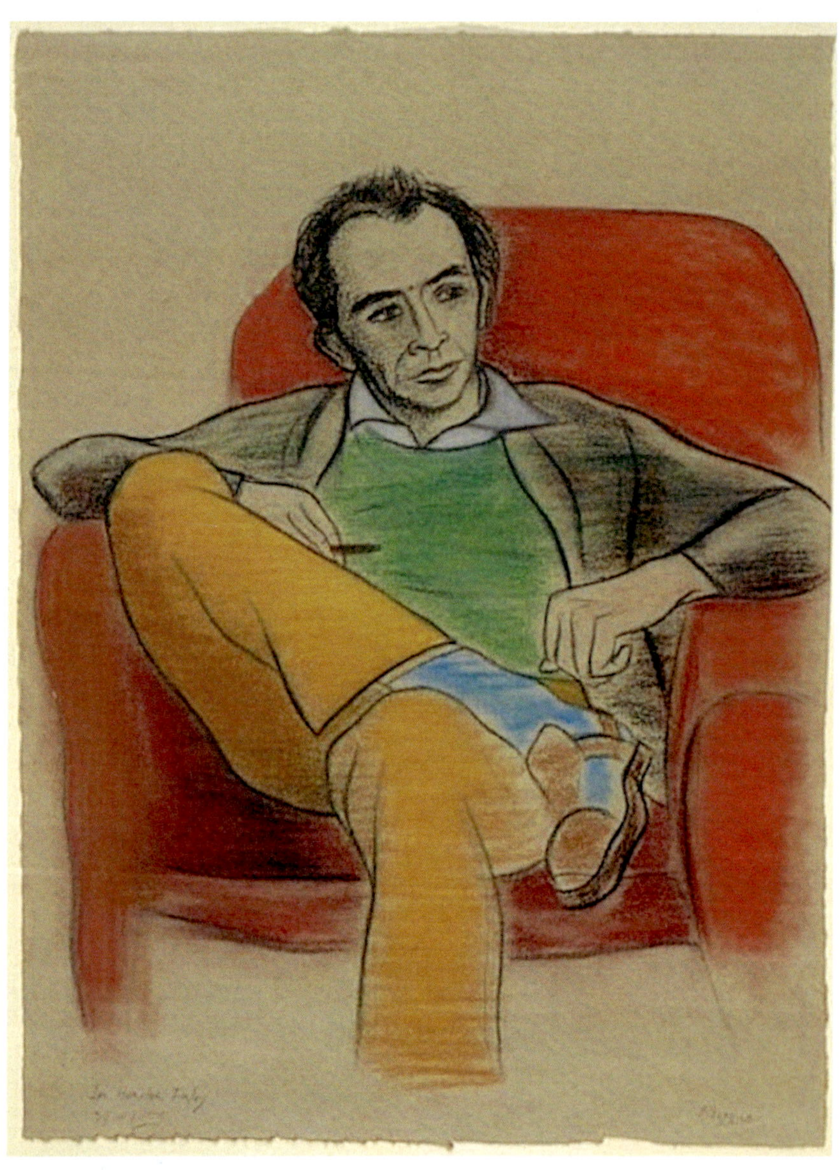

42 *Ian Hamilton Finlay* 1975 pastel on coloured paper 54 x 40 cm (Scottish National Gallery of Modern Art)

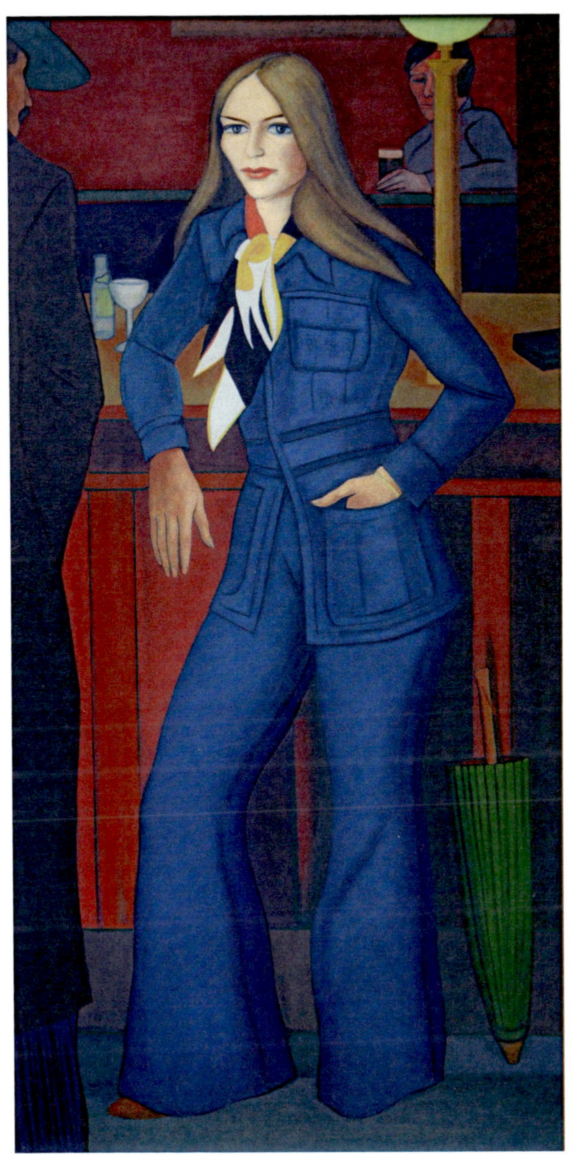

43 *Isabel Hilton* 1975 oil on canvas 157.5 x 76 cm (private collection)

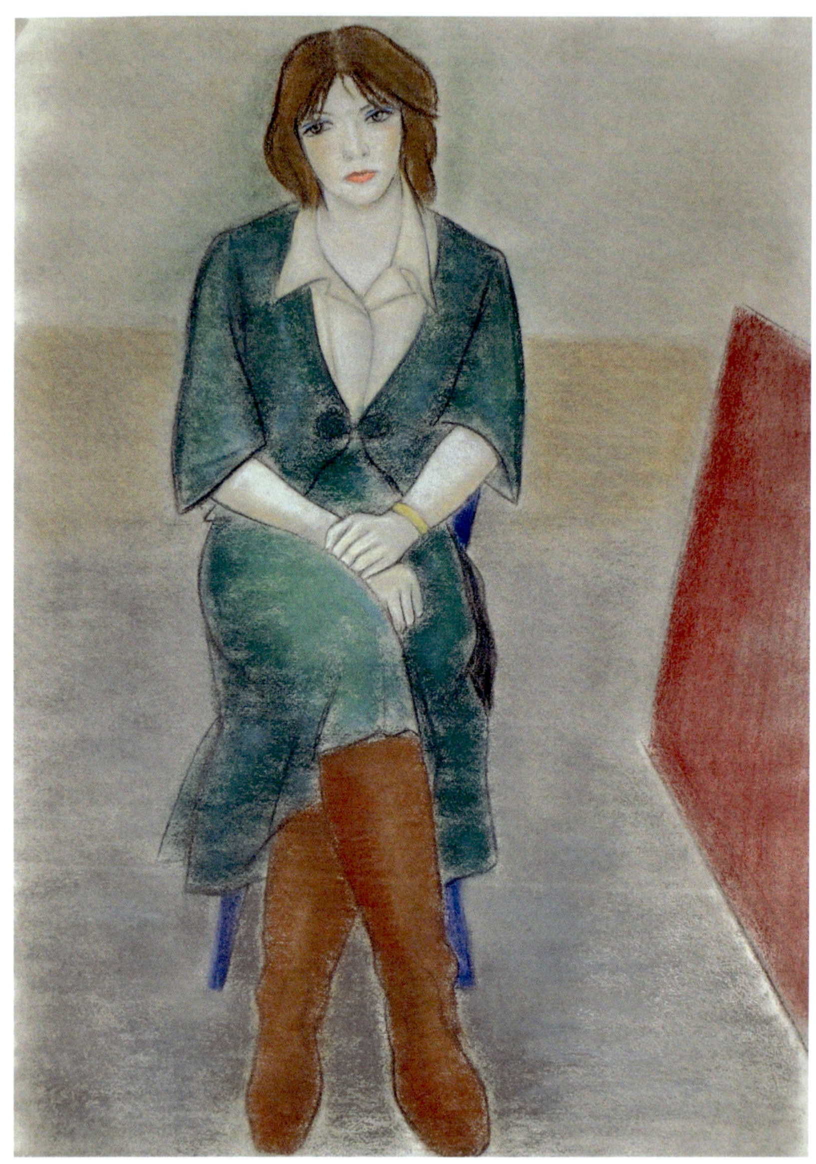

44 *Lynda Myles* 1976 pastel on coloured paper 79 x 57 cm

Hind and – most importantly for his career – Norman MacCaig. It was
not until the later '70s that this particular aspect of his portrait painting
would give him the opportunity to engage seriously with the Scottish
literary community on a more sustained and formal basis. At his own
request, Moffat was commissioned by the Scottish Arts Council to produce
a series of portraits of the poets that were, to varying degrees, part of
Hugh MacDiarmid's Scottish Modern Literary Renaissance. As an artistic
precedent for his literary portraits, Moffat had in mind two inspiring
works by Degas in Scottish collections – *Diego Martelli* (1879) and
Edmond Duranty (1879). By this stage in his career Moffat had become
much more ambitious about the scale on which he could work as a portrait
painter. This can be seen in the *Berliners* series (1977–78, ill. 49) which
was created as a result of his friendship with the renowned journalist Neal
Ascherson who, before returning to Scotland, had been Eastern European
correspondent for the *Observer*. With the large-scale *Berliners* paintings,
Moffat elevated his portrayal of Ascherson into modern history painting
by setting the scene in the decadent night-life of the Weimar Republic
capital of the 1920s, with a range of painterly references to German
artists of that time: George Grosz, Otto Dix and Max Beckmann. This
'expanded' group portrait format, with a biographical and historical
narrative, would be further developed by Moffat in the Scottish literary
portrait series which he embarked upon in 1978.

After leaving Edinburgh College of Art in 1965, Moffat had a
number of jobs, including working in an engineering firm and as a
photographic technician in Edinburgh Public Library. He also ran
the New 57 Art Gallery, taught part time at various art colleges and
eventually was appointed to the painting staff at Glasgow School

of Art in 1979, just about the time he was beginning to work on his *Seven Poets* commission. In the interview with Timothy Hyman for the catalogue published to accompany the exhibition of the *Seven Poets* by Glasgow's Third Eye Centre in 1981, Moffat made it clear that this project was more than a series of individual portraits. He wanted it to be regarded as an epic multi-various portrait of modern Scotland itself. For this highly ambitious and demanding portraiture commission Moffat travelled all over the country to meet and get to know his seven subjects in their particular domains, so that each poet would be placed in the locale or setting from which they drew their immediate inspiration. During these visits Moffat carried out a number of preparatory study drawings in pencil, charcoal, crayon and pastel, and these formed the initial visual information that would be used to formulate the later portrait paintings. These drawings all have their distinctive individual character, but, as Moffat points out in the same interview, 'the drawing and the finished painting are different things'. This, however, is not entirely the case, for the shift in Moffat's approach to drawing, especially with the use of soft pastel, now notably impacted on his method of painting. This can clearly be seen in a comparison between Moffat's painterly rendering of his earlier *Norman MacCaig*, where the impasto is applied in bold conspicuous brushstrokes, and his second depiction of the same sitter for the *Seven Poets* series a decade later. Now Moffat's approach is decidedly more graphic, with strong emphasis on outline and colour applied through the use of a thin fluid staining technique.

Along with the group of individual portraits, Moffat also painted two large-scale canvases which involved highly complex figure compositions centring in both cases on Hugh MacDiarmid. The first, *Hugh*

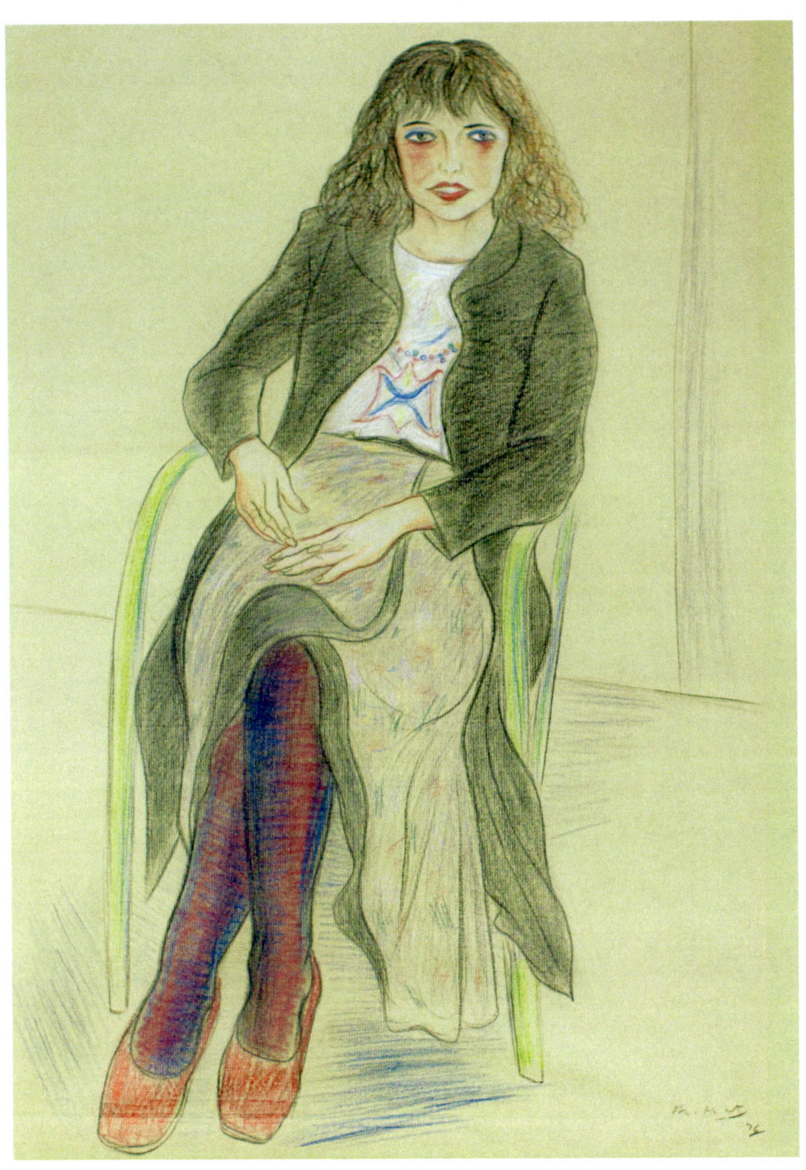

45 *Helen Bellany* 1976 pencil and pastel on coloured paper 70 x 45.5 cm (private collection)

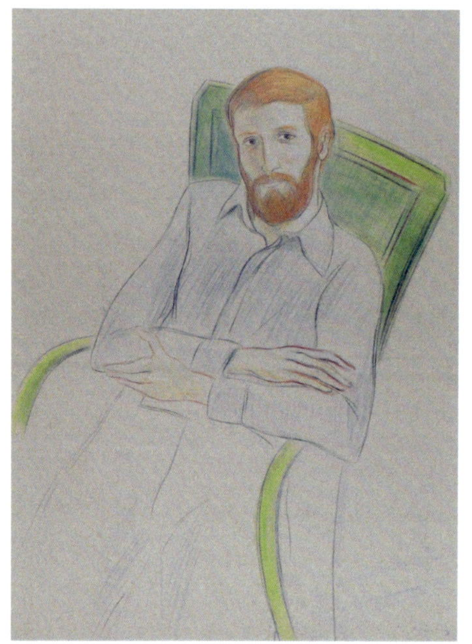

46   *Philip Wright* 1976 coloured pencil on grey paper
68 x 52 cm

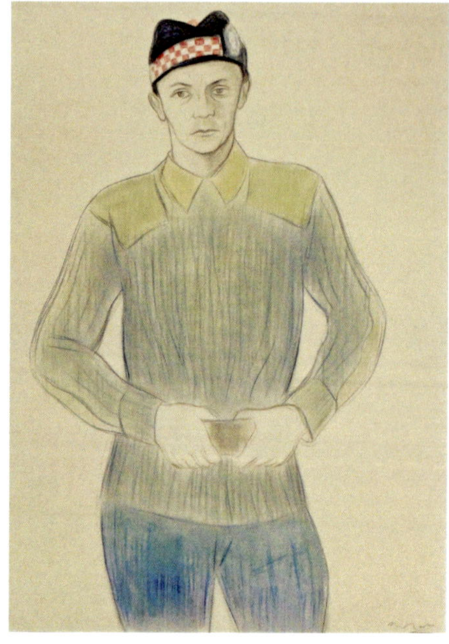

47   *Russell Hunter as 'Jock'* 1976 coloured pencil on paper
69 x 49 cm

MacDiarmid: Hymn to Lenin (1980, ill. 56), is dedicated posthumously
to this man of letters who had died the year before. The frail figure of
the poet is taken from a very moving charcoal and pastel drawing that
Moffat had carried out on his last visit to see MacDiarmid. *Hymn to
Lenin* is very consciously in the mode of epic history painting, yet Moffat
refrains from idealising MacDiarmid into classical hero or isolated
genius – as the poet had been depicted in 1962 by Robert Westwater
in his highly romantic portrait of MacDiarmid as the windswept bard.
Rather, Moffat presents him as frail human being, whose body has
almost run its course, but whose unquenchable spirit and tenacious
beliefs still make him a powerful and dominant personality. The figure

of MacDiarmid, as the great champion of Modernism, is appropriately placed within a collaged composition of associative images and historical figures, from Soviet revolutionaries, such as Lenin, Tatlin and Mayakovsky to their Scottish counterpart, the socialist champion John Maclean. This panoramic scene is set against a fragmented landscape backdrop, made up of different areas of Scotland, all of which had particular personal connections to MacDiarmid during the various stages of his long and expansive intellectual and artistic life. Much of what the great poet had hoped and worked for – political revolution, cultural revival and national independence – had not materialised in his lifetime. So the painting presents him a little like Moses still striving to enter the Promised Land – where the turbulent historical past gives a glimpse of a socialist utopian future. This self-appointed patriarch of the Scottish people is not defeated, nor without hope for the fulfilled outcome of the history of his nation. He raises a toast to his viewers and, looking them straight in the eye, seems to be passing on the baton of radical leadership to the next generation of Scots.

The other large work that was inspired by the portrait project was Moffat's most famous and admired work, *Poets' Pub* (1980–82, ill. 73). Whether these two works, *Hymn to Lenin* and *Poets' Pub*, were planned as a complementary pair, they now appear to work like that – one the sweeping national landscape, the other the local urban interior. Whereas the former is infused with different aspects of international Modernism and is certainly inspired, from Moffat's own confession, by one of the leading modern painters in Britain, RB Kitaj, the latter picture can be seen within a much more Scottish tradition which links back to David Wilkie's genre painting in the first half of the 19th century.

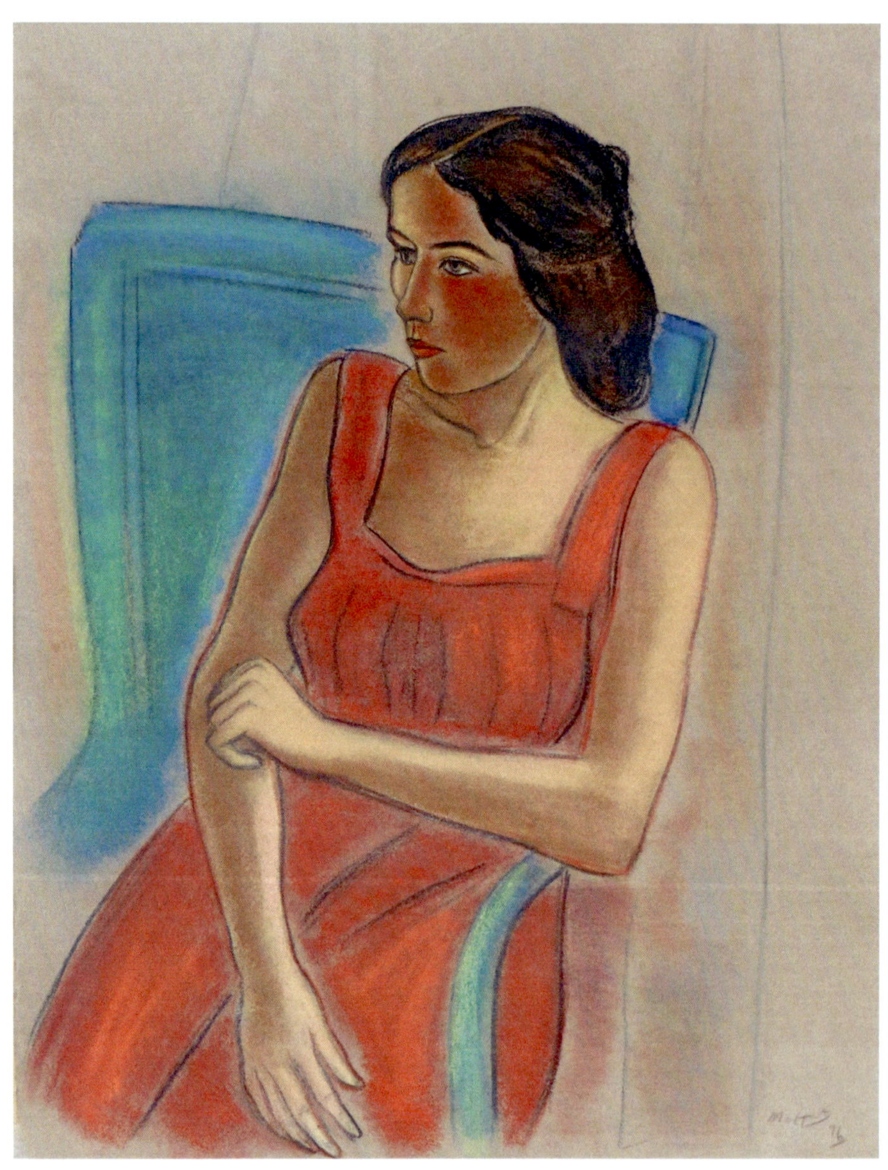

48   *Susan Johnston* 1976 pastel on coloured paper 59 x 47 cm

In *Poets' Pub* Moffat is able to bring together all of the individual portraits of the seven poets and by subtle adaptation and manipulation, unite them in their accustomed convivial grouping in the well-known pub-land of Edinburgh's Rose Street, where Moffat had at one time or another met most of his sitters. While the subject content of the scene is fairly conventional within the combined amalgam of group portraiture and genre narrative, the spatial composition of the picture is fractured by the use of a number of different viewpoints, causing the viewer to experience at second-hand the effects of alcoholic disorientation. Around the tight-knit group of the poets themselves, who engage, or disengage, with the central figure of MacDiarmid, there are isolated individuals who are more loosely connected to this community of poets, such as MacDiarmid's biographer Alan Bold, and the art historian John Tonge; while two anonymous female figures appear to be entirely excluded from the highly exclusive male company. The topics of this pub discussion can only be surmised, but one might be on a political controversy that was still keenly felt, the Spanish Civil War; for Moffat has placed an image on the back wall of Robert Capa's controversial photograph of a falling Spanish Republican soldier. Below that image is another, this time of Delacroix's *Liberty at the Barricades*. Here, however, the flag-waving figure of Liberty appears, not carrying the French tricolour, but rather the Scottish standard. Thus it would be fair to speculate that the poets' heated discussions would certainly involve national issues, both cultural and political. Unarguably these two major highly imaginative and vividly rendered group portraits constitute an important visual discourse on many of the major issues of the 20th century, demonstrating that the theme 'Painting as Arguments' can also make its own contribution to the ongoing discourse concerning the condition of Scotland within the world of international politics.

The works that Moffat produced for the *Scottish Poets* project are seen by many as his greatest achievement as a painter. Yet, at about this time, he was also about to become a leading player in a momentous period for Scottish art. Throughout the '80s, he was a highly influential member of the teaching staff at Glasgow School of Art, and was eventually appointed Head of the Painting Department in 1992. During this period figurative painting came back very much into fashion across the international art scene. A number of young painting students from Glasgow School of Art, under Moffat's guidance and critical/ curatorial promotion through national touring exhibitions, such as *New Image Glasgow* (1985), went on to have very successful careers. These included Steven Campbell, Adrian Wiszniewski, Ken Currie, Peter Howson, Helen Flockhart and Peter Thomson. Moffat struck up lasting friendships with many of his former students and from the mid-'80s began a new series of portraits drawn from his circle of artist friends. This initially ad hoc group of portraits was later pulled together to make another important exhibition at the Scottish National Gallery of Modern Art in 1988. The title of the exhibition was *Portraits of Painters* – a group of sitters with whom Moffat, as a fellow figurative painter, could very much identify. In the case of these portraits of fellow painters Moffat's egalitarian words from our dialogue have a special resonance: 'It's a matter of solidarity too… I very much hope the abilities of the individuals I've portrayed will be taken seriously… that they in their own ways, made a difference in the world.'

As was his long established practice, Moffat would firstly produce

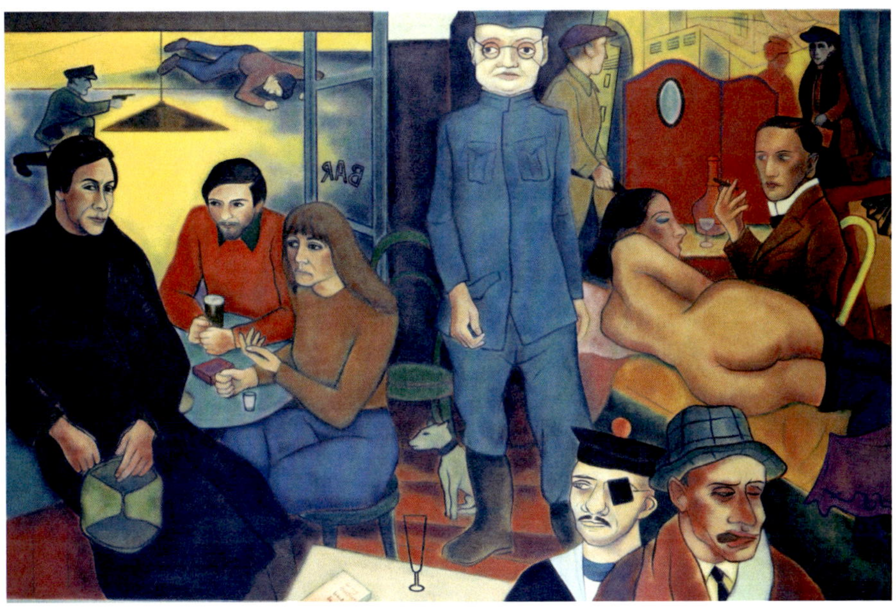

49 *Berliners 3* 1978 oil on canvas 119.5 x 188 cm (private collection)
Neil Ascherson (left) is situated in the 1960s. By him are seated Rudi Dutschke and Ulrike Meinhof, who espoused
violent revolution. The shooting of the student Benno Ohnesorg by the West Berlin police in 1967 is depicted top left.
Other figures include artist George Grosz (foreground) and communist Rosa Luxemburg (top right)

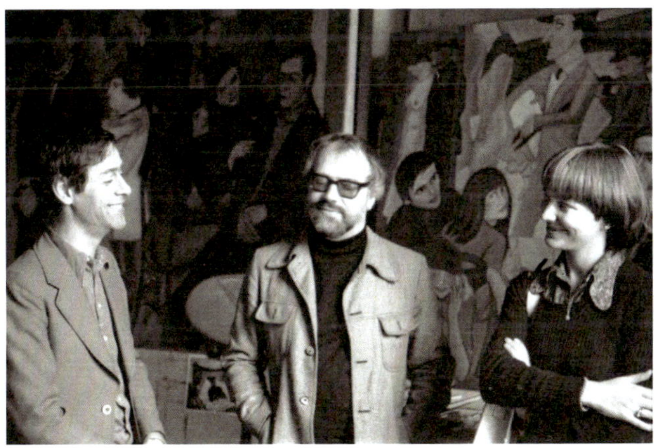

50 Neal Ascherson, Tom Nairn and Isabel Hilton in Alexander Moffat's studio 1977

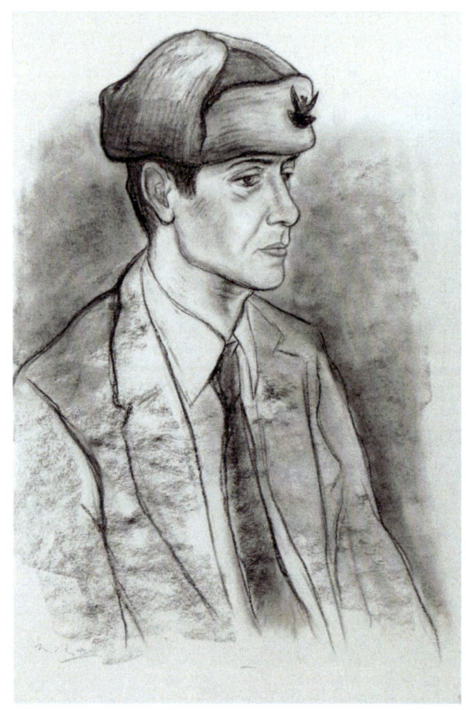 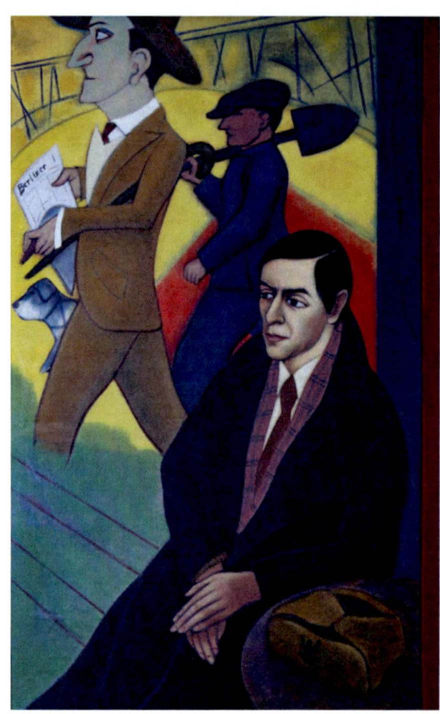

51 *Neal Ascherson (Polish Army Cap)* 1976 charcoal on paper
57 x 39 cm

52 *Neal Ascherson* 1977 oil on canvas 126.5 x 76 cm
(private collection)

preparatory studies of his sitters, with some of these drawings, usually head and shoulders, turned into powerful prints such as the etching *Ken Currie* (1988, ill. 91), and the engraving *Adrian Wiszniewski* (1987, ill. 90). In the spirit of artistic equality, having artists as his sitters, Moffat could forcibly demonstrate his claim that 'all portraits are in a sense collaborations…' For instance, he cites the case of Gwen Hardie – the daughter of one of his Glasgow School of Art colleagues – as an outstanding example of such collaboration. Gwen, a forceful individual in her own right, whom Moffat describes as 'larger-than-life', was

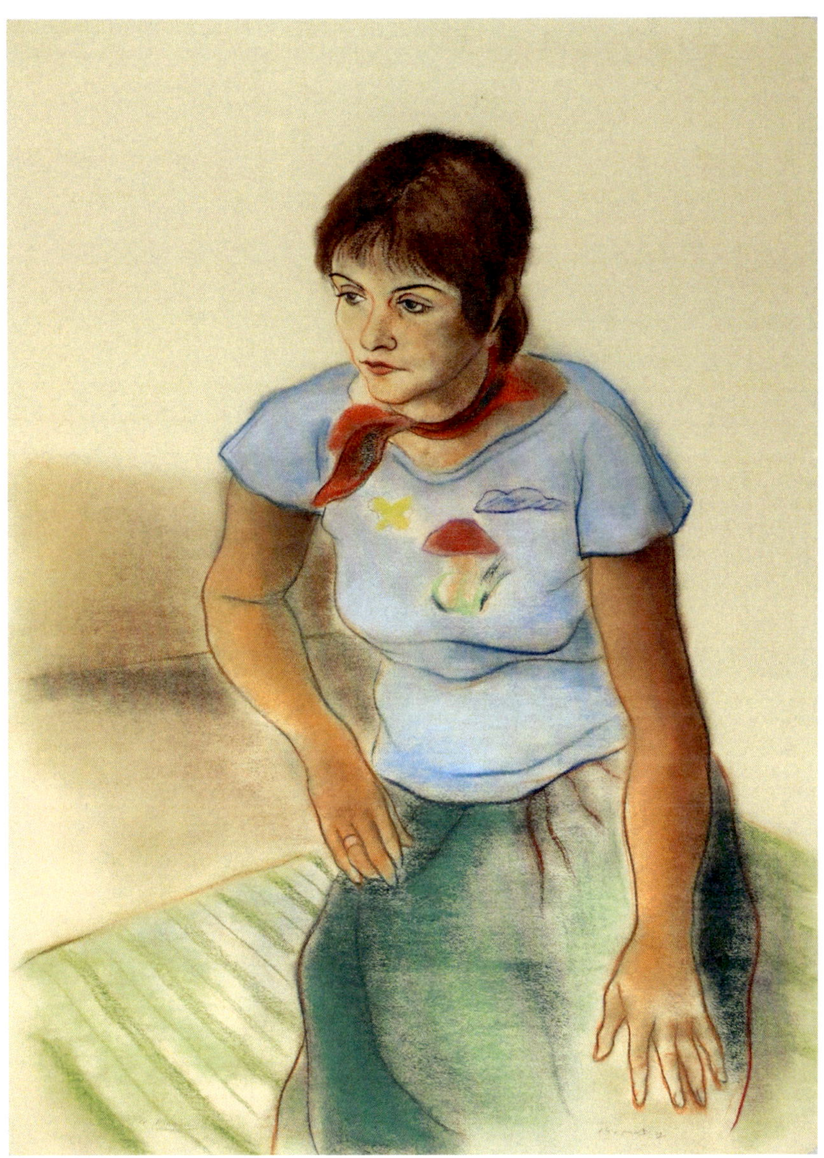

53 *Maggie Mitchell* 1979 pastel on cream paper 75 x 55 cm

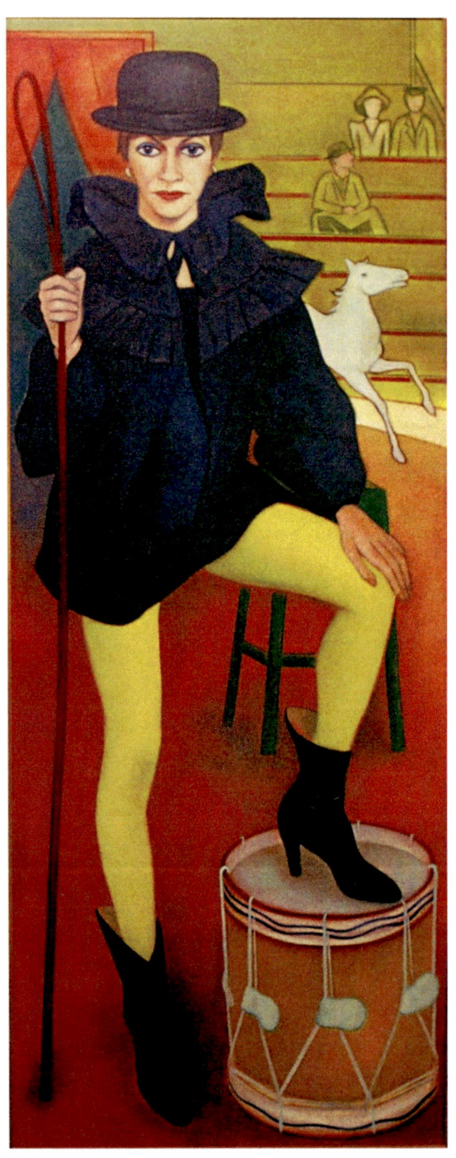

54 *Susie Raeburn (The Ringmistress 2)* 1977 oil on canvas
152.5 x 61 cm (private collection)

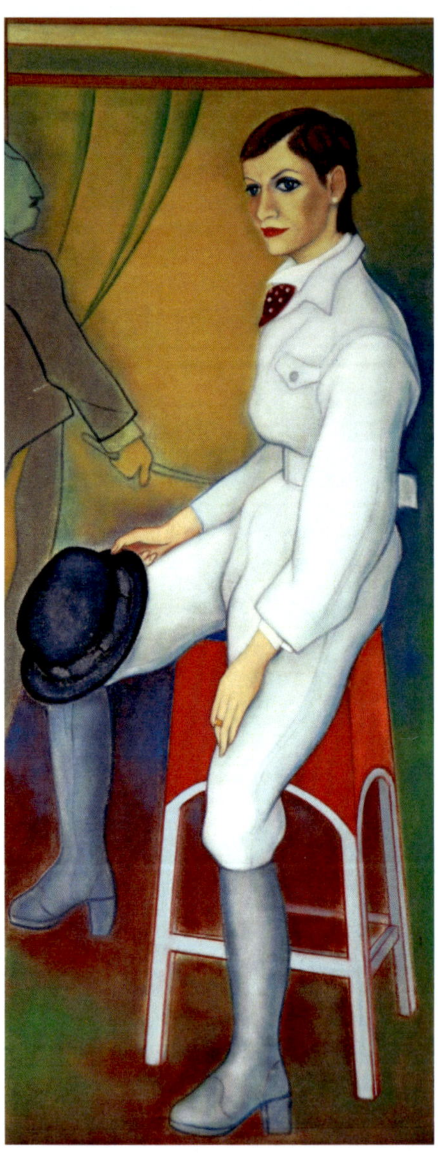

55 *Susie Raeburn (The Ringmistress 1)* 1977 oil on canvas 152.5 x
61 cm (Russell-Cotes Art Gallery & Museum, Bournemouth)

unhappy with his first attempt to portray her, a view with which Moffat concurred, agreeing that it had a 'rather conventional composition that didn't quite work'. The second Gwen Hardie portrait painted in 1987 (ill. 95) certainly captures the assured artistic and feminist persona of the sitter, who seems to fill the canvas with her commanding physique and powerful personality. She is presented in her studio sitting on a stool, her legs defiantly spread wide apart, with one of her own paintings of a monumental Michelinesque female nude floating behind her. The expectant male gaze is suitably challenged and forcibly repulsed!

Moffat had to portray another equally formidable, but very different kind of female sitter a few year earlier in 1984 when he was commissioned by the Scottish National Portrait Gallery to paint a portrait of Scotland's most critically acclaimed contemporary novelist, Muriel Spark. This painting is generally considered one of Moffat's most successful single-figure portraits. During the making of the portrait in Moffat's Edinburgh studio, the writer and the painter seemed to have struck up a good relationship which, according to Moffat, produced 'some very interesting discussions about the nature of art and how the artist must prioritise in order to create'.

The question of prioritising when applied to portraiture is a challenging and complex issue, involving the artist's intention, the sitter's expectations and the viewer's response. With all other kinds of pictorial subjects that a painter may tackle – history, genre, landscape or still life – it is generally assumed that the primary intention is to create a 'work of art'. This, however, might not be so readily appreciated by the sitter when it comes to the role and purpose of portraiture. For it should be remembered that portraiture is the only genre where the subject can talk back to the artist! Thus the relationship between subject and artist is less clear-cut, more fluid than with the other genres: with a portrait there are psychological, emotional and social links and even strains between the sitter and the artist that affect how the artist will represent them. From the viewer's perspective, there is always a pressing need to identify, and identify with, a fellow human subject. This crucially involves the very illusive and contested concept of 'likeness' – visual recognisability. Because portraiture is the genre which is the one closest to the interface between art practice and the conventions of social life – and is most expected to conform to those social conventions – it is more difficult for the viewer to stand back from a portrait and see it as an independent mode of representation with its own history and distinctive artistic conventions. Thus the viewer is probably less ready to take an objective critical position on the aesthetic quality of a portrait, than they would if they were critically engaging with, say, a landscape or a still life picture.

This duality of artistic purpose and social expectation is something the portrait painter has to confront, negotiate and attempt to reconcile. This challenge can be seen in a couple of statements Moffat makes in our dialogue about the nature of portraiture. He states, 'In a sense, a portrait is an affirmation of an individual human being…'; and at another point says, 'I keep coming back to the idea that a portrait must work as a painting.' Of course, these aspects of Moffat's portraiture – the social and the aesthetic – are not incompatible, and in fact this dialectical tension provides a powerful drive to the synthetic development of his work. There is a notable shift in emphasis in his relationship with and treatment of his sitters from his earlier to his later portraits. This can be seen if we compare two female portraits painted more than a decade

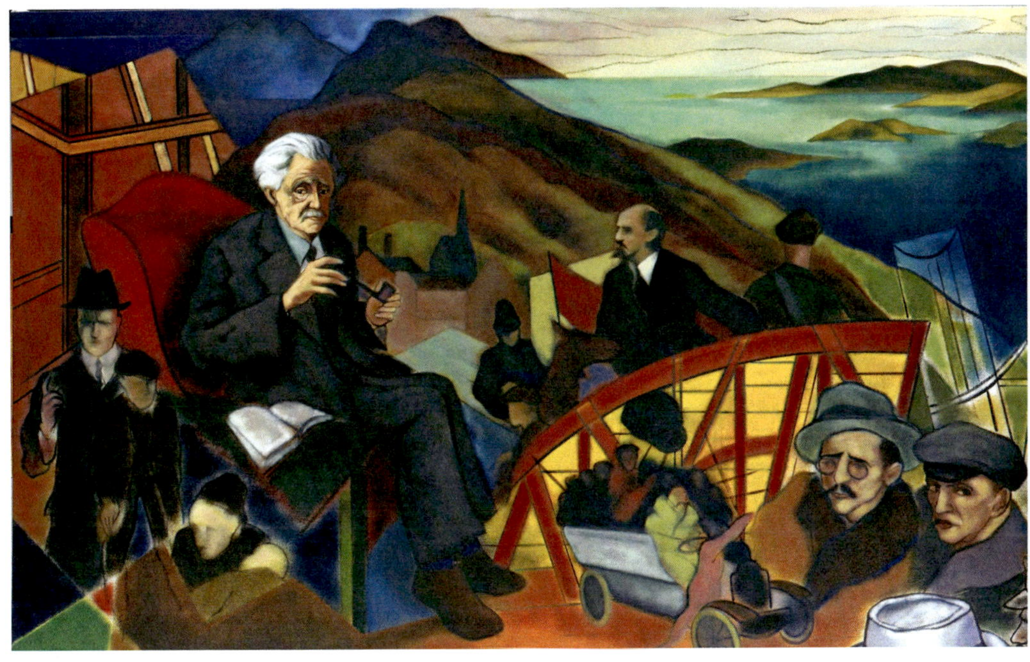

56 *Hugh MacDiarmid: Hymn to Lenin* 1980 oil on canvas 113 x 190 cm (Scottish National Portrait Gallery)

apart: *Helen Grant* (1972, ill. 33) – an image which was used on the
cover of *A View of the Portrait* catalogue – and the celebrated *Muriel
Spark* (1984, ill. 78). Both portraits present an attractive, well-dressed
and intelligent woman seated cross-legged and looking engagingly out
at the viewer. Yet there are also crucial differences – while the figure of
Helen Grant is placed in an actual interior space, Muriel Spark is not
given any specific setting and hovers in an amorphous pictorial world of
'Venetian' blue. Helen Grant is portrayed as a tangible physical presence,
surrounded by personal objects which have a convincing connection to
her as an individual personality – they 'humanise' her; Muriel Spark is

given an almost ethereal aura that sets her persona apart from any ready access by the viewer into a pictorial world in which her wish, 'I only want me', is granted.

Although these two portraits are specific cases, and Moffat is dealing with two different kinds of portrait subjects, there is still a notable shift in his work away from the earlier stage of his portraiture which could be characterised as being markedly portrait/subject orientated, to the later stage where portrait/image predominates. This development has come about for a number of reasons, involving his change in the technical approach to his drawing and painting, and also the changing relationship he has with different types of sitters – from his earlier personal friends and private acquaintances to the later public commissions to portray national figures. This is not to state any critical preference between the earlier and later portraits, but to draw attention to subtle but significant differences between them. In the earlier works, the subjects are set in intimate biographical scenarios, while in the later ones, the carefully considered image of the sitter has more of the feel of a revered painted icon. Both these approaches in Moffat's practice of portraiture are equally capable of producing memorable works of art, all of which still retain his distinctive and recognisable stylistic stamp.

After the *Portraits of Painters* (1988) exhibition, Moffat's artistic interests shifted away from portraiture towards landscape painting and contemporary historical subject matter. In 1992 he was appointed Head of Painting at Glasgow School of Art and such an onerous position, during a period of rapid change in art education – made great demands on his energies. Since his retirement from teaching in 2005 Moffat – an inveterate traveller – has spent a good deal of his time journeying

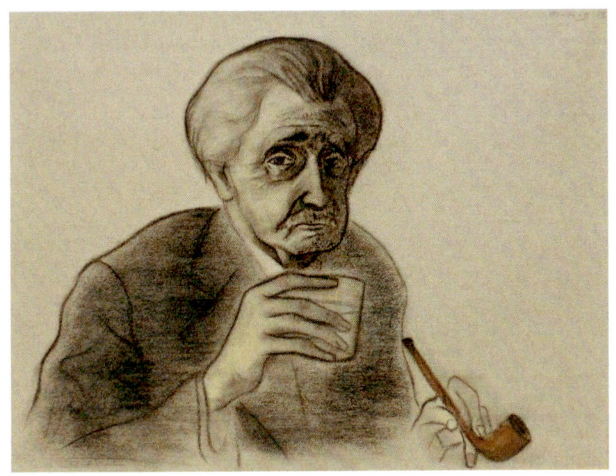

57   *Hugh MacDiarmid* 1978 charcoal and pastel on paper 36 x 47.5 cm

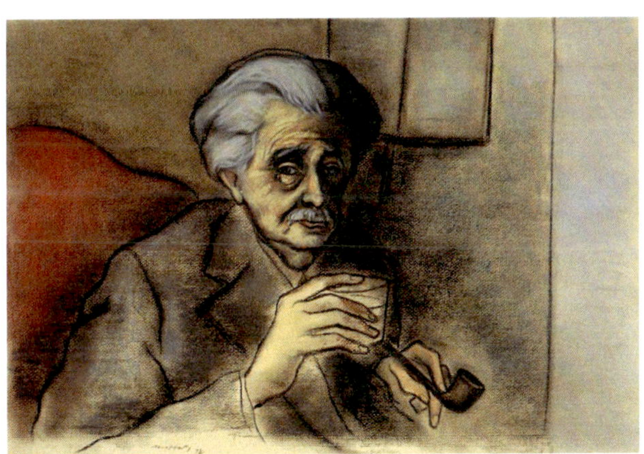

58   *Hugh MacDiarmid* 1978 charcoal and pastel on paper 36 x 47.5 cm
(Scottish National Portrait Gallery)

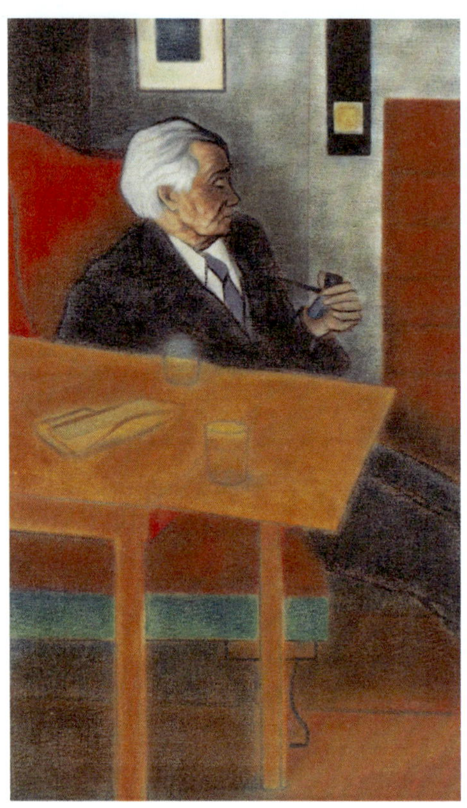

59 *Hugh MacDiarmid: Brownsbank* 1978 oil on canvas
91.5 x 56 cm (private collection)

around the globe, attending innumerable international art events and
promoting the importance of Scottish art and culture. During this period
he has carried out the occasional portrait commission, mainly for the
Saltire Society who asked him to paint three elderly distinguished Scots:
the academic George Davie (1999, ills 112–115), the actor manager
Tom Fleming (2000, ills 119 & 120) and the novelist Robin Jenkins
(2001, ill. 128). His long connection with major Scottish literary figures

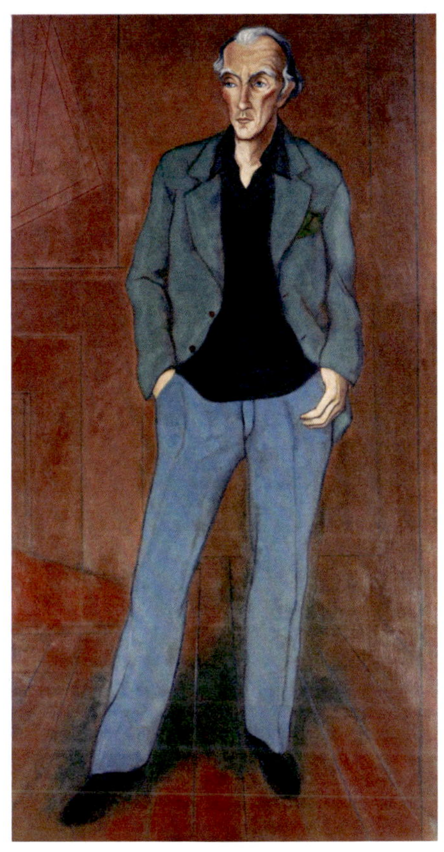

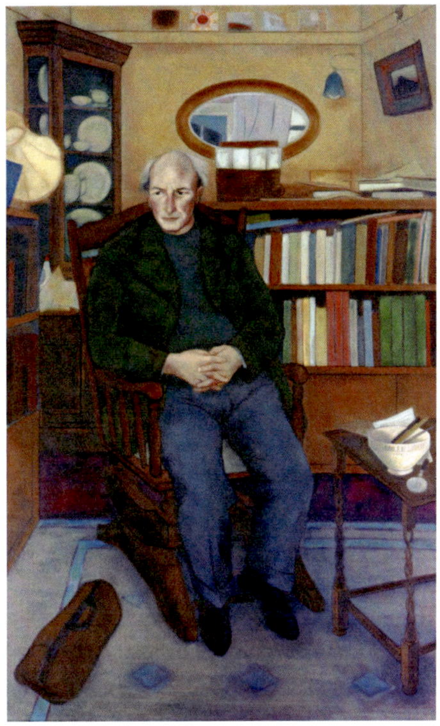

60 *Robert Garioch* 1978 oil on canvas 175 x 113 cm (above)
(Scottish National Portrait Gallery)

61 *Norman MacCaig* 1979 oil on canvas 198 x 106.5cm
(left) (City Art Centre, Edinburgh)

continued when he painted Alasdair Gray (2010, ill. 133), a charming
and very homely portrait of that wonderfully eccentric man of letters.
In this very informal portrait the ever youthful and mischievous
looking author of *Lanark* is seen relaxing, with his arms behind his
head and legs akimbo in his adjustable lounge chair, surrounded by
his library of books and his pictures. More recently, Moffat has again
turned his attention to portraiture with a splendid painting of David

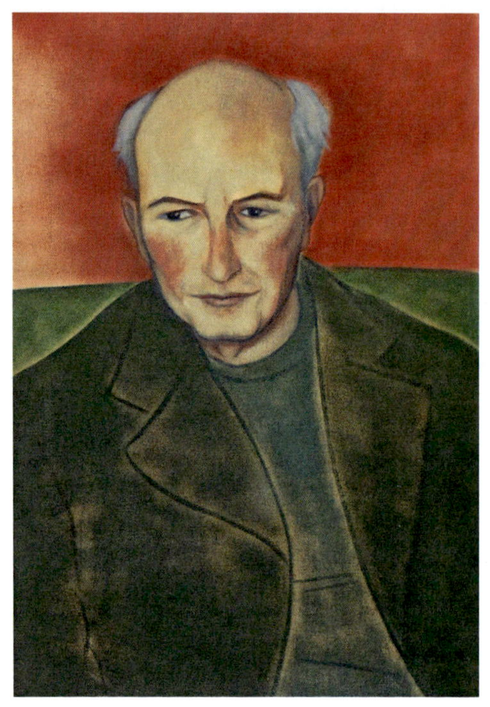

62 *Robert Garioch* 1978 oil on canvas 59 x 42 cm

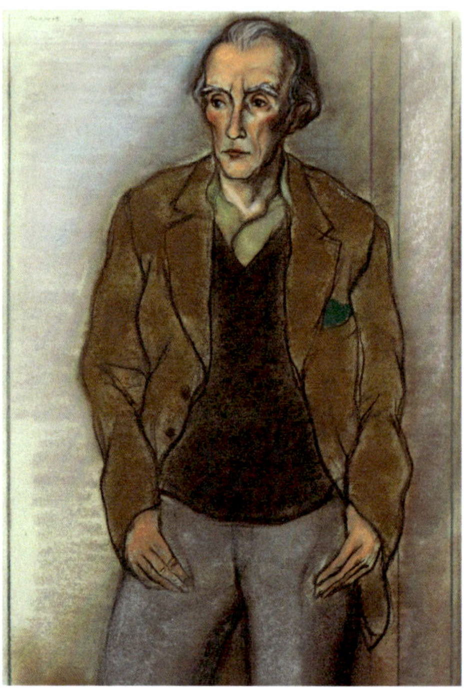

63 *Norman MacCaig* 1979 pastel on paper 63.5 x 45 cm

MacLennan, the influential theatre impresario, who was behind such
radical political touring projects as 7:84's *The Cheviot, the Stag and
the Black Black Oil* and Wildcat, both of which are clearly referred to
in the background of the painting. As Moffat relates in our dialogue,
he has recently completed another major commission, again for the
Saltire Society: a posthumous *hommage* painting, in the manner of his
earlier *Hugh MacDiarmid: Hymn to Lenin*, to the renowned poet and
indefatigable folk song collector Hamish Henderson, entitled *Scotland's
Voices* (2016/17, ill. 149). All of this clearly demonstrates that Moffat's

78

determined task to be the portrayer of individual Scots who have crossed his life, and at the same time to be the chronicler of notable Scottish achievements, is still an ongoing mission.

Let us conclude by returning to a question which would have been a perfectly reasonable one at the time Moffat set out on his career as a portrait painter over half-a-century ago: why should we take portraiture seriously as an art form? As remarked above, the art of portraiture had been under attack since the invention of photography. Portrait painting was critically dismissed as an anachronism, while in other artistic forms, especially literature, it remained a well-respected genre. One only needs to think of such classics as Henry James's *The Portrait of a Lady*, Oscar Wilde's *The Picture of Dorian Gray* or James Joyce's *Portrait of the Artist as a Young Man*, not to mention the innumerable contemporary novels that are basically literary portraits of the main protagonist, to see that the condemnation of portrait painting as a valid art form has not been shared by other creative art forms. In the cinema, the unanimously acclaimed number one film of all time, *Citizen Kane*, is a tour de force in cinematic biographical portraiture. Thus, even if people are not fully aware of it, portraiture has always been and still remains one of the most inspiring and popular genres within the creative arts. This is clearly borne out in the visual arts, where many of the acclaimed masterpieces in the history of art have been portraits, and by the immense attraction that portrait galleries have throughout the world today, and the popularity of the portrait exhibitions that they offer to an eager public. There are endless numbers of masters of portrait painting for these blockbuster exhibitions to call upon for, as Moffat points out, despite whatever critical hostility there has been to portraiture, most major

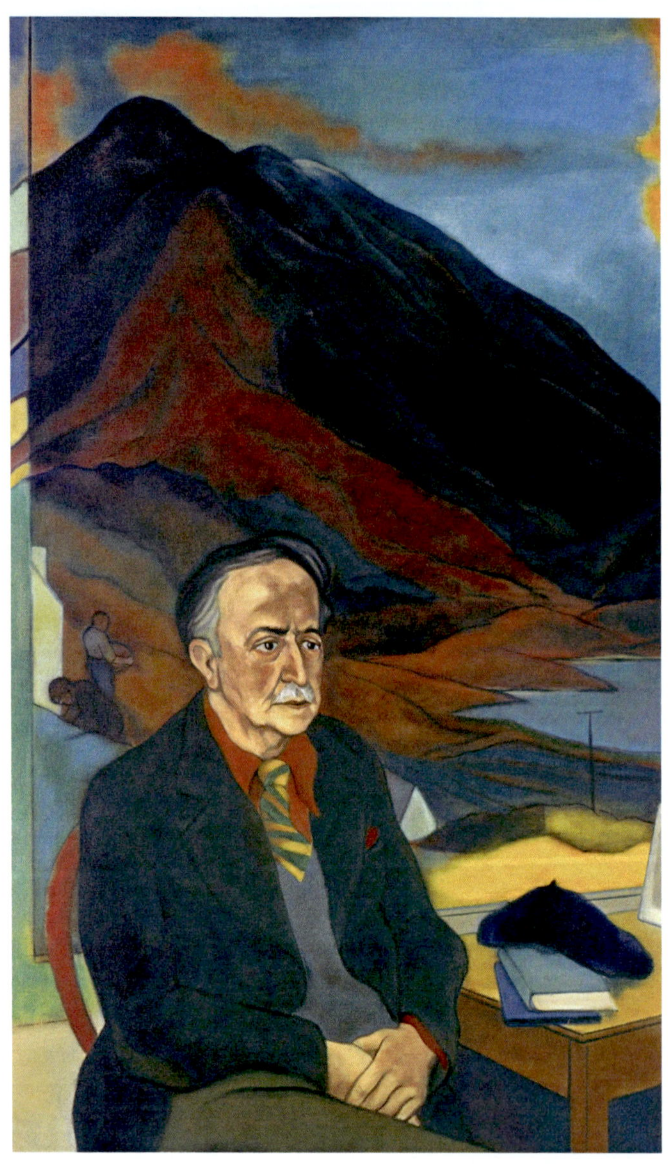

64   *Sorley MacLean* 1979 oil on canvas 152.5 x 91.5 cm (Museum of the Isle of Skye)

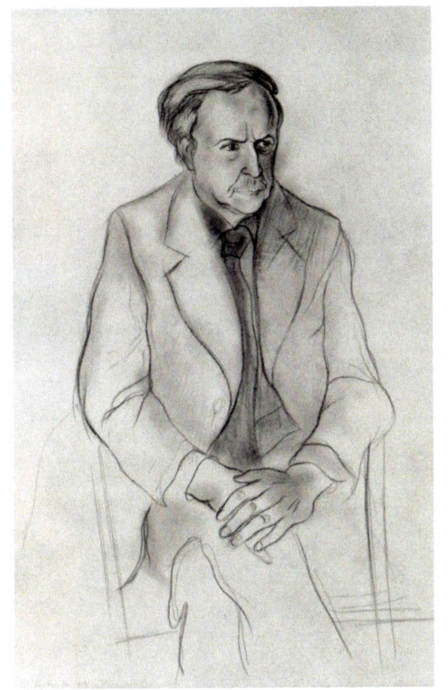
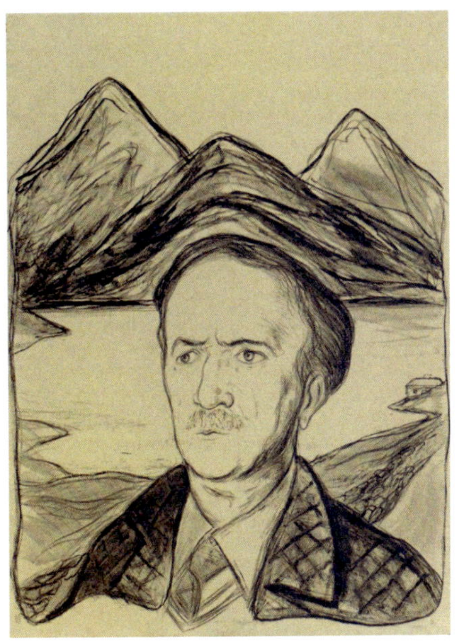

65 *Sorley MacLean* 1979 pencil on paper
59 x 40 cm (private collection)

66 *Sorley MacLean* 1984 lithograph 78 x 57 cm
(paper size)

modern artists have made their own contribution to that 'continuing portrait tradition'.

Unfortunately, after the great achievement of Scottish portrait painting during the Enlightenment, the standard of artistic excellence markedly declined. Therefore it is not surprising that when Scottish artists began to turn to Modernism as a way out of Victorian picture making, they should take little interest in portraiture, turning to landscape and still life as the genres that best accommodated pictorial innovation and aesthetic experiment. In our dialogue, Moffat identifies a 'tradition' in Scottish modern portraiture, citing James Cowie, Edward Baird and William McCance as having made 'significant contributions'.

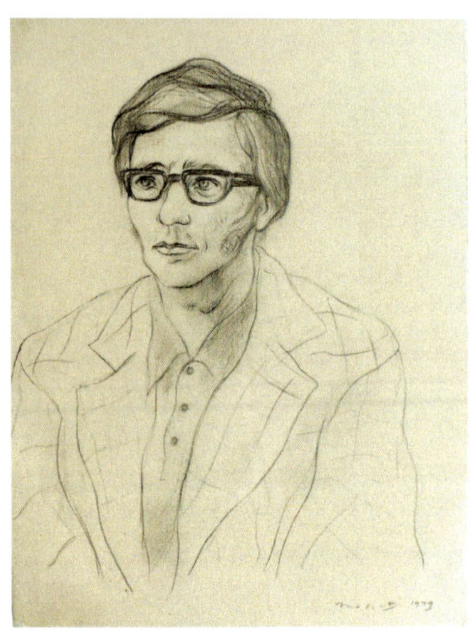

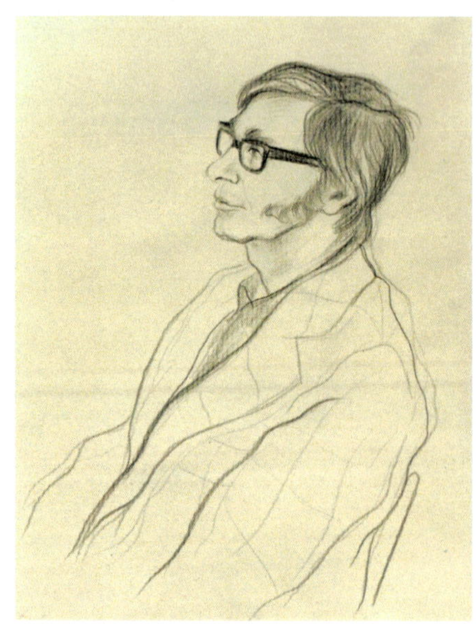

67 *Edwin Morgan* 1980 pencil on paper 27 x 21 cm
(private collection)

68 *Edwin Morgan* 1980 pencil on paper 27 x 21 cm
(private collection)

Whether that claim is valid is arguable, but certainly by the time Moffat began to focus his ambitions on portraiture as a serious form of artistic expression in the early '60s, its standing was at a very low ebb. Yet, despite such a discouraging critical attitude at the outset of his career, Moffat has, with outstanding creative skill and sustained determination, forged a distinctive artistic oeuvre in the seemingly unrewarding and 'flawed genre' of portraiture.

How has he achieved this? The answer may lie in a personal assessment he made of himself as an artist, in an interview he gave for the catalogue of his *Seven Poets* exhibition. Here he observed, 'I suppose that is my own dilemma, a series of contradictions with which, like many artists, I have to live with.' He was talking about the way that, although he saw himself as having a rational, humanist outlook, he

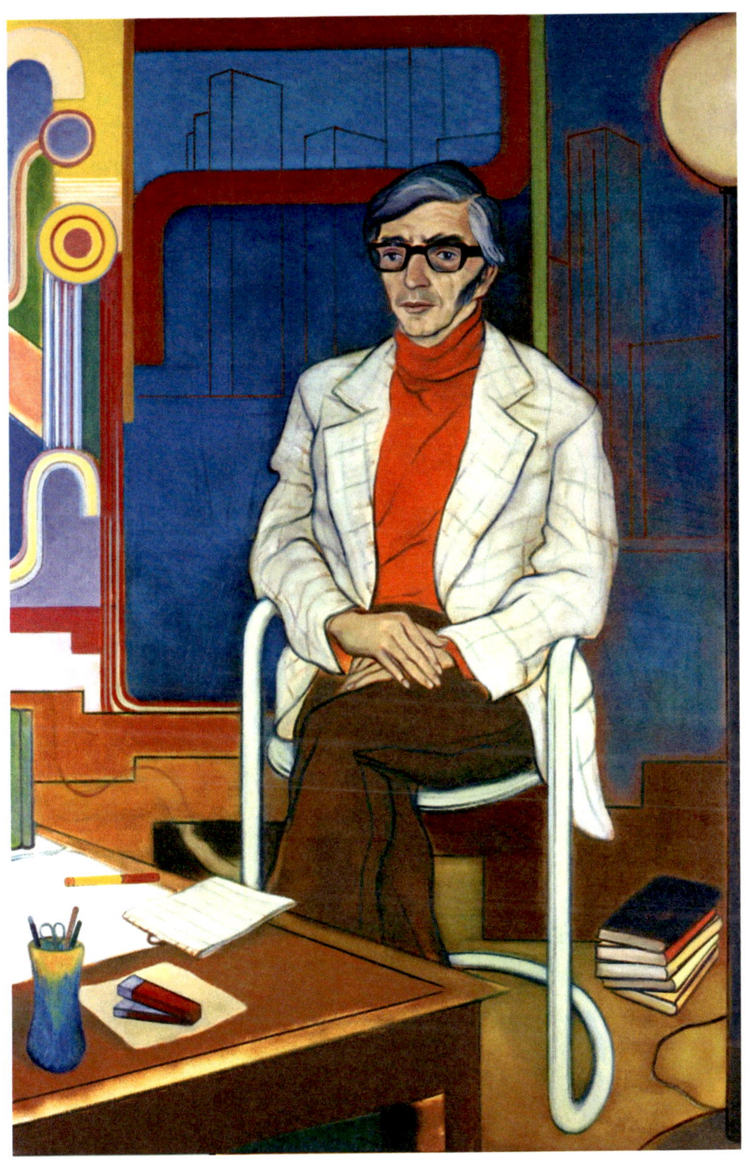

69   *Edwin Morgan* 1980 oil on canvas 153 x 101 cm (Scottish National Portrait Gallery)

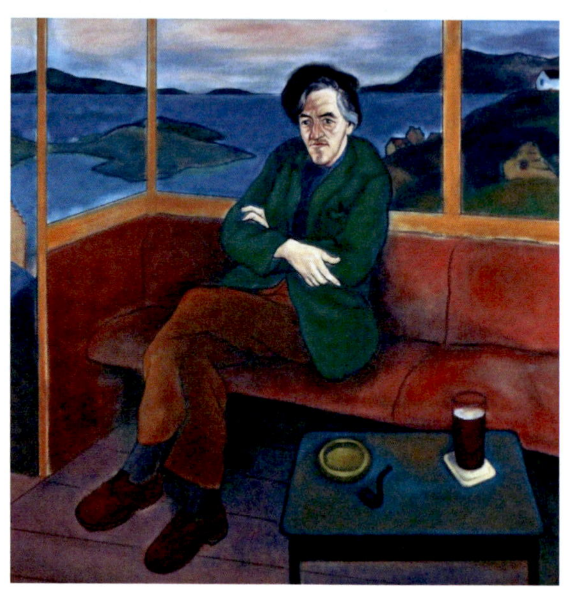

70   *George Mackay Brown* 1980 oil on canvas 152.5 x 152.5 cm
(Stromness Academy, Orkney)

was nonetheless influenced in his art by such mystical and anti-rational
movements as abstraction and Expressionism. Yet these supposed
'contradictions' have not manifested themselves in any detrimental
way in his portraiture; there has been, on the contrary, a consistent
and rational development throughout his career. In fact, it has not been
contradiction, but rather, consistency, along with intelligent flexibility
and accommodation, where form adapts to the specific demands of
content, that have been the hallmarks of Moffat's success as a portrait
painter. From his solid academic training at Edinburgh College of Art
in the early '60s he quickly developed a reliable studio practice in his
approach to making portraits which he has retained throughout his
career. This has been the foundation for a recognisable 'Moffat style'

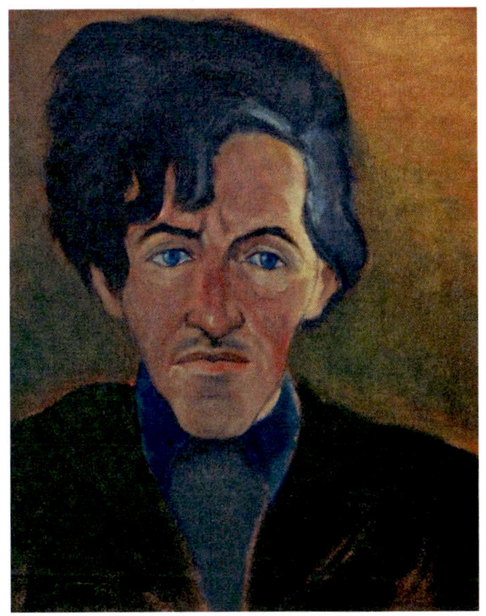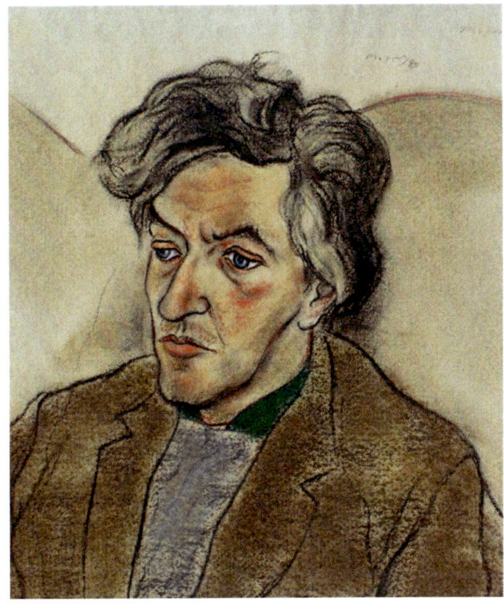

71 *George Mackay Brown* 1980 oil on canvas 37.5 x 30.5cm

72 *George Mackay Brown* 1980 charcoal and pastel on paper 55 x 37.5 cm (private collection)

that gives his work such a marked organic unity.

In his early portraits Moffat experimented with a range of stylistic influences, including aspects of Expressionism, Realism and Modern Classicism, but never allowed this stylistic experimentation to become an end in itself. Moffat, who believes that a portrait is a 'creative collaboration' was careful to strike a balance between the subjective point-of-view of the painter, and the objective expectations of the sitter, and the viewer. This feeling of 'collaboration' and trust between artist and his early subjects, where personal and intimate aspects of appearance and character are examined, places Moffat's portraits of friends and acquaintances within an important strand of modern portraiture. In these portraits there is a special bond between artist and

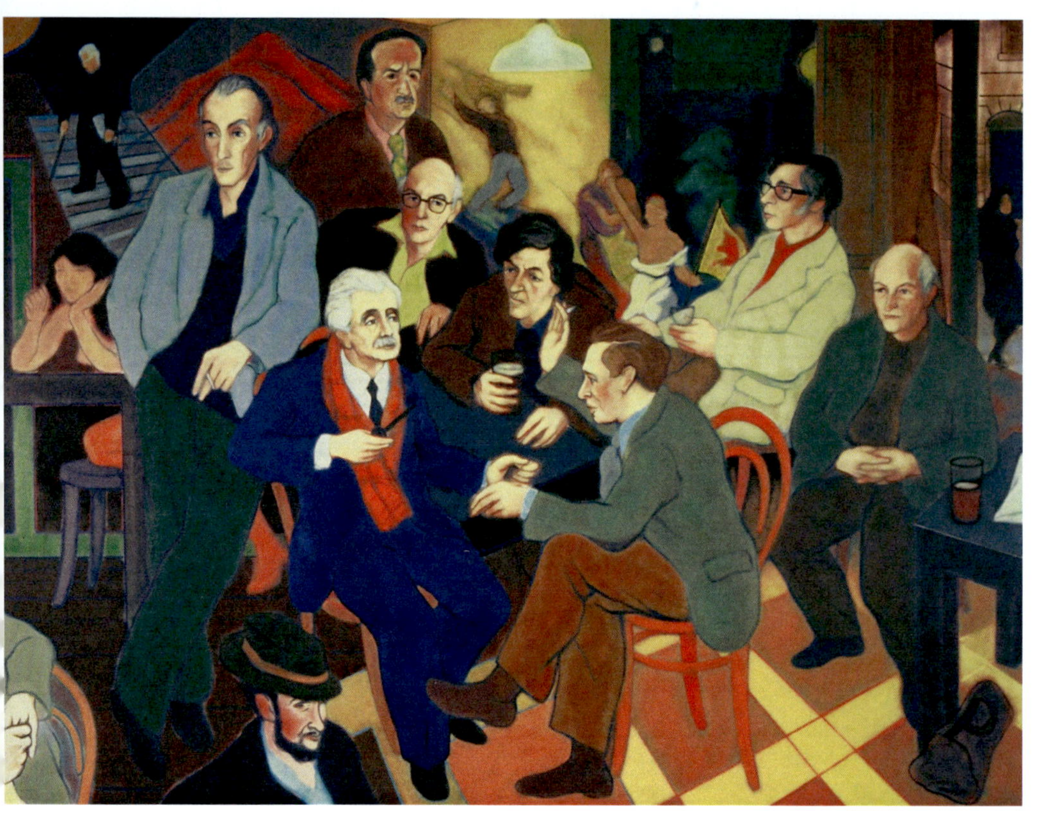

73 *Poets' Pub* 1980/82 oil on canvas 183 x 244 cm (Scottish National Portrait Gallery)
Left to right: JA Tonge (descending steps), Norman MacCaig, Alan Bold (foreground),
Hugh MacDiarmid, Sorley MacLean, Iain Crichton Smith, George Mackay Brown,
Sydney Goodsir Smith, Edwin Morgan and Robert Garioch

sitter through the artist's intimacy with his subject. By circumstance
and necessity, once Moffat began to attract commissioned portraits, his
relationship to his sitters had to change. The image and public persona
of the sitter became a more pressing consideration. Yet while Moffat
rises to the challenges of this type of portraiture and gives well-known
sitters the kind of iconic image the public expects, he still seeks to express

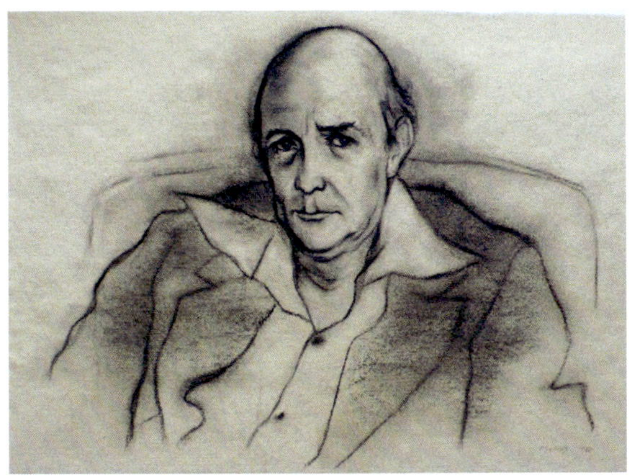

74   *Iain Crichton Smith* 1980 charcoal on paper 38 x 53 cm

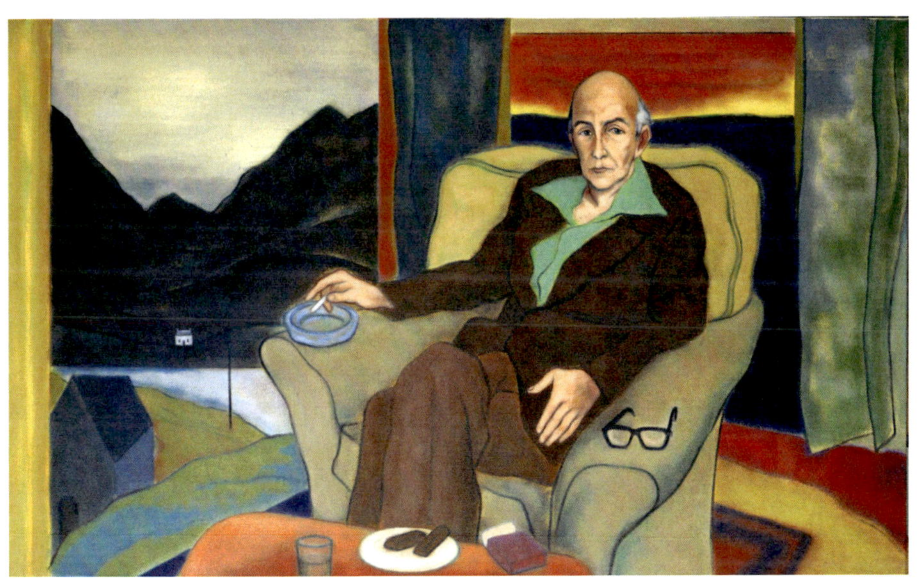

75   *Iain Crichton Smith* 1980 oil on canvas 91.5 x 152.5 cm (Scottish National Portrait Gallery)

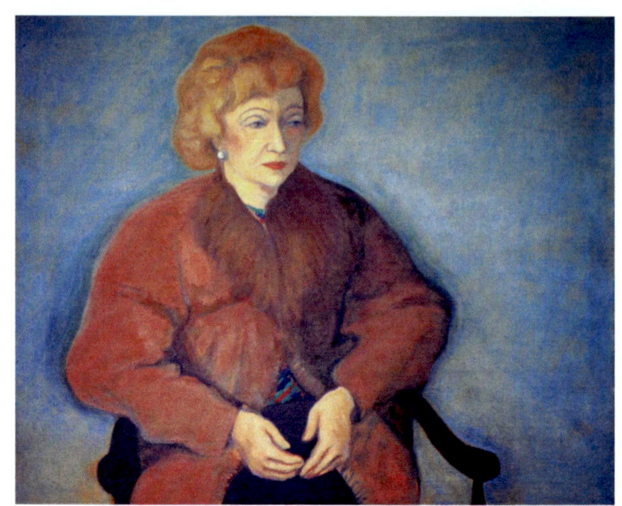

76   *Muriel Spark* (study) 1984
oil on canvas 76.2 x 106.5 cm

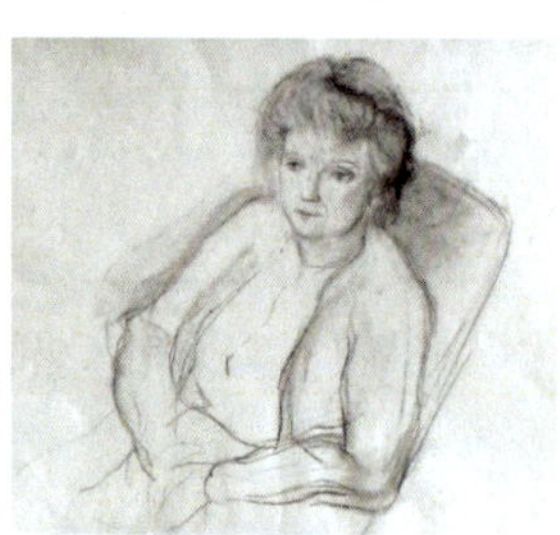

77   *Muriel Spark* 1984
charcoal on paper 53 x 60.5 cm

the distinctive individuality and vital human personality of each of his
subjects. In all of his portraiture, Moffat aims to find a balance between
emotional expression and compositional order. Over the last 50 years or so,
almost single-handed, he has upheld the importance of modern portraiture
in Scotland. A determined champion and outstanding practitioner of
modern portrait painting, he has produced a body of work not only of high
artistic quality, but also of national and historical importance.

A Portrait of the Artist as a Portraitist

Bill Hare in conversation with Alexander Moffat

BH Do you think of yourself as a portrait painter or as a painter who sometimes paints portraits – along with other types of subjects such as landscapes? What position does portraiture hold within your work as a whole?

AM A painter who often paints portraits, with portraiture occupying a central position within my work.

BH What is the relationship between portrait painting and the rest of your work?

AM Most of my paintings include the human figure and painting a portrait is closely related to that main activity. I was once asked if I thought everything was really there in the face? I do think it is. When Braque was asked if he believed painting was enough, his reply was simply 'Yes'. I've recently come across an essay by Siri Hustvedt where she's discussing Picasso's *Weeping Woman*. She writes, 'the face is the locus of identity – the place on the body to which we give our attention. We do not recognise people by their hands or feet, even those intimate to us'. And she elaborates: 'To some degree at least, while we are looking at someone in life, in a photograph, or in a painting, we have her face. The face we perceive supplants our own.'

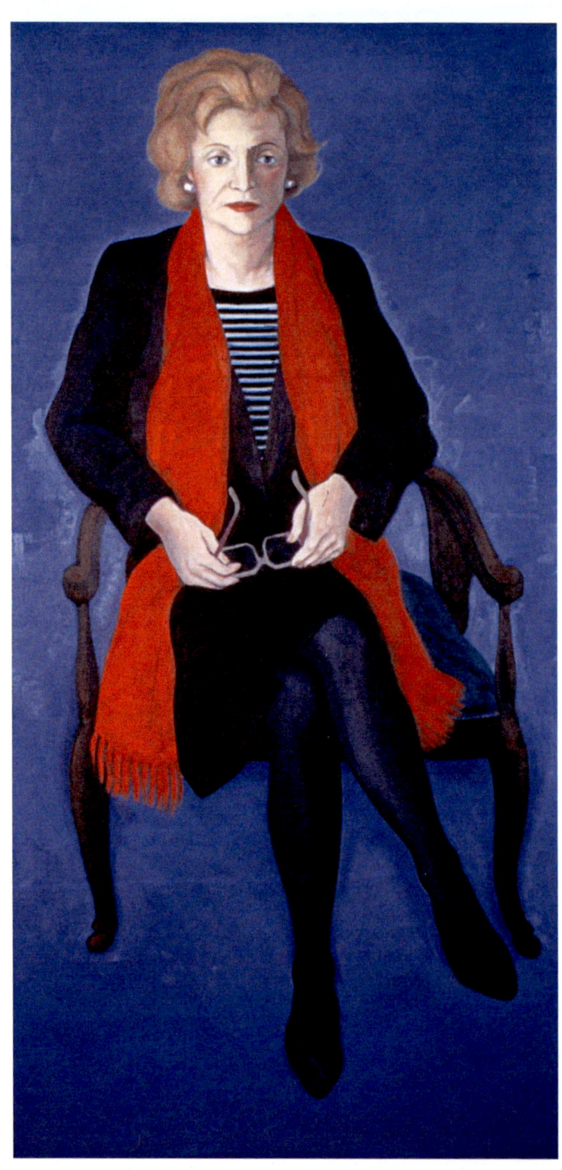

78   *Muriel Spark* 1984 oil on canvas 183 x 91.4 cm (Scottish National Portrait Gallery)

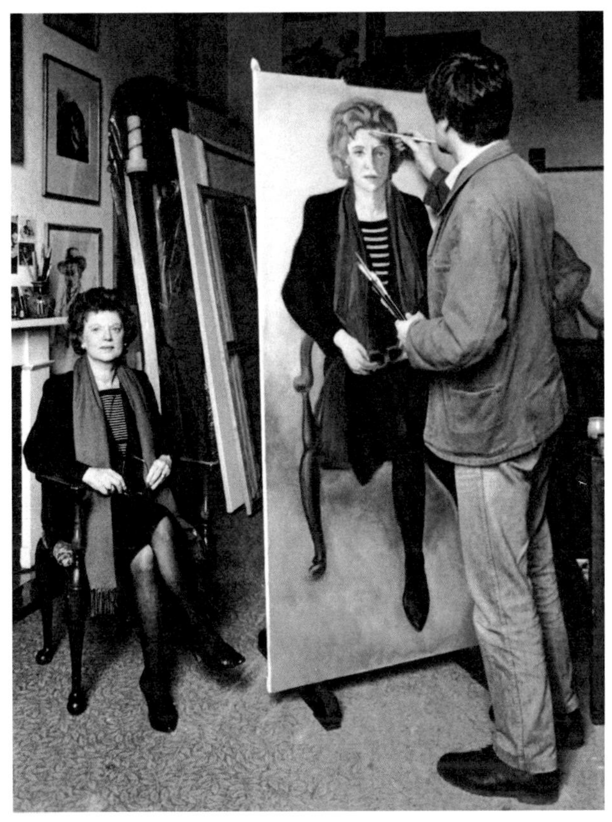

79 Muriel Spark sitting for her portrait (photograph: *Scotsman*)

BH   What drew you to making portraits in the first place?

AM   As a human-centred figurative painter I guess it was inevitable that
I would be drawn to the individual portrait in one way or another.
It all began during my student years when along with John Bellany
it became necessary to move on from an experimental abstract
period towards a language of figuration that would take on board

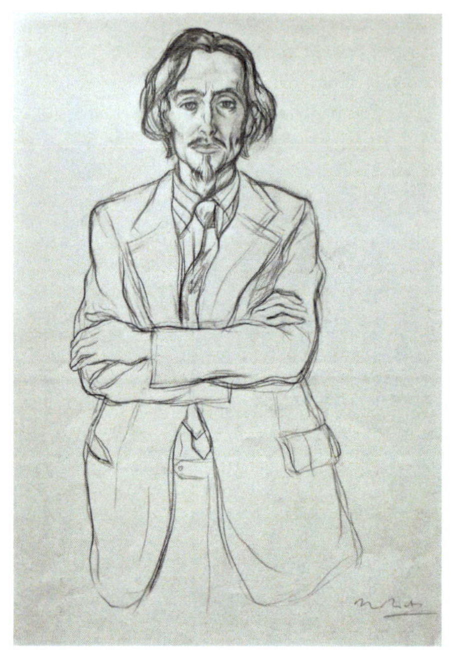

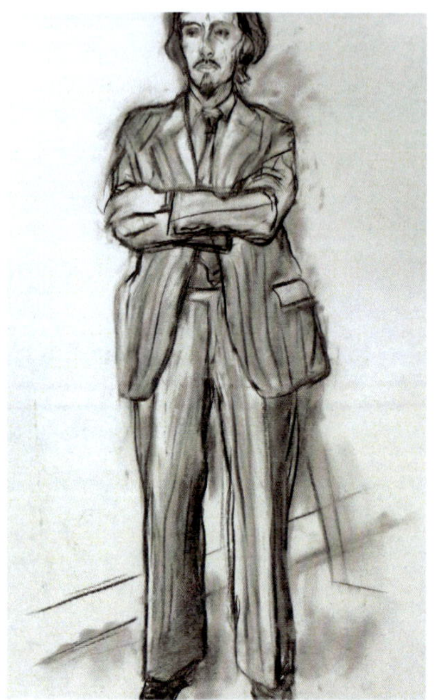

80 *Duncan Thomson* 1981 pencil on paper 46 x 32 cm

81 *Duncan Thomson* 1981 charcoal on paper
50 x 32 cm

the modernist viewpoint developed in the early years of the 20th
century. The catalyst for what was a momentous decision was
both political and aesthetic, a combination of hearing Hugh
MacDiarmid speak at the Edinburgh International Festival's
Writers Conference and seeing a large Kokoschka exhibition at the
Tate, both in the summer of 1962. Kokoschka's humanism struck
a chord and his youthful portraits of Adolf Loos and Herwarth
Walden, painted in Vienna in that special era before 1914, were
the works that first convinced me that painting portraits was
consistent with my desire to be a modern artist.

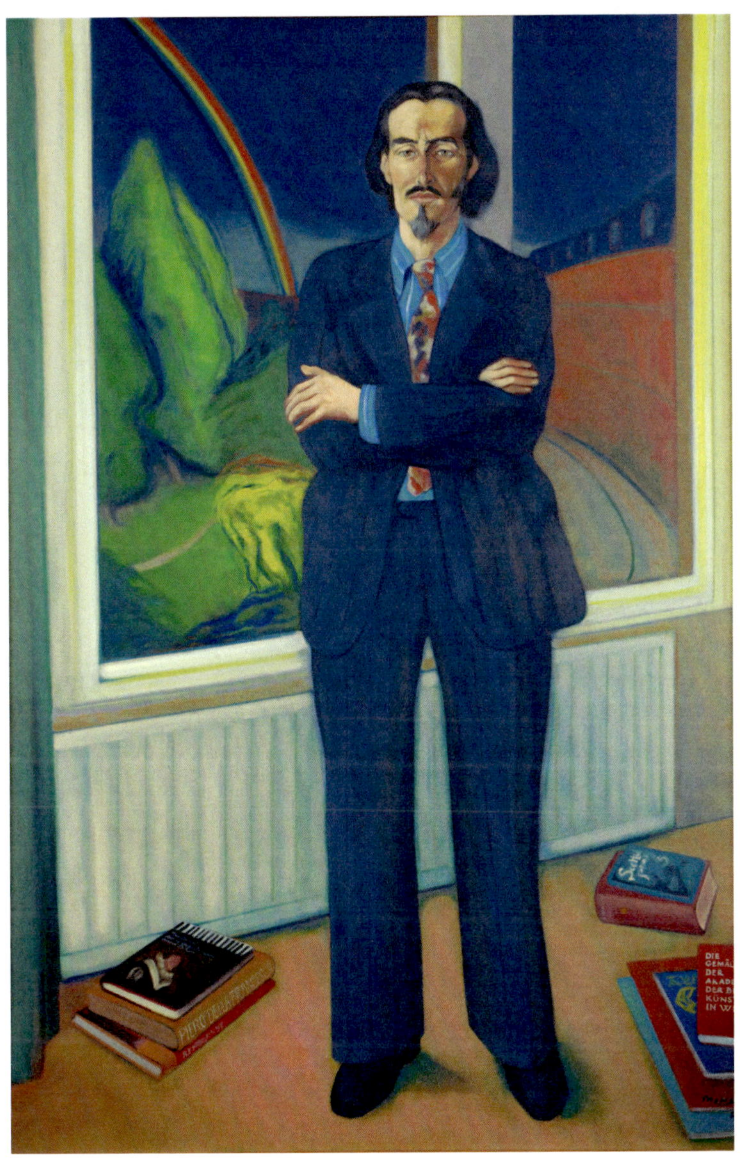

82 *Duncan Thomson* 1981 oil on canvas 183 x 123 cm (private collection)

BH   So you see the genre of portraiture as having a significant relationship with Modernism?

AM   I do, but the relationship needs careful explanation. Modernism took many different directions in the first half of the 20th century in all of the arts. In music, the main directions stemmed from national traditions… Stravinsky and Prokofiev/Russia… Bartok and Kodaly/Hungary… Debussy and Ravel/France… Schoenberg and Webern/Austria… Vaughan Williams in England and Erik Chisholm in Scotland. In the visual arts there was a huge difference in what happened in Paris as opposed to Berlin, but portraiture was never neglected by any of the main modern movements wherever they were. Within the various arenas of Cubism, Futurism, Surrealism, German Expressionism, *Neue Sachlichkeit*, and so forth, portraits of distinction emerged. Scotland's pioneering abstractionist, William Johnstone, painted portraits of his friends and fellow borderers Hugh MacDiarmid and Francis George Scott.

Of course, there were other groups of artists who rejected figuration, most famously centred on the Bauhaus, in their desire to create an art that was independent of history and tradition. With the arrival of Walter Gropius in America in the mid-'30s these views gained the high ground. During the Cold War art became politicised with figuration strongly associated with Stalinist socialist realism. Clement Greenberg announced that 'abstraction is the major mode of expression in our time' and a hard-line dogma emerged intent on projecting a 'proper

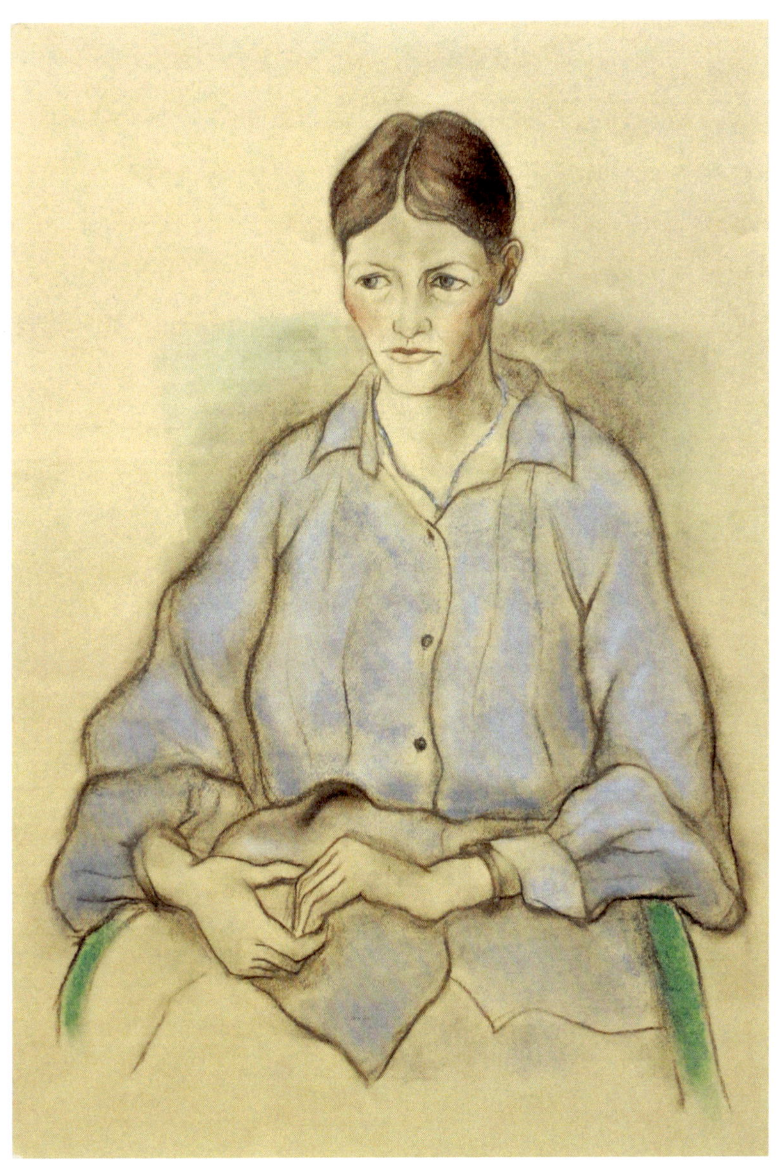

83 *Susanne Dunbar* 1980 pastel on coloured paper 49 x 34.5 cm

modernist style' that discarded the work of many of the most creative and individual artists of the century. Modernism became 'Americanised' with the autonomous 'art object' its main goal. Ideology, tradition and history, all fundamental to European culture, were ignored and rejected. By the mid-'60s art schools had caved in and promoted this version of Modernism, but for better or worse there was resistance in Scotland. This was the situation I found myself dealing with as I began to make my way as an artist.

It's taken time, but we now seem to have moved on from that kind of narrow inclusiveness, while gaining a greater awareness of the importance of local circumstances and tradition. The work of many of the great modern painters from Picasso onwards has been reassessed, with portraiture rightly regarded as a key component of their oeuvre. We no longer consider Modigliani or Balthus less modern because they painted portraits. Above all, we now clearly understand that never again should one single version of history be accepted as the truth.

BH   Let's move on to a more general question – what do you think is the status of portraiture today? Recently there have been several major portrait exhibitions in London, with Picasso and Cézanne at the National Portrait Gallery and Hockney at the Royal Academy. Do you see this as a revival in the critical and public interest in portraiture as a distinct art form in its own right? If so, what do you think has brought this about?

AM   Cézanne is rightly regarded as the 'father' of modern portraiture

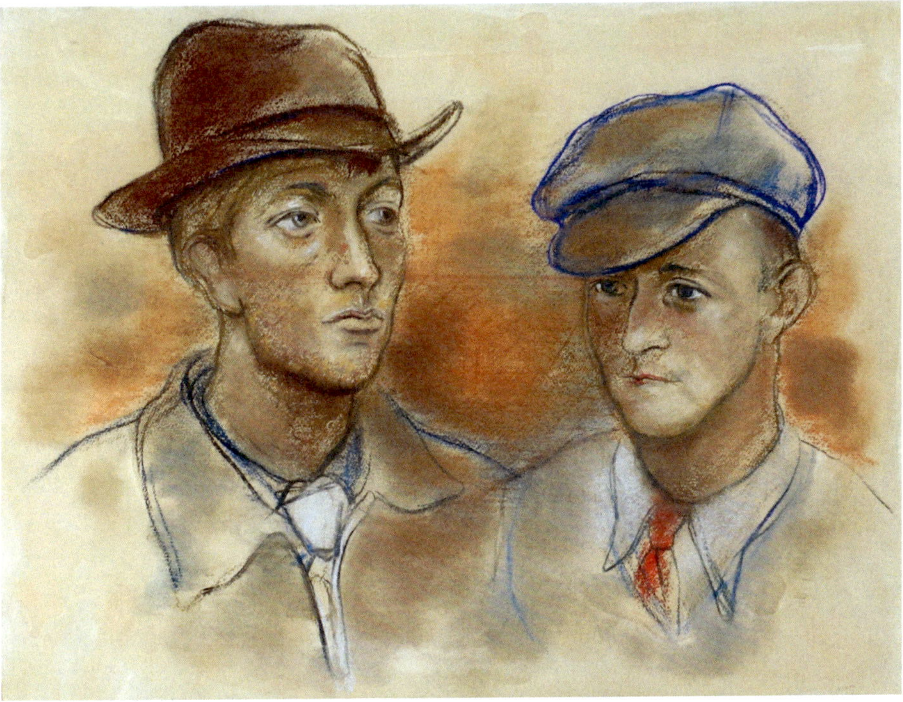

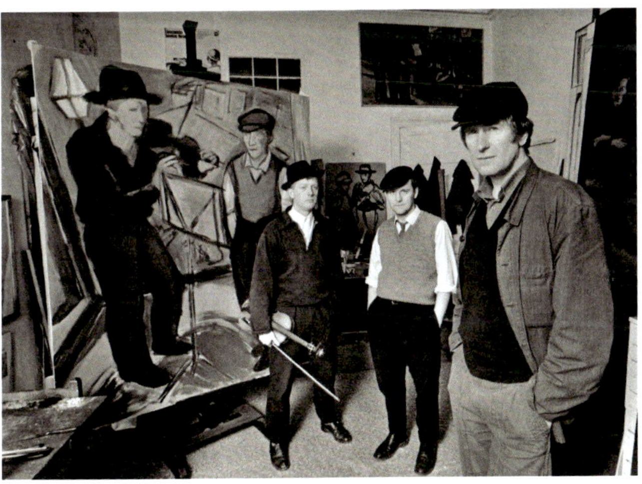

84 *Graham Durward and Brian Gibb (The Two Musicians)* 1985 pastel on paper 49.5 x 66 cm

85 Graham Durward and Brian Gibb with Alexander Moffat (photograph: Sean Hudson)

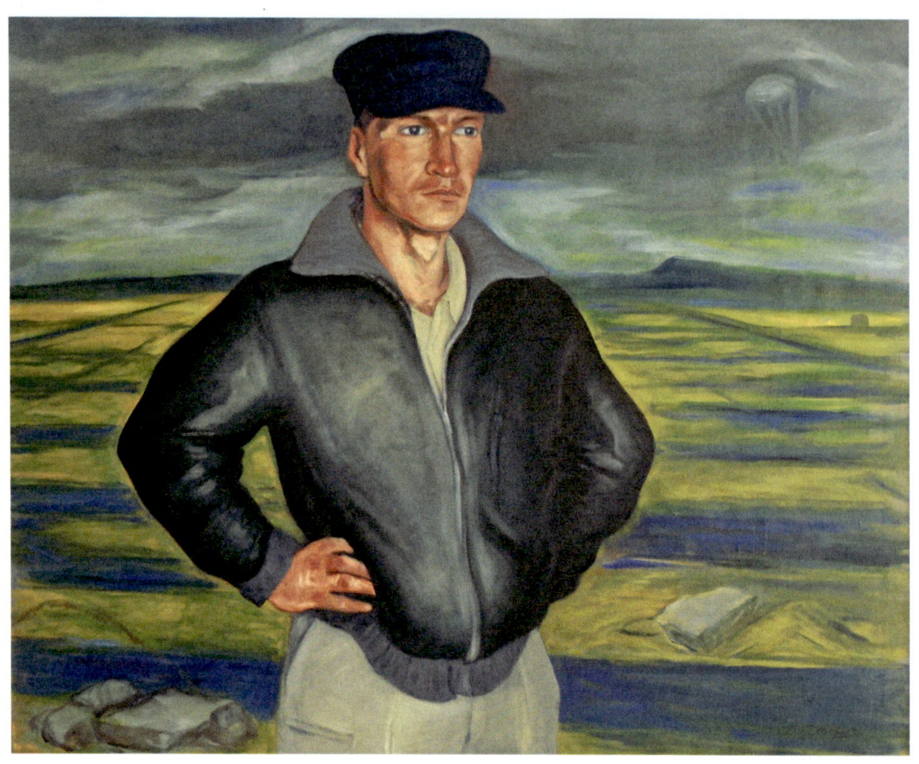

86   *Stephen Barclay* 1987 oil on canvas   122 x 152.5 cm

and both Picasso and Hockney painted wonderful portraits, but
I'm not sure if they actually reflect the status of portraiture right
now although I wish they did! There has always been a popular
interest in portraiture, but critical opinion, on the other hand, is
much more divided. In the '60s when I made my first portraits,
portraiture was critically suspect, regarded as a deeply flawed
genre. This state of affairs was largely historical in origin. In the
18th and 19th centuries the fashionable priorities of gentility

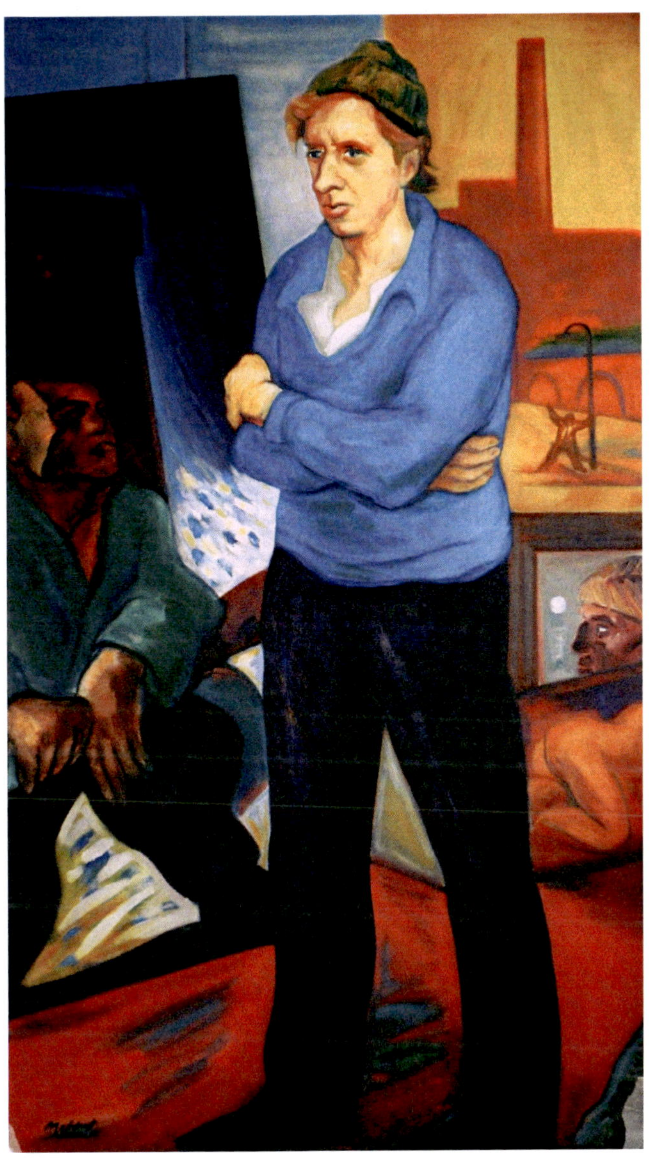

87 *Peter Howson* 1987 oil on canvas 183 x 91.5 cm (private collection)

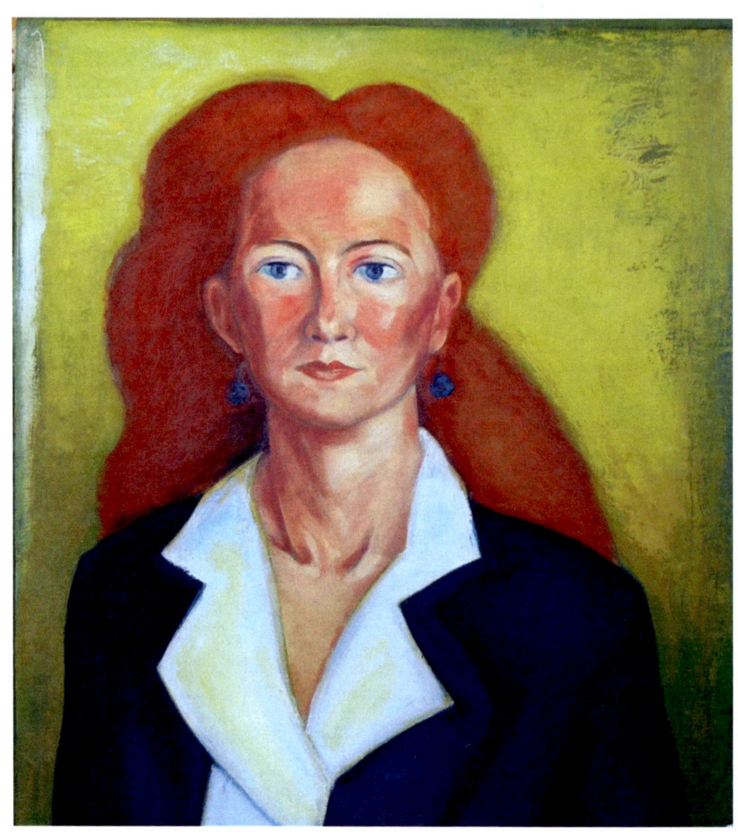

88 *Fiona McLeod* 1987 oil on canvas 57 x 52 cm

throughout Europe generated unquantified numbers of portraits
of rich people, the nobility, dukes and duchesses, flattering
representations of the utmost banality. I saw portraits like that
in the Royal Scottish Academy during my student period, hack
work with no relevance to modern life or painting. At the time a
critical voice such as John Berger questioned the very nature of

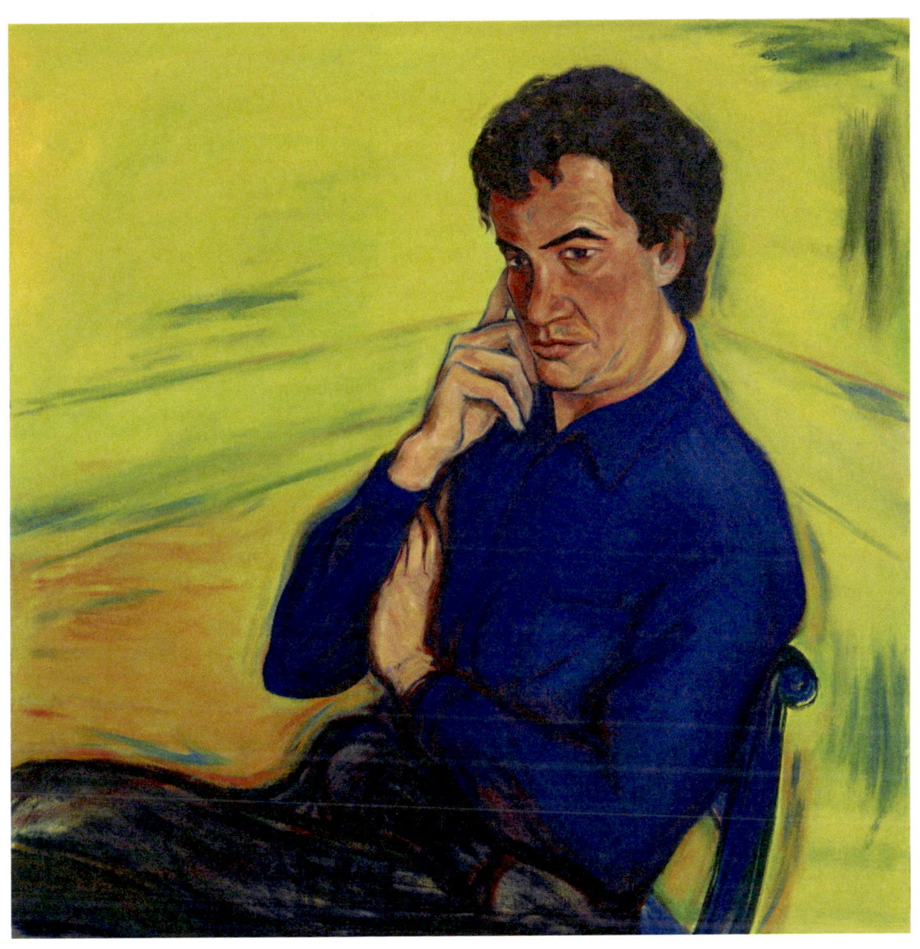

89 *Jim Birrell* 1987 oil on canvas 122 x 122 cm

portraiture – 'it seems unlikely that any important portraits will ever be painted again' – arguing that after Géricault portraiture degenerated into servile and crass flattery. He qualified this by making reference to 'those sincere artists' – Corot, Courbet, Degas,

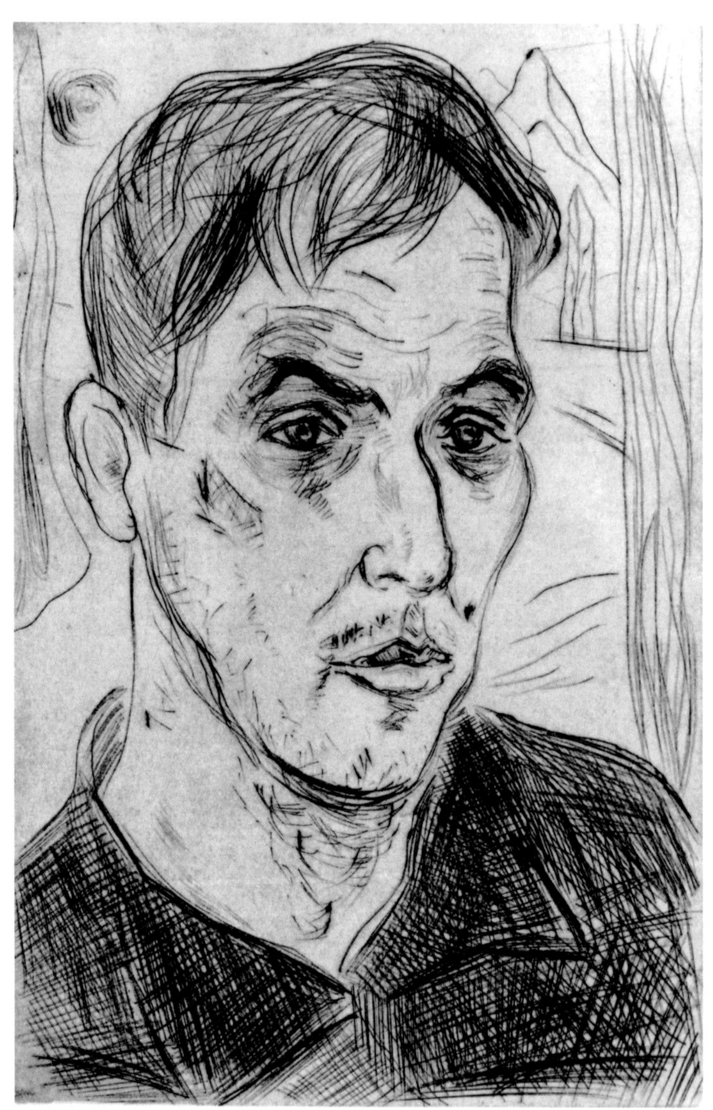

90   *Adrian Wiszniewski* 1987 drypoint 22 x 14.5 cm (plate size)

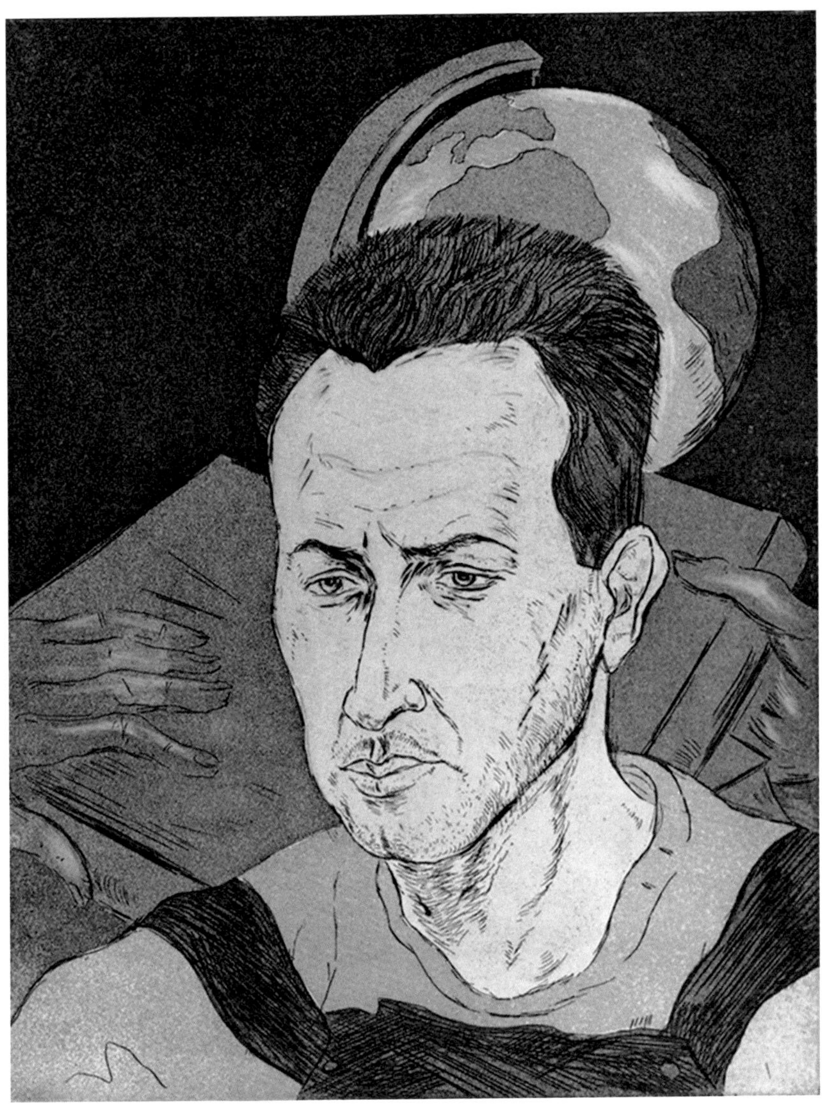

91   *Ken Currie* 1987 etching 32 x 24.5 cm (plate size)

Cézanne and Van Gogh – who made intimate portraits of their friends. It was this aspect of portraiture that had an immediate appeal for me.

BH   We might take up Berger's infamous death sentence on portraiture later, but can I ask you – what do we mean by portraiture now, compared with the past? For instance, I just read in a Howard Hodgkin obituary by a curator at the National Portrait Gallery that Hodgkin's abstract paintings should be considered as poetic portraits – where it is distant memory rather than direct observation that is involved. Do you not think that is stretching the notion of portraiture too far? How would you define what constitutes a portrait in the 21st century?

AM   I'm unsure as to what's meant by portraiture now. A lot of what I see has nothing to do with painting, but is more concerned with copying the surface information of a photograph. It all appears quite reactionary and academic.

Putting current fashions to one side, defining what a painted portrait is in the 21st century shouldn't be too problematic. After all, we humans haven't changed much over the past thousand years in terms of visual identity, nor in other ways as well. It seems we were much more equal in the middle years of the 20th century, in the aftermath of two terrible world wars, but now we are much more unequal again. Portraits should tell us about all of these things. Indeed, most of the great portraits of the past century do precisely that, with time and place right there in the portraits

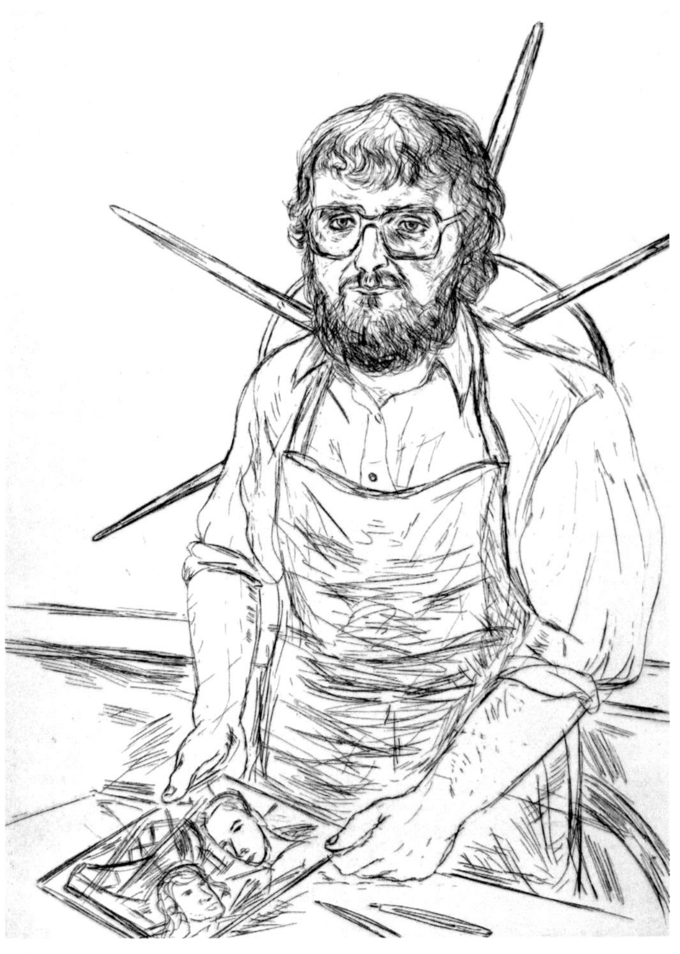

92 *Alfons Bytautas* 1987 etching 45 x 33 cm (plate size)

of Beckmann and Dix, as well as in the portraits of very different
artists such as Klimt, Spencer or Warhol. Hodgkin's paintings
have little in common with the conventions of portraiture, but the
so-called School of London produced several outstanding portrait

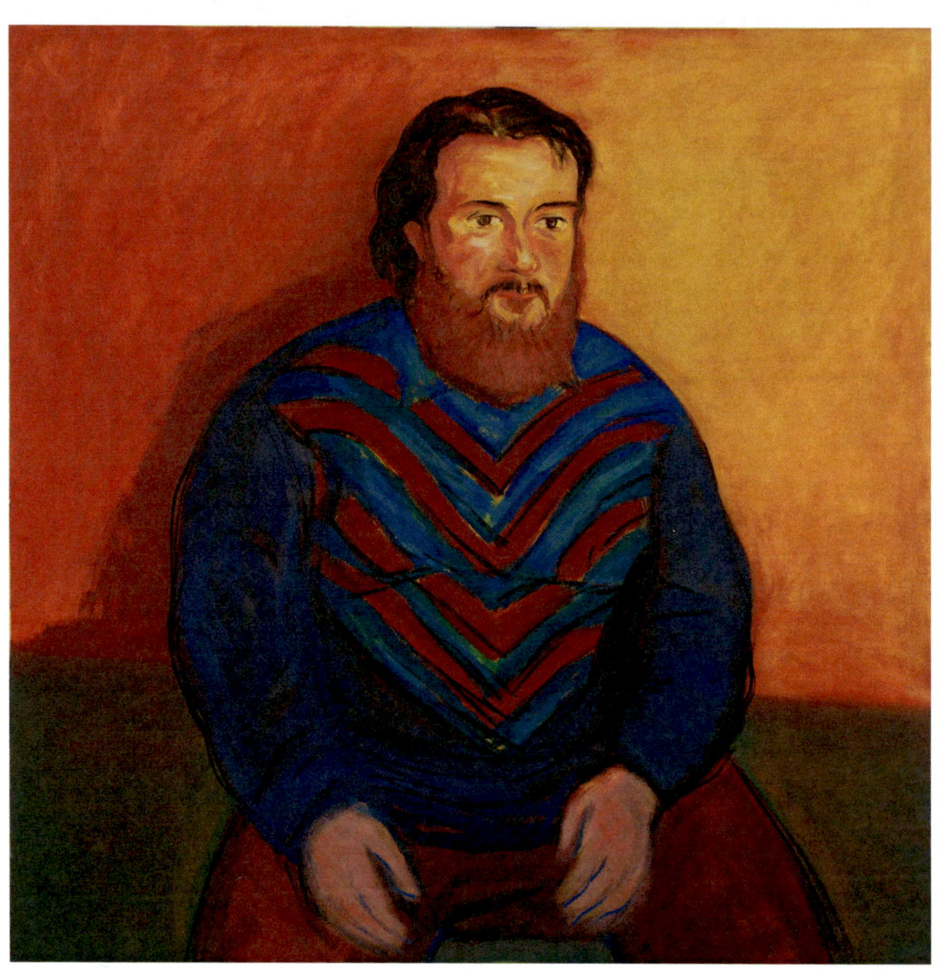

93 *Arthur Watson* 1987 oil on canvas 137 x 137 cm

painters – Bacon, Freud, Auerbach, Kitaj and Hockney – and we should add Paula Rego to the list. We've also recently seen the portraits of Alice Neel in Edinburgh. All of these late 20th-century painters provide models for a continuing portrait tradition.

 You just mentioned the allure of the photographic image, and of course photography has dogged portraiture since its invention. Does photography play any part, either directly or indirectly, in your attitude and approach to making portraits?

AM I worked as a photographer for several years after leaving art college and I continue to take lots of photographs, but for me painting and photography are quite separate activities. Of course, there's been a continuing and fascinating dialogue between them from Delacroix and Degas onwards and we mustn't forget the influence of painting on photography.

There are a number of photographers I particularly admire – Paul Strand, Edward Weston, Walker Evans, August Sander and Manuel Alvarez Bravo are particular favourites, and I've more than likely been influenced by specific aspects of their work. The photographs of a painter like Edvard Munch interest me greatly too. His experiments with double exposures, hand-held self-portraits, etc, fed into his painting, but when asked to explain the difference between painting and photography his reply was straight to the point: 'The camera cannot compete with painting as it cannot be used in heaven or hell.'

We live in an age obsessed by the photographic image and I agree with Wim Wenders when he says the task of the artist is to retrieve the image from its present degraded condition. According to Wenders, there are so many images circulating the globe with ever increasing speed that we look at all the time, but we no longer appear to have the means or the skills to see. He regards the

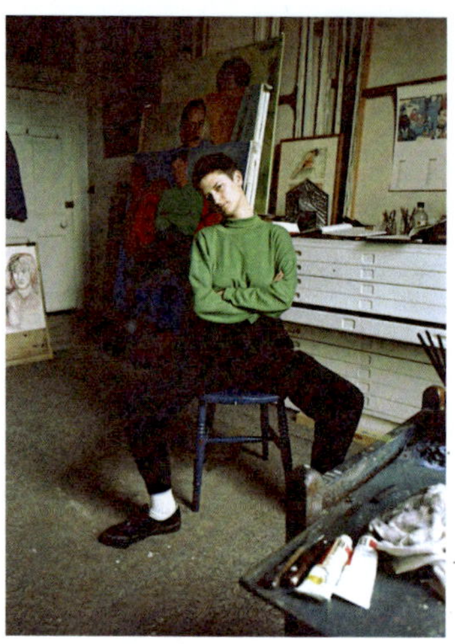

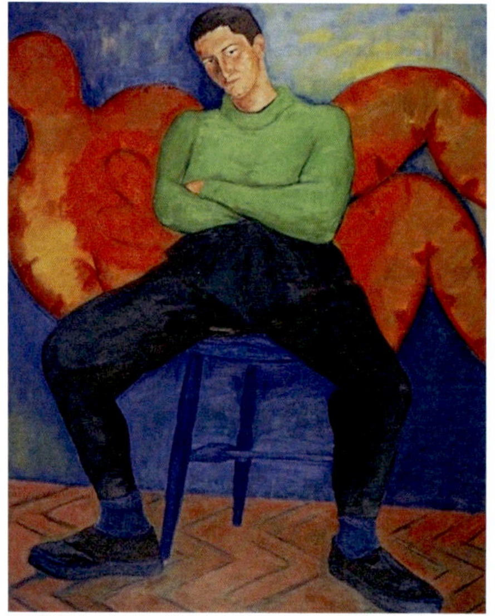

94   Gwen Hardie sitting for her portrait (photograph)

95   *Gwen Hardie* 1987 oil on canvas 152.5 x 122 cm (Scottish National Gallery of Modern Art)

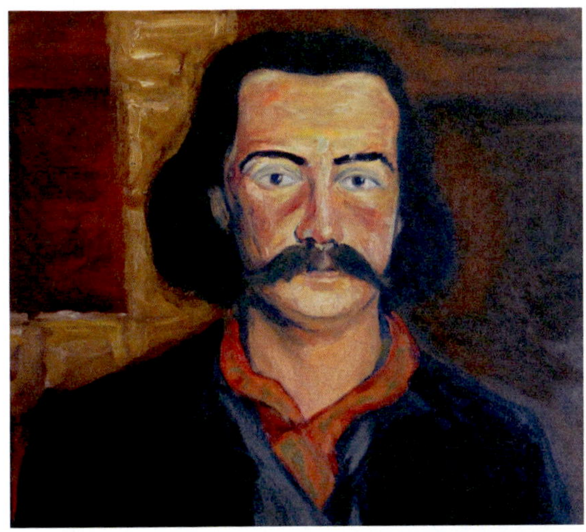

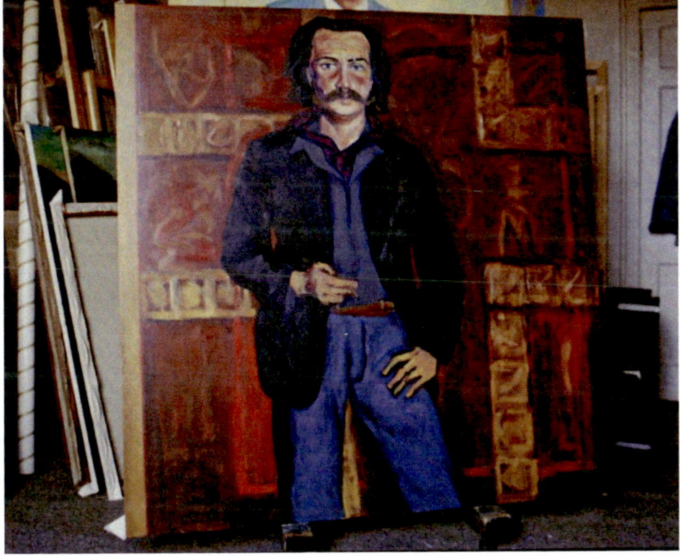

96   *Stuart MacKenzie* 1987 oil on canvas 61 x 71 cm (cut down version)

97   *Stuart MacKenzie* 1987 oil on canvas 152.4 x 152.4 cm (original portrait)

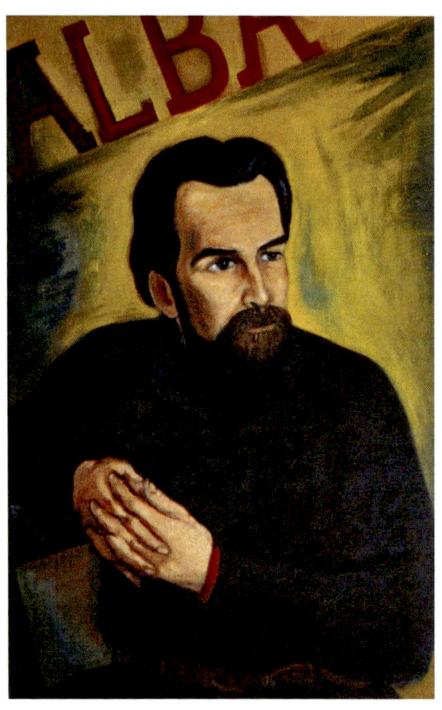

98 *Peter Hill* 1989 oil on canvas 91.5 x 61 cm
(private collection)

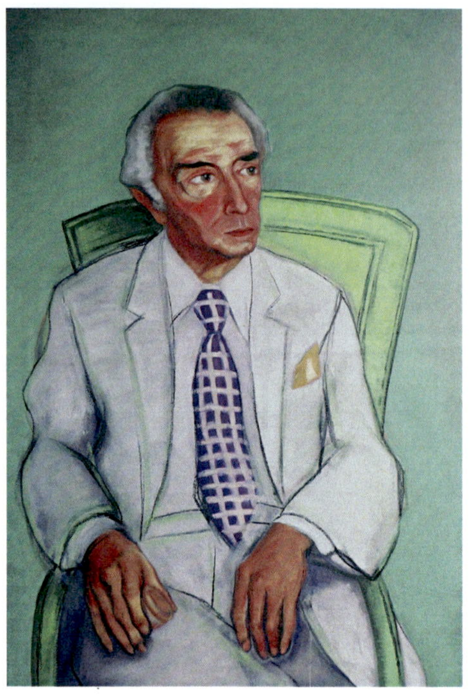

99 *Emilio Coia* 1989 oil on canvas 91.5 x 61 cm
(private collection)

'recovery' of the image as an ethical and moral task essential for
the future of all visual art.

BH Despite the loosening of firm generic categorisation and the
ubiquity of the photographic image, most people still seem to
feel that the painted portrait should involve the depiction of
visual resemblance of another person. How important to you is
individual 'likeness' in your practice of portraiture? It seems to

me that a mimetic correspondence is more of a concern in your preparatory drawings than in the finished painted portraits.

AM   Likeness is important – there's no point in denying that simple fact. All of the great portrait painters, from Titian and Velázquez, to Manet and Degas and even Picasso, insisted upon likeness and that was why they were so admired. I'm always conscious of the need to capture a likeness, but this has to be balanced against the desire to make a good painting. I usually feel I can't really get to grips with the painting aspect until the sitter has gone. The encounter with the sitter is the starting point but other ideas quickly come into play. Painting a portrait is a subjective business linked to stylistic and aesthetic concerns with likeness at the mercy of those conflicting elements. My preparatory drawings are all about getting to know the sitter, attempting to gain a kind of visual understanding that can be used during the painting process to go beyond what might be referred to as mere appearance – perhaps in the same way that a musician must first get the notes under his or her fingers before going on to develop a personal interpretation of the score. I like the way Max Beckmann put it: 'The identification with the object must be perfect… but I do not have to tell you there can be no question of thoughtless imitation of nature.'

BH   Or Matisse's statement 'exactitude is not truth'. Of course, 'likeness' is not a very stable concept. So what other aspects – over and above resemblance – should the portraitist be seeking out in the sitter?

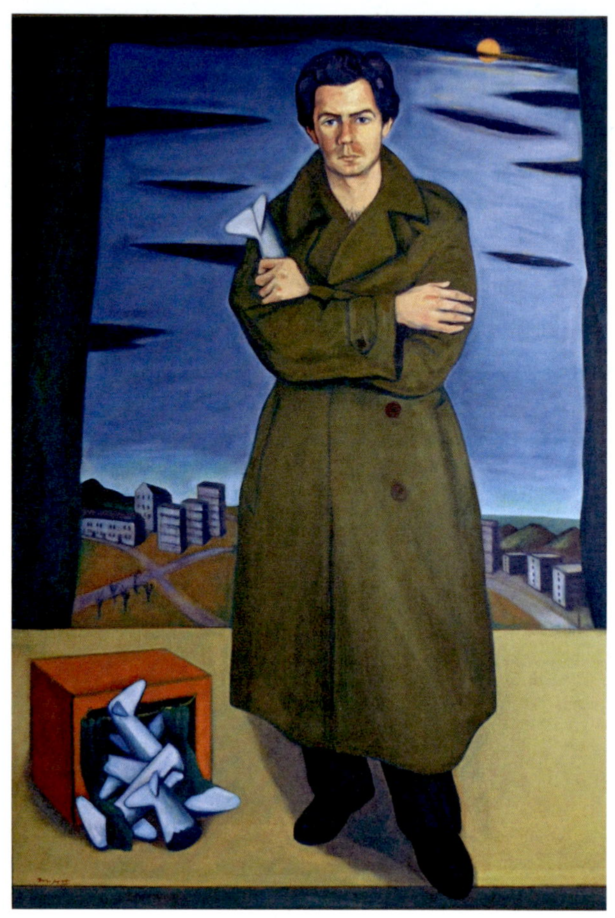

100 *David Hosie* 1988 oil on canvas 175 x 122 cm

AM   I agree that likeness is an elusive concept, but the painter seeks permanence. I'm with John Berger on this when he says, 'Painting is, first, an affirmation of the visible which surrounds us and which continually appears and disappears. Without the disappearing,

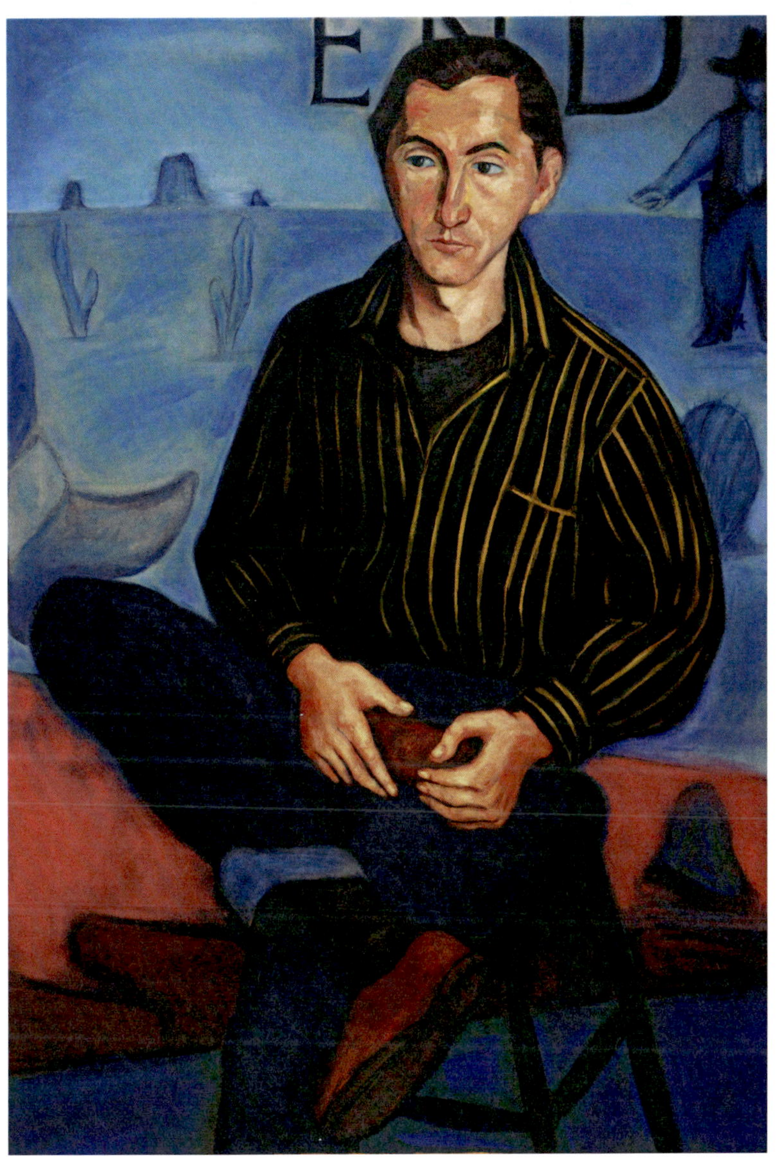

101 *Henry Kondracki* 1987 oil on canvas 152 x 106.5 cm

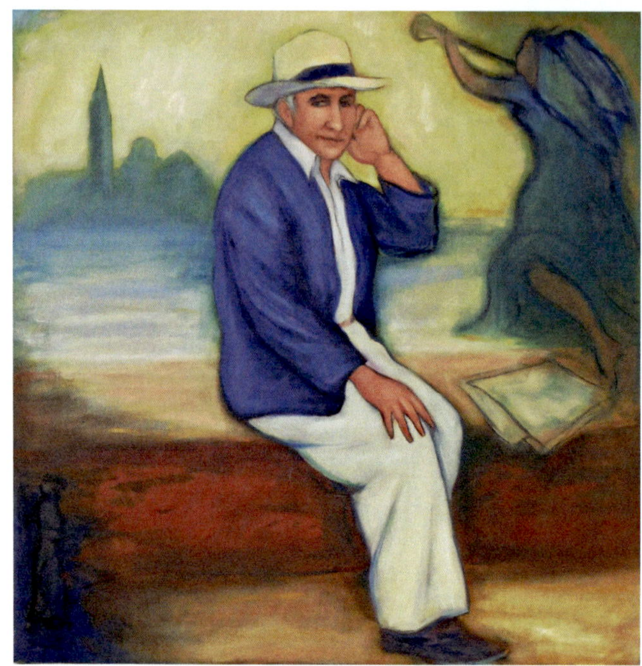

102 *Richard Demarco in Venice* 1988 oil on canvas 137 x 137 cm

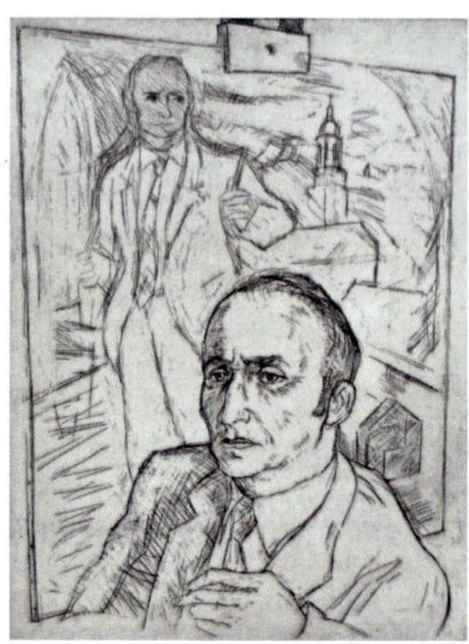

103 *Richard Demarco* 1987 etching
33 x 25 cm (plate size)

there would perhaps be no impulse to paint, for the visible itself would possess the surety (the permanence) which painting strives to find. More directly than any other art, painting is an affirmation of the existent, of the physical world into which mankind has been thrown.' So in a sense, a portrait is an affirmation of an individual human being.

BH   Would you say that these other qualities are of a more general nature – involving social status, intellectual attitude and sexual

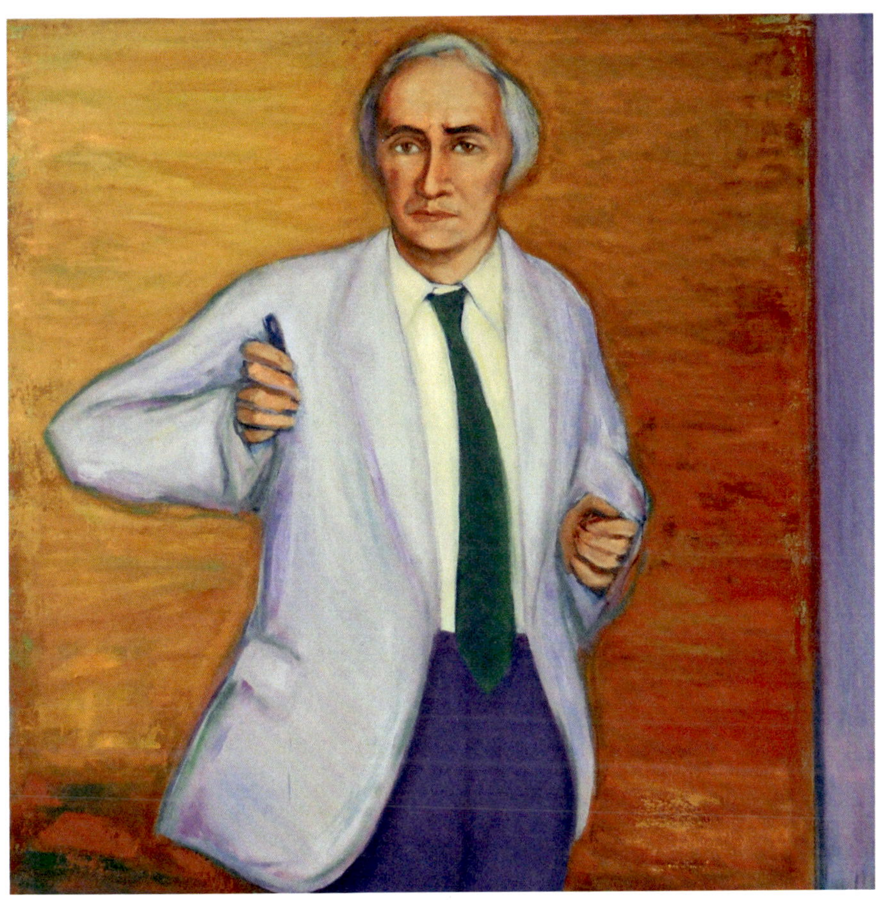

104 *Richard Demarco* 1988 oil on canvas 122 x 122 cm

identity, for example? Here we are dealing with something more akin to the typical rather than the individual, are we not?

AM   Social status is certainly one way of analysing a portrait, but would an artist really describe painting a portrait in those terms?

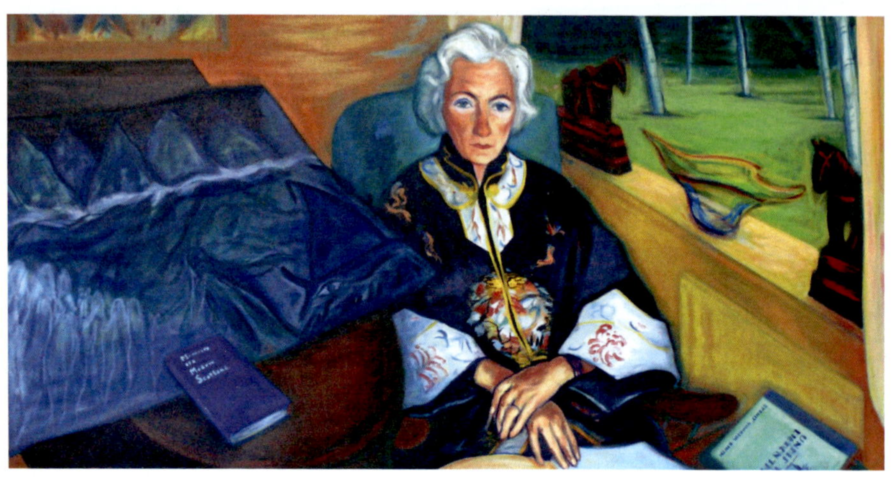

105 *Mary MacIver* 1988 oil on canvas 76 x 152 cm (Richard Demarco Archive)

I'll call on Cézanne (in a letter to Henri Gasquet) to explain:

'If you think it's easy to do a portrait… between you and me, Henri, I mean what makes up your personality and mine, there is the world, the sun, what's going on, what we see in common. Our clothes, our bodies, the play of light, I have to dig through all that. That's where the slightest misplaced brushstroke spoils everything'. And he continues: 'If I weave around your expression the entire network of little bits of blue and brown that are there, that combine there, I'll get you to look as you look, on my canvas. One stroke after the other, one after the other. And if I'm unemotional, if I draw and paint as they do in the schools, I'll no longer see anything. A mouth, a nose, by the book, always the same, with no soul, no mystery, no passion.' For nearly all of the artists I admire, mystery, passion, soul, come first, rather than social status or sexual identity.

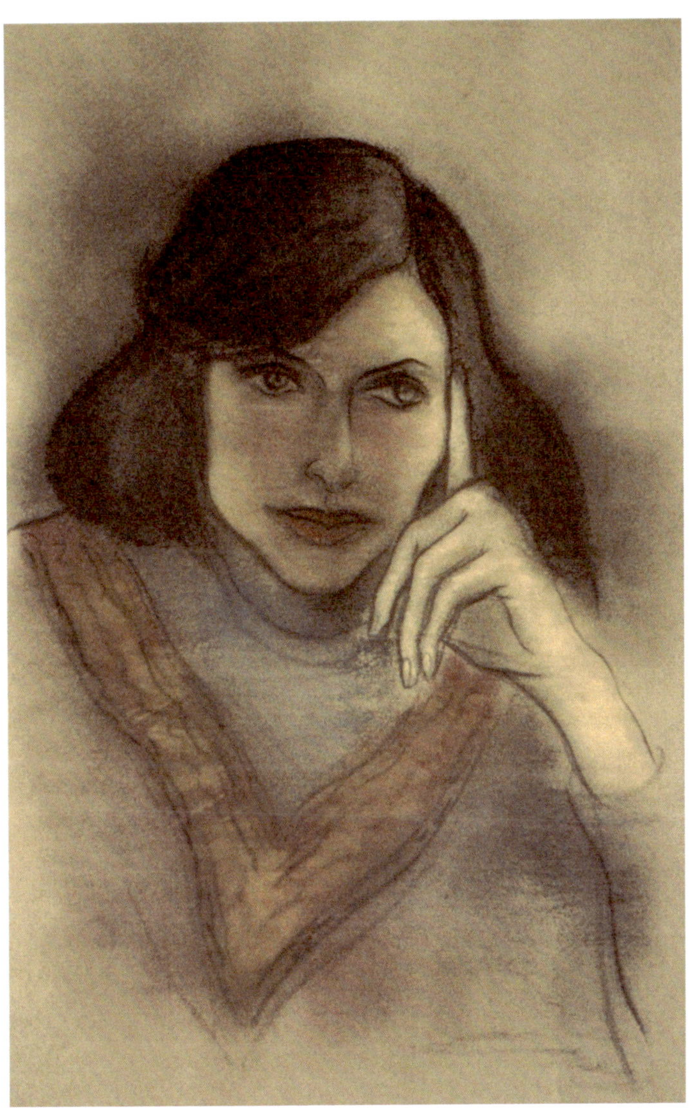

106 *Sandra Fisher* 1991 pastel on coloured paper 48 x 34 cm (private collection)

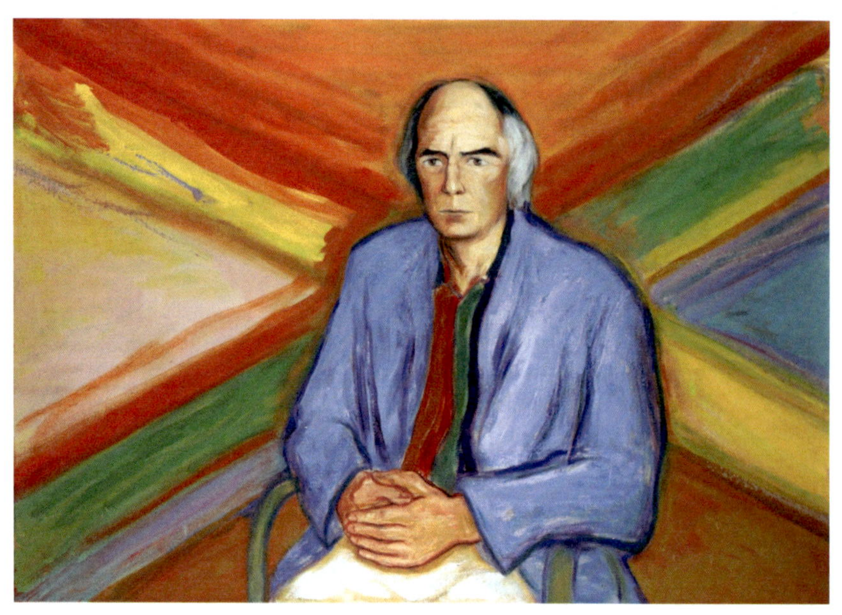

107 *Albert Irvin* 1989 oil on canvas 106 x 152.4 cm

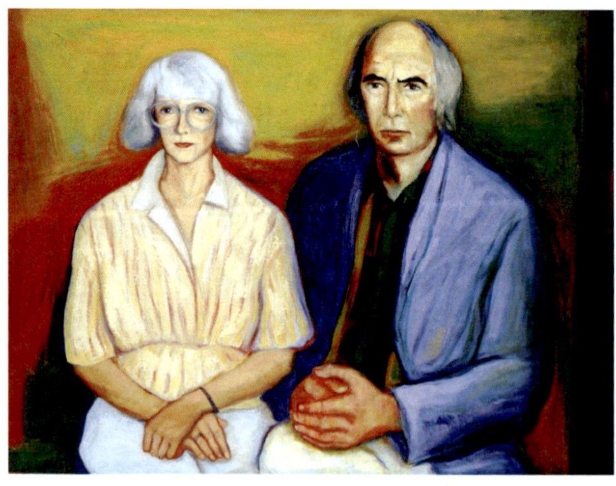

108 *Albert and Betty Irvin* 1989 oil on canvas 91.5 x 122 cm (private collection)

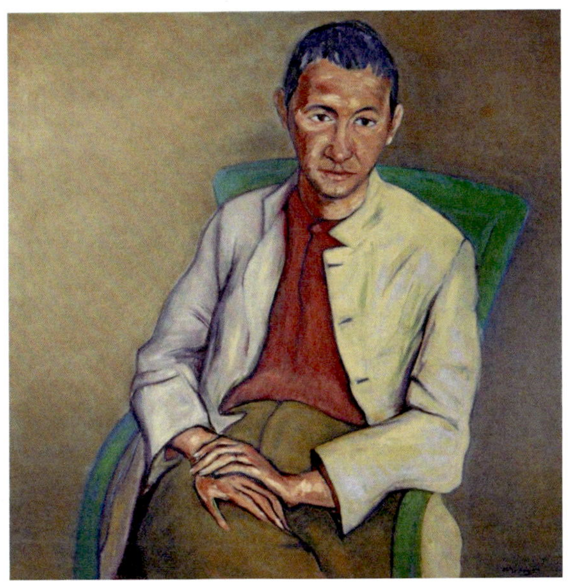

109 *Timothy Hyman* 1987 oil on canvas 122 x 122 cm (Kirkcaldy Galleries, Fife)

BH   This seems to echo some of the concerns that Professor Ernst
Gombrich raises in his essay 'The Mask and the Face', where
the truly enquiring portrait painter must see past the transient
and the superficial and uncover the permanent and profound
visual character of the sitter. Is that what you are seeking in your
painting, and how is that achieved?

AM   That's what I'm after… but how is it achieved? I wish I knew,
for that's the crux of the matter – how to penetrate beyond the
superficial and achieve profundity? One has to keep on trying. We
can see what Gombrich is talking about in the late self-portraits

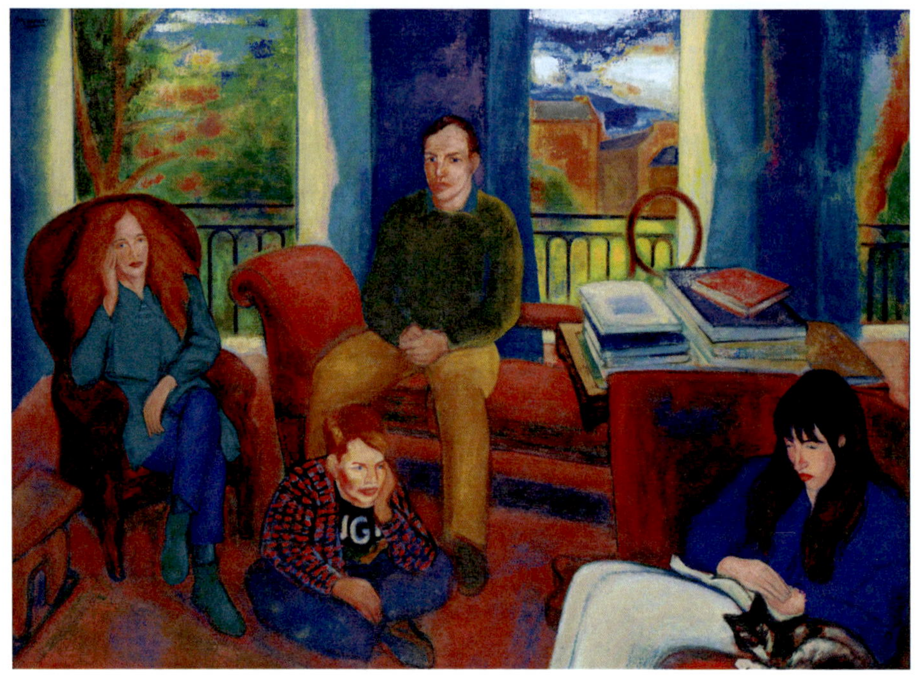

110 *The Munro Family* 1994 oil on canvas 107 x 152.5 cm (private collection)

of Rembrandt and that's a kind of benchmark. No wonder
Beckmann always referred to him as the 'chief'. I think too, that's
what I recognised in those early Kokoschka portraits, critically
acclaimed by his Viennese contemporaries 'as x-raying the soul of his
sitters'. He didn't achieve that depth of insight in his later portraits
which reveals just how difficult it is to do so.

BH   Of course, these two central concerns of portraiture – individual
likeness and general type – are not mutually exclusive; in the best
portraits, they are successfully integrated by the artist. In your own

practice, how do you accommodate the twin demands of likeness
and type – which of them do you prefer to emphasise?

AM I always concentrate on the individual in front of me. That for me
is the most important part of portraiture. It's about attempting
to capture the humanity of my sitters. If one can make a good
painting on that basis then the twin demands you speak about
should take care of themselves. I keep on coming back to the idea
that a portrait must work as a painting, not simply as a likeness of
some type or other.

BH This brings us to another concept that has come to the fore,
especially in the modern era – the idea of 'self'– which for many
is the core of personal identity. To deal with this challenge of
how to show this sense of self in the sitter the portrait painter has
to decide whether to take a detached objective approach or an
involved subjective one. What pictorial strategies do you employ
to reveal the inner character or personality of your sitters? Do
setting, dress, props, etc, play a part in this?

AM It's perhaps impossible to decipher another person's sense of self
and put that down on canvas – the idea of self is probably only
truly resolved in a self-portrait. I'm thinking now of a self-portrait
of around 1970 I have by John Bellany in which he depicts himself
as a skeleton, literally. It's a revealing and powerful statement, but
would I really be able to portray one of my subjects in this way?
I doubt if such an interpretation would be considered acceptable

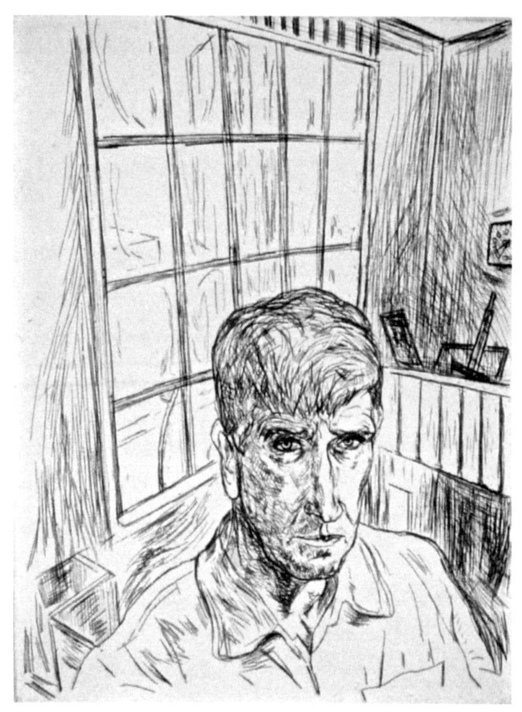

111 *Self-Portrait in Studio 40* 1987 etching 28 x 20 cm (plate size)

or meet with approval. Otto Dix regarded the self-portrait as a
'confessional' and the self-portraits of Rembrandt, Munch and
Beckmann certainly fall into that category, as do those of Bellany.
I've rarely attempted a self-portrait and apart from a number of
efforts during my student years, they are few and far between. The
self-portraits I greatly admire are those late pictures of Bonnard
where he looks at himself in the bathroom mirror and comes up
with something that is both poignant and visionary. In his book
on Bonnard, Tim Hyman talks about the disappearing self with

regard to these paintings, noting that the emotional timbre shifts from reverie to something approaching tragedy.

The setting, clothes, props, etc, do play a part and can be important at times. MacDiarmid's pipe, Neal Ascherson's Polish army cap, Robert Garioch's little bag, all contain the potential for additional storytelling. But painting a portrait usually means the artist has to deploy both a degree of objectivity in an intense study of an individual and subjectivity in his or her distinctive painterly process.

BH   Do you ever use symbolic meaning in your portraiture, say through the use of colour, or the placement of significant objects as clues to the sitter's character?

AM   In my earliest portraits, there's only the sitter, nothing more, as nothing more was needed. Colour became increasingly important, but I'm not sure I used it symbolically at that stage. Then in 1976 I painted a portrait of Neal Ascherson incorporating quotations from George Grosz, and setting Neal in Berlin where he had worked as the *Observer*'s East European correspondent throughout the '60s. I further developed this idea in a series of three large group portraits entitled *Berliners* with Neal placed amidst a collage of images of Berlin in the '20s as well as the '60s. It was this concept of the 'expanded portrait' that provided a starting point for the *Seven Poets* series I embarked upon in 1978.

In the portrait of Hugh MacDiarmid, subtitled 'Hymn to Lenin', I used imagery from the Russian revolution of 1917, a

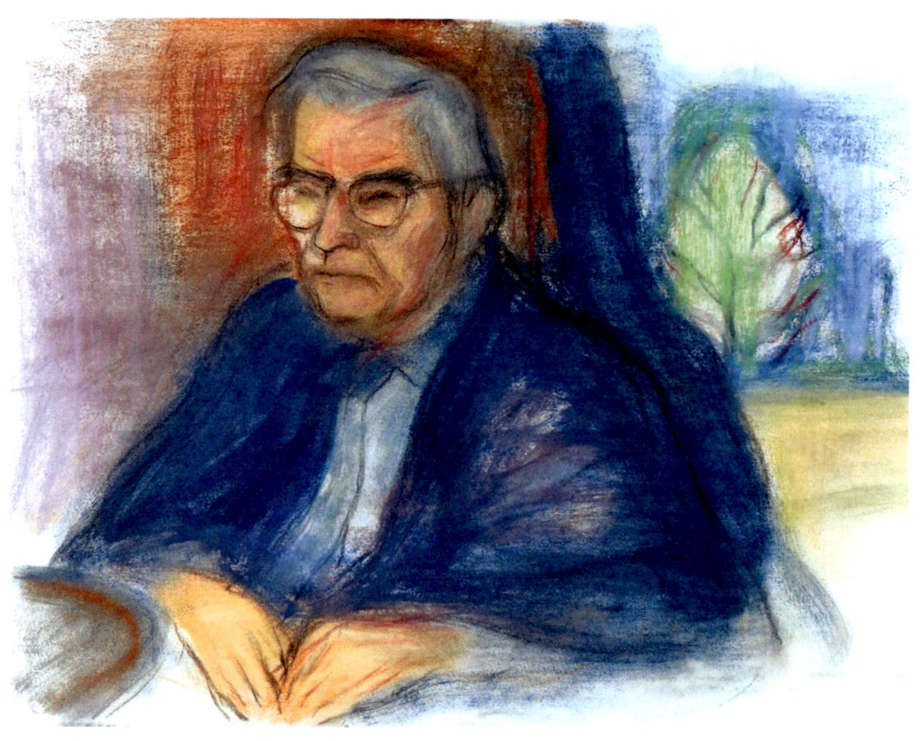

112 *George Davie* 1999 oil and pastel on paper 46 x 61 cm

crucial event for MacDiarmid with Mayakovsky and Tatlin's tower in the foreground. I placed the Scottish socialist leader John Maclean at MacDiarmid's side, while the landscape element, which symbolises Scotland, moves from the Borders where MacDiarmid was born to Shetland where he lived in the '30s. In the portrait of Sorley MacLean, the mighty Cuillin perhaps become a symbol for all Gaelic history and culture. So colour, as well as imagery becomes increasingly symbolic in those works.

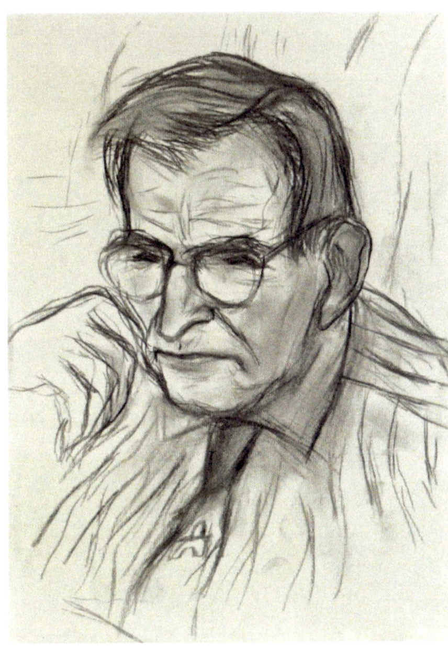

113 *George Davie* 1999 charcoal on paper 34 x 24 cm

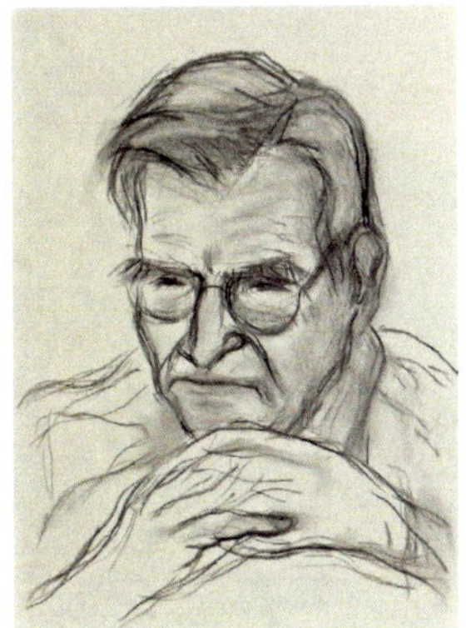

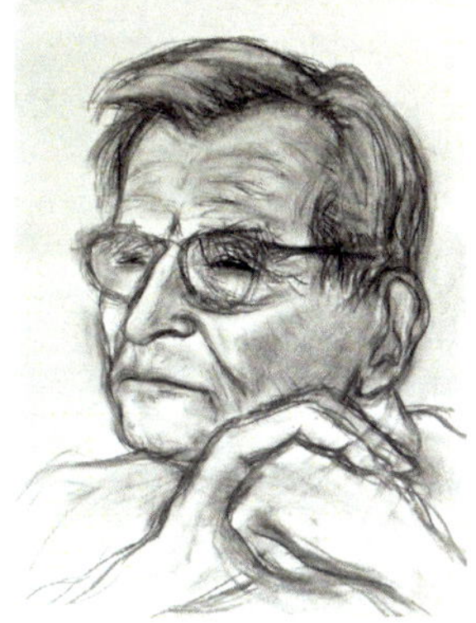

114 *George Davie* 1999 charcoal on
paper 34 x 24 cm

115 *George Davie* 1999 charcoal on
paper 24 x 28 cm

BH   During the ritual of portrait painting, do you not think that the portraitist is in a privileged, even powerful position, in relationship to the sitter, who must feel vulnerable and exposed as you intently examine and scrutinise them? How do you gain their confidence and trust in such a peculiar relationship?

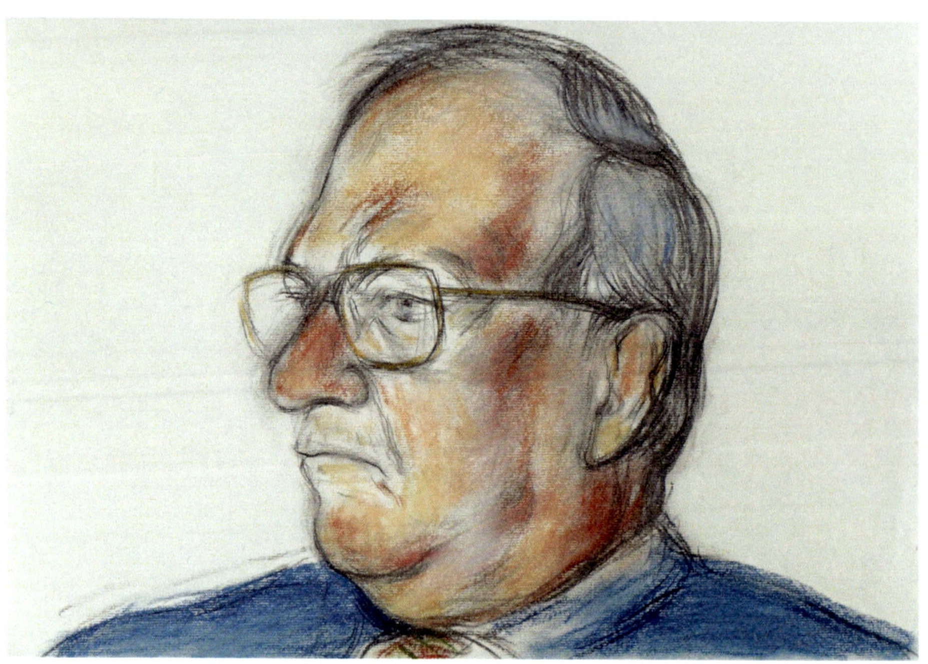

116 *Paul Henderson Scott* 2000 pastel on paper 30.5 x 45 cm

AM   The relationship between painter and sitter can either be perfectly
straightforward or exceedingly complex. Rather than the painter
being all powerful at all times, in many instances the painter is
the vulnerable one. Many sitters are completely ignorant of how
painters work, and making changes, altering the position of the head
or hands, tends to spook them. If they think you're not up to the
task then it's almost impossible to gain their confidence and trust.
There are intimidating sitters and given that one's initial drawings
can go badly wrong adds to the pressure. So yes, the painter might
appear to occupy a privileged position, but this is misleading.
We know that Picasso struggled for months over his portrait of

Gertrude Stein. The privileged part is when the sitter opens up and takes you into their confidence, almost like the patient on the couch and starts to tell their life stories. This often happens, and with Norman MacCaig and Muriel Spark I was able to eavesdrop on a wealth of fascinating and highly personal revelations.

BH   So do you think that to be a successful portrait painter you also require other skills – such as being an engaging conversationalist, as Allan Ramsay was reputed to be, and a sympathetic listener, as I am sure Henry Raeburn was?

AM   This certainly corresponds with my experience of painting portraits. I may not be an engaging conversationalist but I've tried my best and as for listening, I've found that essential. I was painted on several occasions by John Bellany, who issued strict instructions such as 'no talking for the first 25 minutes'. After that initial period of silence we launched into conversation. I could always tell, though, when it was best to keep quiet during the later stages of the portrait.

BH   As a portrait painter, over many years you must have had many different kinds of people as sitters. In all that time have you ever been tempted to caricature someone you disliked – or, on the other hand, flatter one you admired?

AM   I hope not... flattery is the reason portraiture got such a bad name! On the other hand, caricature, often derided, is an essential part of portraiture and is a starting point for many portrait painters. I've always admired James Gillray, and Hogarth of course, is one of the greats. Daumier packed a punch in his lithographs and spent time in prison for his efforts. He's one of my favourite painters. Perhaps I should have taken caricature more seriously rather than try to avoid it as something that only cartoonists did. In my early

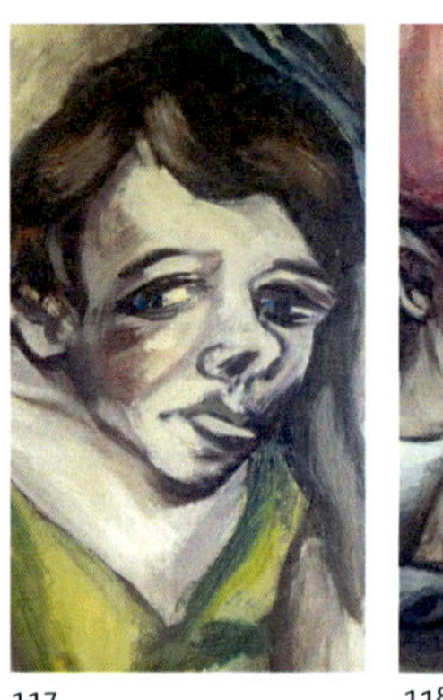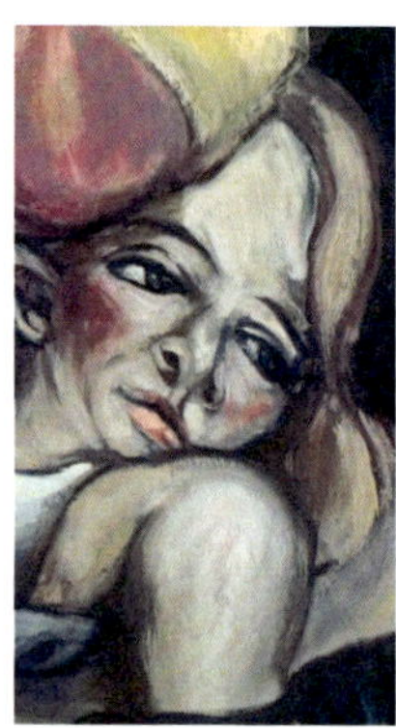

117   118

Details from *Concerning the Arrest of Poor EK* 1967 (City Art Centre, Edinburgh)

days I made 'comic' drawings of friends and enemies and in several of my paintings from the '60s there's evidence that caricature played a bigger part than I had previously remembered.

BH   What is the difference for you between painting a picture of a friend you have known for many years and a commissioned portrait of a relative stranger?

AM   It's basically a question of the intimate visual knowledge one builds up in connection with close friends allowing a greater

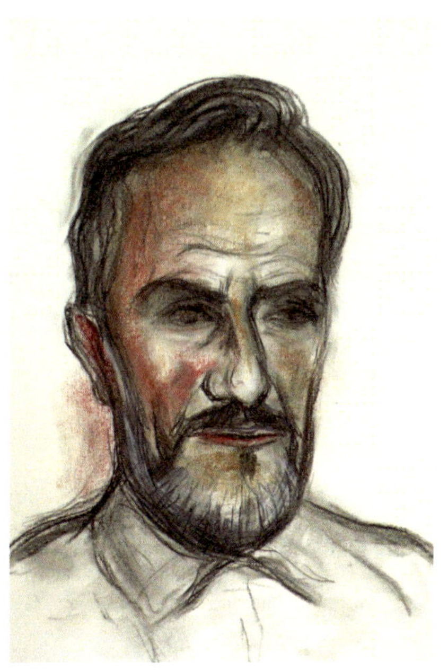

119 *Tom Fleming* 2000 charcoal and pastel on paper 44 x 30 cm

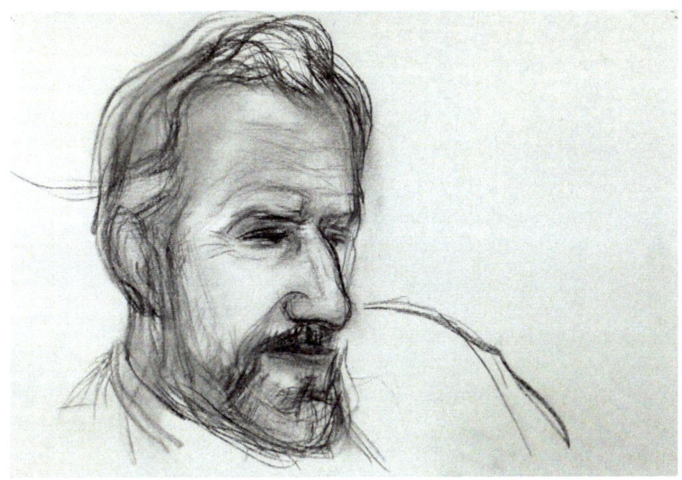

120 *Tom Fleming* 2000 charcoal on paper 30 x 44 cm

freedom of action from the onset. With a sitter you don't know
so well, there's always a period of 'finding-out', of careful study
of physical features, etc, before one can truly launch into the
painting.

BH   This brings us to the question as to the selection of the sitters for
your portraits. How do you decide who you want to portray, and
what portrait commissions you are going to accept?

AM   To begin with I simply asked a number of friends such as Alan and
Alice Bold, John Bellany, Tam White, if they would sit for their
portrait. They all seemed to like the results and so I continued to
invite my fellow artists and their wives and a few literary figures
from Milne's Bar to come to the studio and sit and all of a sudden,
I found myself painting dozens of portraits.

Before this, my first attempts at portraiture were during my
student days at Edinburgh College of Art. These were mainly
drawings of models in the Head Life class and of my fellow
students when the models failed to turn up. Then there were
paintings of Alan Bold and Ken Harrold in 1962 and 1963. Bold,
sitting in his mother's kitchen reading the cantos of Ezra Pound,
very much the work of a student.

The portrait of Ken Harrold, titled *Portrait of a Young
Workman* – he was an apprentice electrician – was exhibited on
the railings at Castle Terrace during the Edinburgh Festival as part
of the first open-air exhibition that John Bellany and I staged in
1963. It was bought by a young German couple and I didn't see it

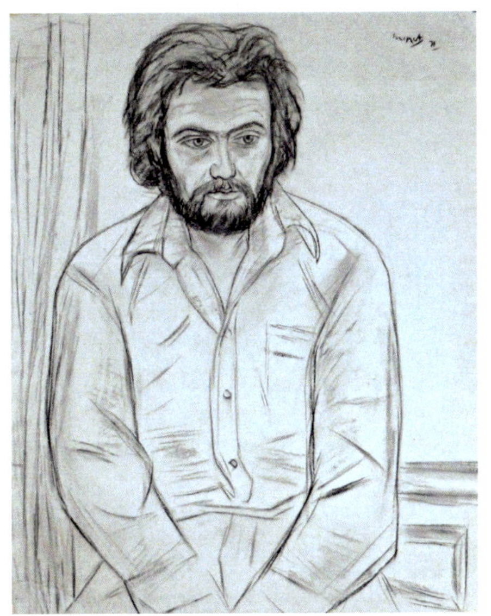

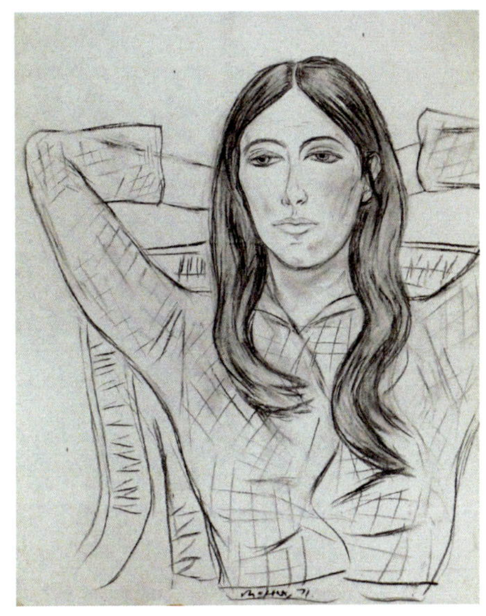

121 *Ian McLeod* 1971 charcoal on paper 53 x 50 cm

122 *Mary McLeod* 1971 charcoal on paper 58 x 45.5 cm

again until 2012 when I visited them in their home near the Dutch
border. I now recognise it was a key work for me, a first step on
the road to making a convincing modern portrait.

Of course, as a student I made other portraits, of girlfriends,
etc, some of which were 'chucked out', but there was a good
one of my grandfather that has stood the test of time. After art
college I worked in an engineering factory in Abbeyhill. During
the nightshifts there was a lengthy break when I set about drawing
and painting small portraits of my 'comrades'. There must be
dozens of those little pictures scattered around somewhere or other.
Astonishingly one of them turned up a couple of years ago in the

123 Jimmy Jones 1965 ink on paper
7.2 x 9 cm

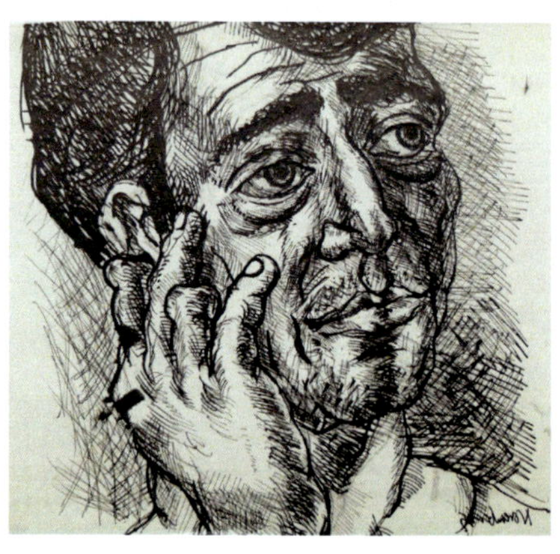

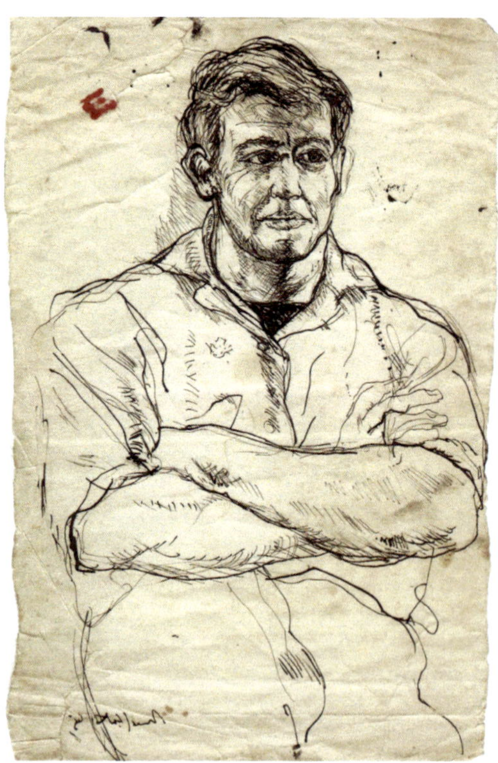

124 *Albert Renwick* 1965 ink on paper
29 x 20 cm (private collection)

usa – a small drawing of Bert Renwick – in Georgia of all places!

There were few commissions in my early days and I accepted them willingly as I had to make a living. My first major commission came as a result of *A View of the Portrait* in the Scottish National Portrait Gallery when Edinburgh University asked me to paint their Principal and Vice-Chancellor, Sir Michael Swann, on his retirement. Swann was a scientist and we both agreed there should be no gowns or mace, none of the traditional trappings of high office. This would be a modern portrait. Many years later I was delighted to read in *The University Portraits* (Second Series 1986) that my painting was considered 'the most important portrait the Court has commissioned in recent years'.

At much the same time, W Gordon Smith made a film for bbc television of me painting a portrait of the poet Alan Jackson, a risky business, but all went well. After painting Alan, my next portrait was of his wife Margaret. The portraits were the same size, vertical in format, and linked by compositional means such as the angle of the carpet and the division of the space between floor and wall with both sitters wearing sleeveless tops. A double portrait, though on separate canvases.

In the mid-'70s I began to use soft pastels, influenced by both Kitaj and Degas, for my portrait drawings. I should emphasise they were not conceived as sketches or preparatory works but as drawings in their own right. Working with pastels liberated my use of colour, allowing a significant move from a darker palette to a lighter one. I made a number of portraits of women at this stage – Lynda Myles, Susan Johnston and Isabel Hilton – and the use of

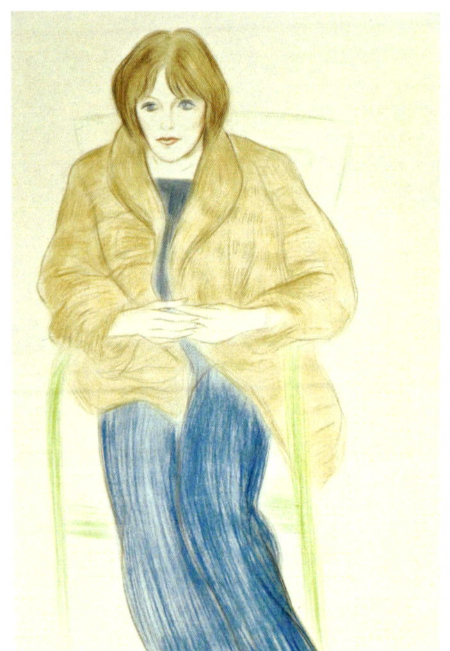

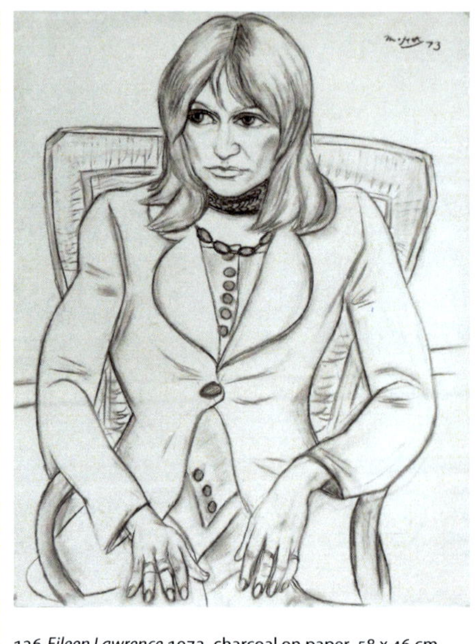

126 *Eileen Lawrence* 1973 charcoal on paper 58 x 46 cm

125 *Lynda Myles in fur jacket* 1976 coloured pencil on paper
70 x 50 cm

pastels was an important factor in the success of these works.

The portraits in both pastels and oils of Susie Raeburn (*The Ring-mistress 1 & 2*) that followed were collaborative efforts – she loved dressing up and we were able to find references to 19th-century French masters such as Seurat and Lautrec in the costumes she wore and the poses she adopted. I've always welcomed this kind of involvement from the sitter in the setting-up of a pose.

BH   Who do you feel you are painting your portraits for – yourself (surely first and foremost it should be readily recognised as a

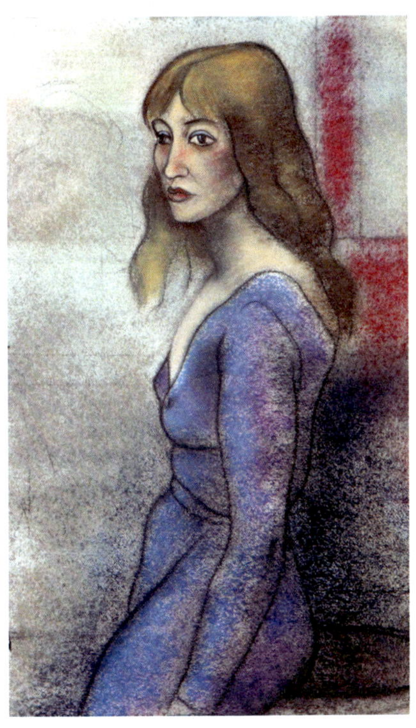

127 *Susan Moffat* 1979 pastel on paper 57 x 39 cm

'Moffat portrait'), the sitter, whoever commissions the portrait or the viewer? Who has priority? Whose judgement is most crucial in deciding the merits of your portraits?

AM   In a way, all of them. That's what makes painting a portrait different from my other works where I do, first and foremost paint for myself and I have priority. With a portrait other factors come into play, but of course my judgement is crucial during the painting of the portrait.

As I've just referred to with the portraits of Susie Raeburn, it's often productive to establish a creative collaboration with the sitter. This normally happens with fellow artists when suggestions are made as to how they wish to be portrayed. These are usually straightforward matters concerning what the background might contain or should the sitter stand or be seated. When painting *Gwen Hardie*, for instance, I completed a large seated portrait first of all, but Gwen felt it was too polite. It simply wasn't her... something more was needed. In a second portrait, her pose was more assertive and the inclusion within the composition of one of her own works provided a dramatic context. There's no question that our collaboration produced a far more successful and memorable portrait.

I was also able to work successfully with David MacLennan's widow, the actress Juliet Cadzow. After showing her some initial sketches we discussed how the portrait might proceed. Her suggestions regarding the pose, the colour of jacket and the Sutherland landscape with fishing boat, added greatly to the overall conception of the portrait. At the end of the day, all portraits are, in a sense, collaborations. The sitter prepares himself or herself for the occasion and the artist responds.

Where the portrait is actually made – in my studio or in the sitter's living room is also important. With Robert Garioch it seemed essential to capture him at home surrounded by his own furniture, including items he had made himself. I've just discovered an old sketchbook containing several sheets of detailed studies, plus written descriptions of the various objects in his study.

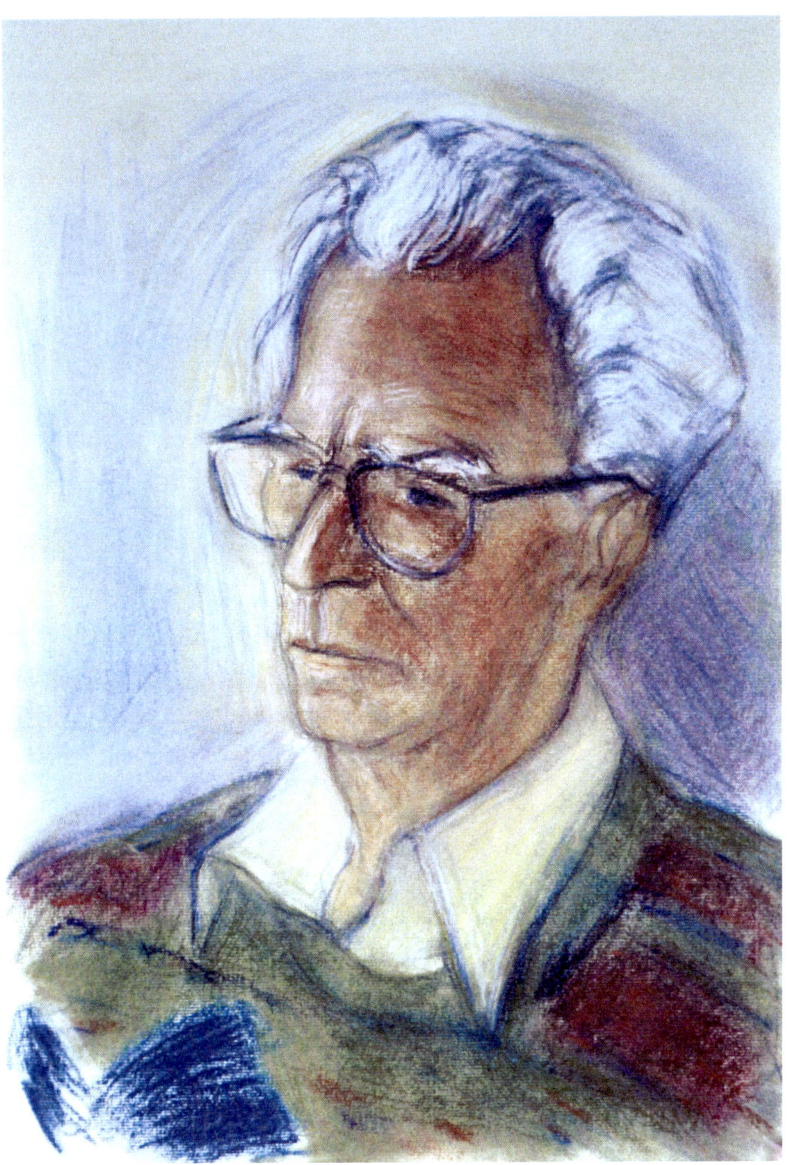

128 *Robin Jenkins* 2002 pastel on paper 50 x 35 cm (private collection)

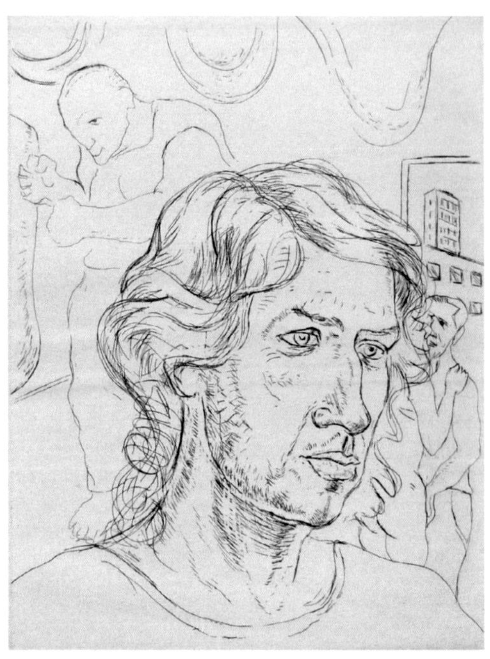

129 *Peter Howson* 1987 etching 32.5 x 25 cm (plate size)

My pastels of Ian Hamilton Finlay were done in the kitchen at
Stonypath and similarly, the George Mackay Brown portrait began
in his council house in Stromness and finished in the bar of the
Braes Hotel because he was barred from the bar in the Stromness
Hotel!

The large portrait of Peter Howson was painted in his studio
in the east end of Glasgow and my small drypoint of Adrian
Wiszniewski was made in a corner of the Edinburgh Printmakers
Workshop. The pastel portrait of Sandra Fisher came from a series
of drawing sessions that took place in her Chelsea studio.

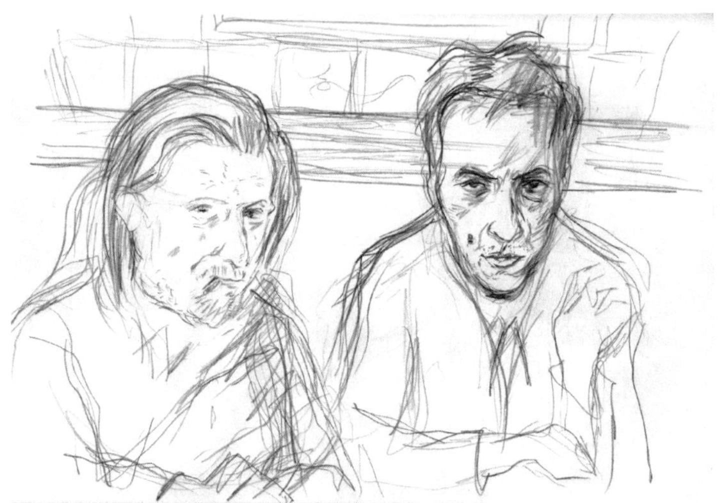

130 *Steven Campbell and Adrian Wiszniewski* 1987 pencil on paper 20 x 27.5 cm

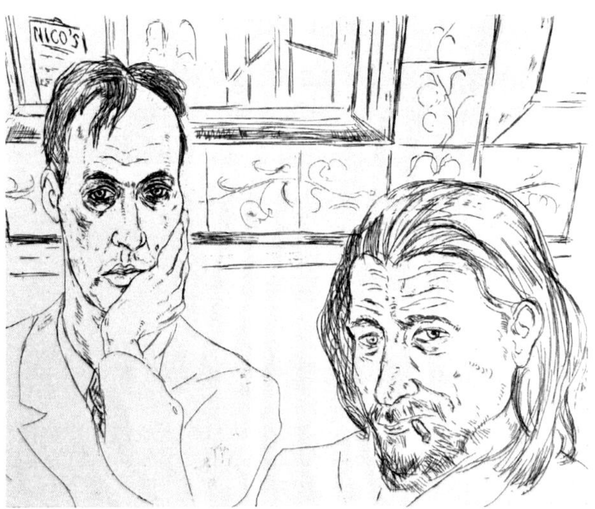

131 *Steven Campbell and Adrian Wiszniewski in Nico's* 1987 etching 24.5 x 32 cm
   (plate size)

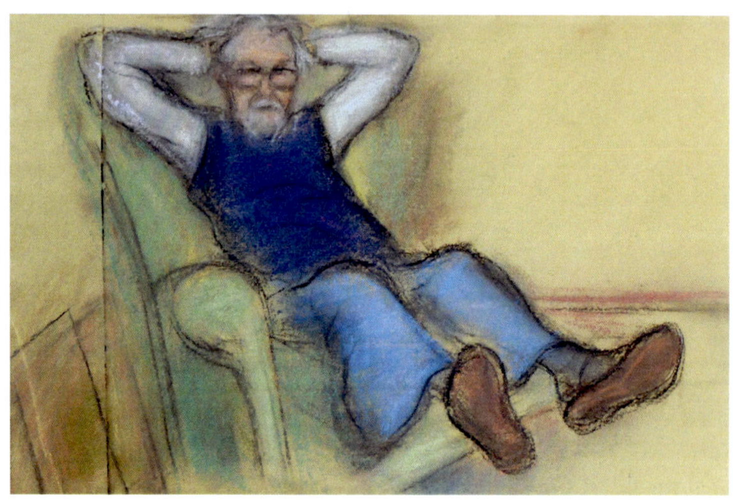

132 *Alasdair Gray* 2010 pastel on paper 35 x 56 cm

Actually, when I think more about it, many of my best portraits began on location and have been inspired by location. All of the poets for instance and most of my more recent portraits from George Davie to Chris Smout and Jim Swire. I'm no longer studio-bound, and more aware of the sitter's wider surroundings and how that forms part of their story.

With Alasdair Gray, working in his large living room/studio proved an ideal location for both of us. He sat in a splendid big chair and at the touch of a button a platform emerged for his legs and feet. He sat back and relaxed before launching into lengthy descriptions of the novels he admired, the painters he adored and so forth. When I told him that the film of Joyce Cary's *The Horse's Mouth* had inspired me to become a painter, he recited the final pages of the novel from memory, before jumping up and

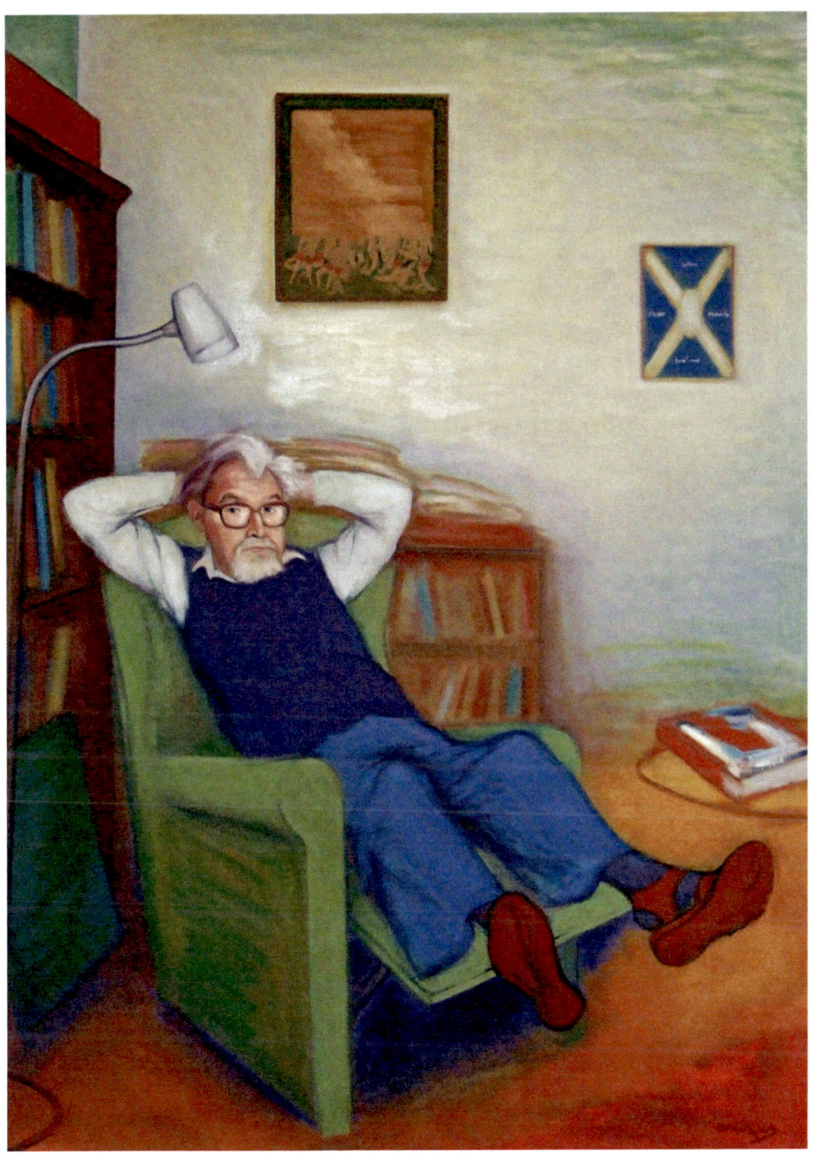

133 *Alasdair Gray* 2010 oil on canvas 137 x 107 cm (Òran Mór, Glasgow)

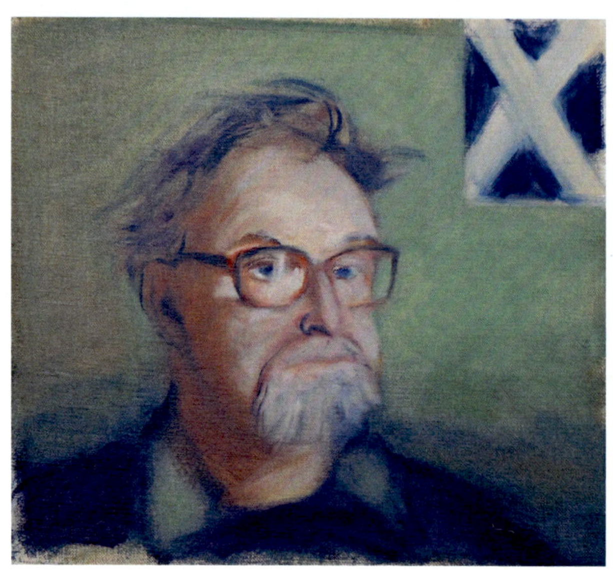

134 *Alasdair Gray* 2010 oil on canvas 42 x 46 cm

presenting me with the Penguin Classics edition, pointing out that the film had a different ending from the novel.

BH   Ultimately, what do you feel is the purpose and role of your portraits?

AM   I hope they will be seen as human documents. In an age obsessed by triviality and celebrity perhaps it's essential to think differently about power and prestige. It's a matter of solidarity too. I very much hope the abilities of the individuals I've portrayed will be taken seriously and that they have in their own particular ways, made a difference in the world. What I'm saying is that all people are equal.

BH   Can I focus on the role of the viewer of your portraits for a
      moment? To go back to Gombrich again, he invented the phrase
      'the beholder's stare', meaning the degree of ambiguity – areas
      open to speculation – the artist leaves in the work for viewer to use
      their own interpretive imagination. Do you feel you allow your
      viewers an opportunity to assess the character and personality of
      your sitters?

AM   This is an important one. How does the artist allow the viewer a
      way into the painting? It's something one slowly becomes aware
      of, so to speak. As a student one has to work through an obsession
      with 'correctness' and 'detail', and only afterwards can one
      begin to see the wood from the trees in terms of what needs to be
      emphasised and what is better left alone. It takes time, a long time
      and practice. I often think of those late, great paintings by Titian
      The Death of Actaeon and *The Flaying of Marsyas*. Were they
      'unfinished' or not? The point is, of course, they do leave room
      for the viewer's imagination. Nothing could be further from the
      academic idea of 'finish'.

BH   This question of the role of the viewer in reading your portraits
      must involve the issue of technique – that is, how much 'finish' do
      you give to your painting?

AM   Another interesting question that makes me think about the
      approaches to teaching drawing I experienced first in Edinburgh
      and then in Glasgow. In the art college in Edinburgh there was

an emphasis on solidity of form and detail, a classical approach
if you like, with drawings of the antique casts and life models
mainly carried out carefully in pencil. In the art school in Glasgow
drawing classes were very different. What I would describe as a
romantic approach was favoured over a classical one and drawings
were mainly made with soft charcoal. The Glasgow students were
often instructed 'don't finish it' or 'take a rag to that', with blurring
and smudging playing a major part in the process of both drawing
and painting. Atmosphere rather than precision was the goal. I
remember taking this up with David Donaldson when he was Head
of Department only to be told that he longed for more objectivity
in the students' drawing: 'we should be more like Edinburgh in
that respect'. This is worth further consideration given the kind
of drawing, meticulous and objective in style, that emerged from
Glasgow in the '20s and '30s when Cowie and Baird and then
Colquhoun and MacBryde set the pace. It seems that in the '40s
– the war years perhaps playing a part – a darker, more romantic
'Glasgow aesthetic' emerged, best exemplified by the early work of
Joan Eardley. Not that precision and line were entirely abandoned;
rather, they were merged with tonal and expressive gestures to
create richer and more dramatic effects.

BH   Looking at the sitters in your portraits, they appear to fall into
distinctive groups and this seems to be borne out by three important
exhibitions you have had for your portrait painting. Your early
portraits, as shown in *A View of the Portrait* at the Scottish
National Portrait Gallery in 1973, were mainly of your own

personal acquaintances. In 1978 you were given the *Seven Poets* commission which resulted in your next major portrait exhibition at the Third Eye Centre in Glasgow in 1981. Then in the '80s, you moved on to painting portraits of young emerging painters, which lead to your exhibition *Portraits of Painters* at the Scottish National Gallery of Modern Art in 1988. Was that 'grouping' process something you were aware of, and planned at the time, or did it emerge through the circumstances of your career?

AM   You're right to draw attention to these three exhibitions and their contents. *A View of the Portrait* was an ad hoc collection of portraits of my closest friends and acquaintances. The *Seven Poets* exhibition comprised portraits commissioned by the Scottish Arts Council of the generation of great post-Second World War poets and the *Portraits of Painters* in 1988 was exactly that, a bunch of painters who I knew well, some of whom I had taught as students at Glasgow School of Art. In the latter two, the groupings were planned, though of course they emerged through the circumstances of my career and specific interests as an artist. The main difference between *A View of the Portrait* and *Seven Poets* was that the portraits of the poets were conceived as public paintings, to be viewed in public spaces, as opposed to the intimacy of the earlier paintings.

BH   Undoubtedly your most renowned portraits are of celebrated literary figures. Does that type of sitter set you a particular challenge? How do you go about conveying their creative power, their intellectual personality and their public profile?

 There was a sense of responsibility involved in portraying people like the poets who shaped and contributed in such an important way to the art and culture of modern Scotland. Had it not been for them, I probably wouldn't be painting, or believing art to be important.

MacDiarmid's status as the poetic peer of Eliot, Pound and Yeats was initially intimidating. How does one put that into a painting? George Davie, an equally formidable character, posed a different set of problems. How does one deal with the fragility of extreme old age? Throughout the many sessions I spent drawing him, I was aware of Giacometti's comments on drawing the old and ill Matisse: 'I was drawing, and at the same time observing what cannot be captured by drawing'. And with Sorley MacLean, Robert Garioch and Edwin Morgan I was aware they had all survived the battlefields of the Second World War, something outwith my own experience and again the question arose: how does one paint about that? But there was fun too...

When I began my portrait of MacDiarmid in the summer of 1978 I knew he was battling cancer and hadn't long to live. Once the bottle of whisky was opened, however, there was a stream of good-natured banter about the other poets I intended to paint and whether or not they might prove suitable subjects for a portrait, when suddenly Valda came in and scolded him for not having his false teeth in. He laughed and said there was no need for that as the artist would simply see to it with the stroke of a brush. Of course, painting great poets like MacDiarmid or Sorley MacLean or Edwin Morgan is tremendously inspiring and giving one's

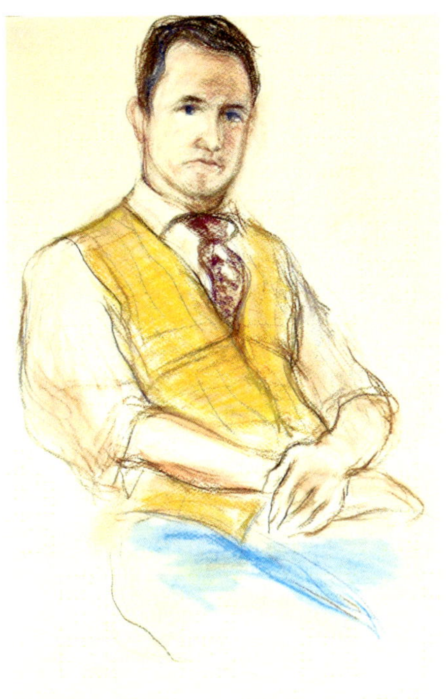 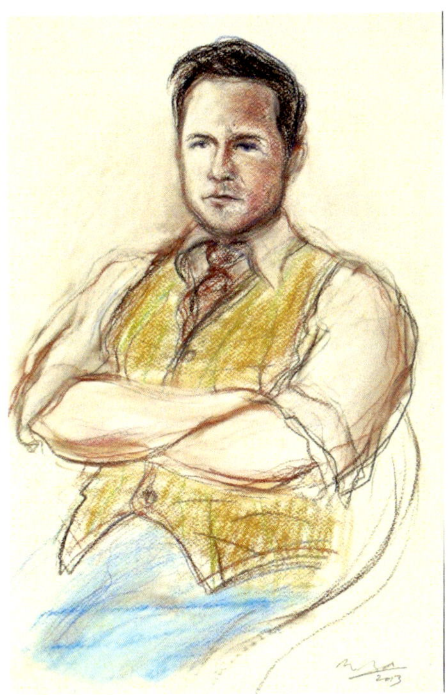

135 (left) *Alan Bissett* 2013 pastel on cream paper 50 x 32 cm

136 (right) *Alan Bissett* 2013 pastel on cream paper 50 x 32 cm (private collection)

best in these circumstances, although never guaranteed, is always possible.

BH   How much does the gender of your sitter affect your approach to painting a portrait? Do you try to bring out different qualities in a female sitter from those of a male one?

AM   Observing the physical differences between male and female models in the life studios and anatomy classes at Edinburgh College of Art – and I'm not making a statement of the obvious here – was an important learning process. How to capture those differences with a pencil or a brush? As was studying the masters. How did Vermeer or Watteau or Goya achieve such revealing and dignified images of both men and women, young or old? How did Suzanne Valadon or Alice Neel represent their female and male subjects? And if we're talking exclusively about female portraits, then Raeburn comes into his own as a supreme interpreter of women. His portrait *Mrs Robert Scott Moncrieff*, for example: 'pre-eminently a portrait of sensibility and sexuality' is how Dr Duncan Thomson describes this wonderful painting. I'll come back to that.

So what kind of qualities would I try to bring out in a female sitter? Certainly, painting Muriel Spark was a very different experience from painting the group of male poets. Although she shared many similarities to her male counterparts – much the same age, intellectually formidable and with an uncompromising seriousness about art and the role of the artist – what was immediately different was her elegance, her feminine allure. When I asked if she wanted me to include additional imagery in the background, 'No, no, I only want me' was her reply.

I do, however, think of the blue background space as a homage to the Venetian painters, alluding to Italy where she spent the final years of her life. There was a problem of sorts, though, in that every time she arrived at the studio she had a different hairstyle – she would visit the hairdresser before each sitting. That's something I never had to contend with in any of my male subjects!

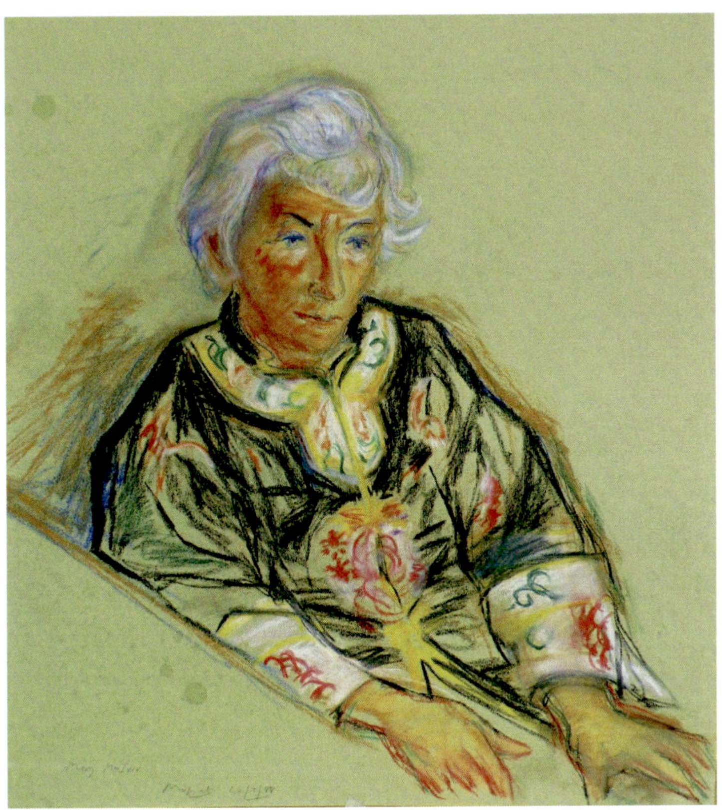

137 *Mary MacIver* 1988 pastel on coloured paper 54 x 47 cm

Painting Mary MacIver, widow of Hector MacIver and close
to several of the male poets, again demanded a different kind of
portrait. She and Hector had lived next door to William Gillies
in the small village of Temple and she had many stories to tell of
those days, including a famous drunken night with Gillies and
MacDiarmid dancing around the room. I made some initial studies
in her house at the foot of the Braid Hills before completing

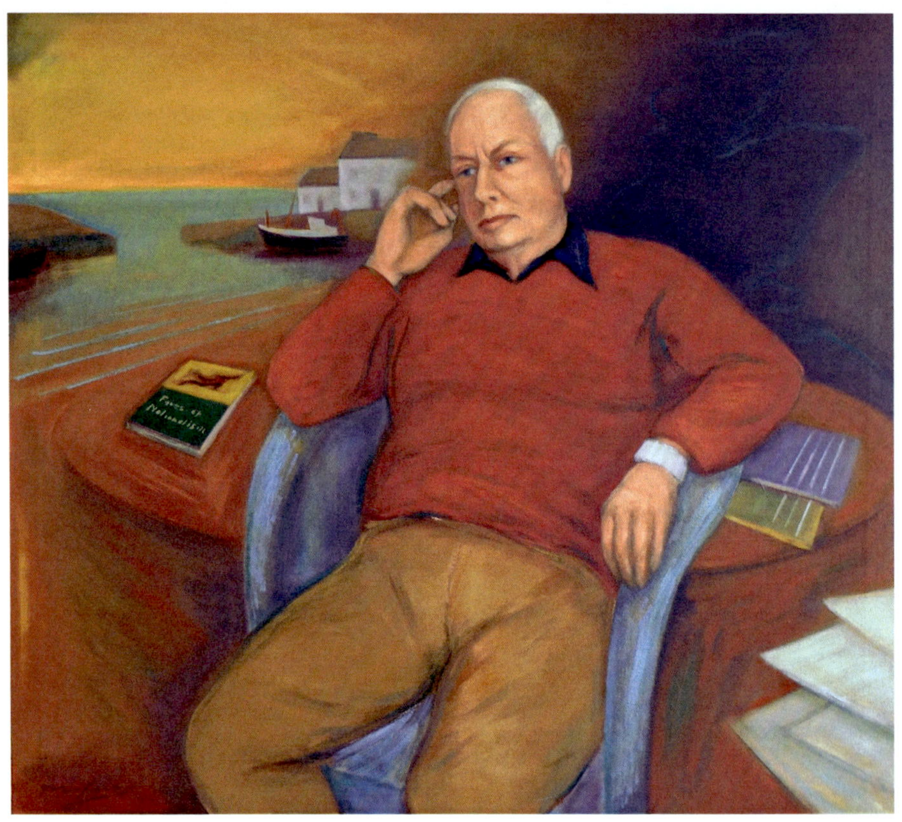

138 *Tom Nairn* 2012/14 oil on canvas 107 x 122 cm (Dundee Art Galleries and Museums Collection, Dundee City Council)

the portrait in my studio. So sensibility and sexuality are in the foreground in my portrayal of women. A more painterly, less forceful approach is needed.

BH   When you are painting a double or group portrait, are you concerned to show through such features as gesture and body language not only the physical, but the psychological relationship between the figures?

AM Certainly with double portraits, usually husband and wife in my case, the psychological relationship plays a big part in the success of the portrait. I can observe and even feel these things during the painting process, but making sense of it with paint is fraught with difficulties. The double portrait offers the possibility of interesting compositional arrangements, as well as the human interaction between two people and that's why I've always liked to take them on. Looking back at those double portraits I did in the late '60s and early '70s, I think they stand up well – Ian and Patsy Croal, Graham and Eileen Martin, and Ken and Margot Duffy. And Harro and Anna Rösing, though on separate canvases, combine to make another double portrait I still feel good about.

Group portraits and big compositions are a challenge, full stop. Back to Poussin and Géricault. I first became aware of the idea of the great 'machine' on a visit to Paris with John Bellany in the spring of 1963 – that's when the huge paintings of Courbet and Delacroix were hanging in the great central gallery of the Louvre. That was a defining moment for both of us; we realised we would have to be more ambitious in terms of scale and content and on returning to the art college we made a start in the mural room under the guidance of Jimmy Cumming. My first attempt ended in disaster, but the second, although far from fully realised led to further developments, culminating in a successful group of large paintings completed during the summer months of 1963 and shown during the Edinburgh Festival.

I've been working on a large group portrait entitled *Scotland's Voices* for the past year – the legendary folklorist Hamish

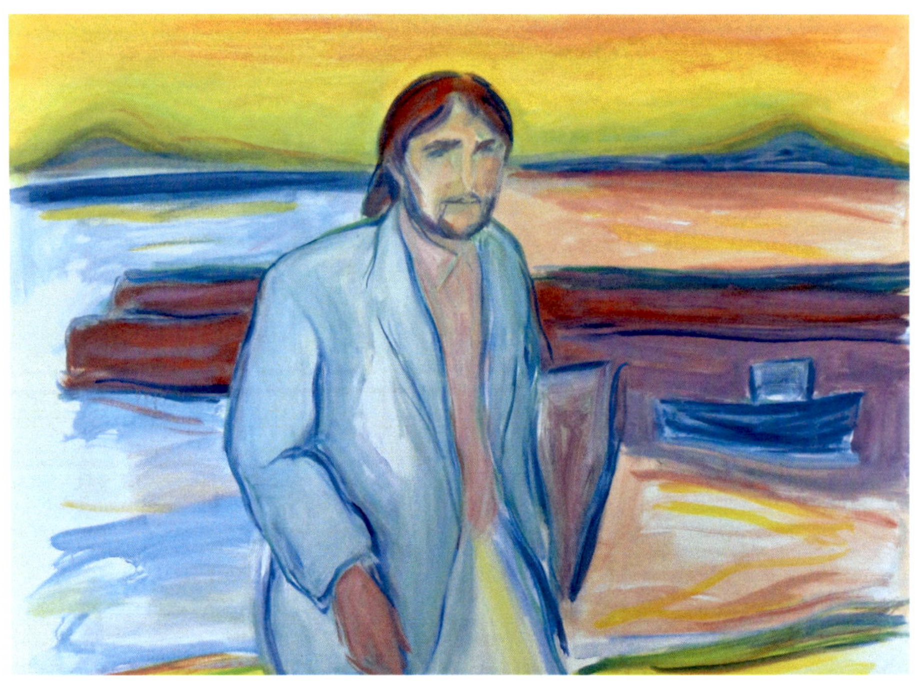

139 *Port Seton Man (John Bellany)* 2023 oil on canvas 91 x 122 cm

Henderson surrounded by many of the singers and musicians
he 'discovered' and recorded in the years after the Second
World War. It was a struggle on a number of fronts – gesture
and body language, the relationship between the figures has to
be convincing – get that wrong and the whole thing fails. It's all
about unifying the various parts – landscape, figures, instruments,
while making explicit the various 'portraits' within the painting.
Scotland's Voices is a kind of 'history painting' set in the '50s
when Henderson was travelling across the north of Scotland on
a motorbike, armed with a large tape recorder. Most of the main

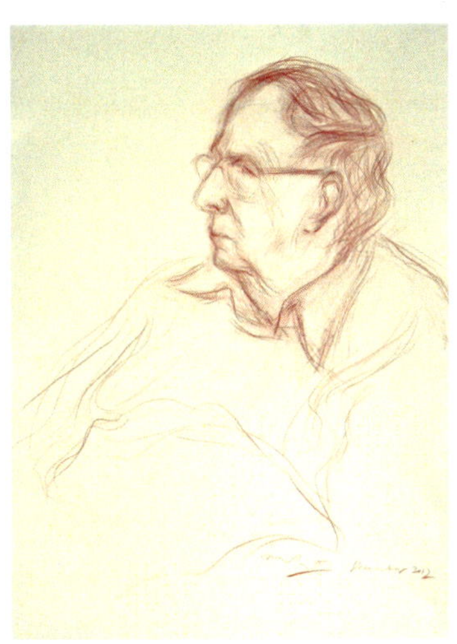

140 *TC Smout* 2012 conte on cream paper
53 x 34 cm (Democratic Left Scotland)

players are no longer with us and so I've used a number of old photographs as a starting point for their portraits. I found the best way to proceed was to make as many drawings as possible in order to establish a closer understanding of the various characters – and they were all big personalities. Slowly but surely, I'm re-inventing them in painterly, as opposed to photographic terms. The idea for the painting came directly from an old friend, the film-maker Douglas Eadie. As the producer of a new film on the life and work of Hamish Henderson, he suggested I make a painting as well. What he had in mind was a companion piece to *Poets' Pub*. I protested, saying that I didn't really know enough about the great figures of the Folk Revival, but he brushed that aside and made a list of who should be in the painting. When I read that MacDiarmid, Gramsci and Heinrich Heine were to be included,

I was ready to go. So this was another creative collaboration
and over the past year I've had visits from a number of Hamish's
friends and fellow musicians, such as Dolina MacLennan and Aly
Bain, who both feature in the painting.
Also, I enjoyed conversations with Raymond Ross, author of *On
the Radical Road*, a play about Hamish, and Ian MacGregor,
a grandson of Belle Stewart. Their insight, advice and personal
memories all proved invaluable in the development of the painting.

BH   Can we now turn to the stylistic aspect of your portraiture? You
have said that your 'favourite portraits all come from the first half
of the 20th century'. That would seem to indicate that you see
your work within the distinctive tradition of modern portraiture.
Would that be correct, and if so, what are the stylistic qualities of
modern portraiture that particularly appeal to you as a portrait
painter yourself?

AM   First of all, let me bring in Cézanne, because the modern
portrait begins with him. That visit to Paris in 1963 was my
introduction to his paintings and portraits. Dissatisfied with the
flimsiness of Impressionism, he sought a more solid structural
and compositional base for his paintings; back to Poussin, as it
were. His late portraits are full of humanity and that was often
overlooked, especially by certain influential English critics, in
favour of dull aesthetic analysis, carefully avoiding the emotional
side of his work. It's this aspect of Cézanne, along with his
emphasis on painting as an intellectual construction that seems to

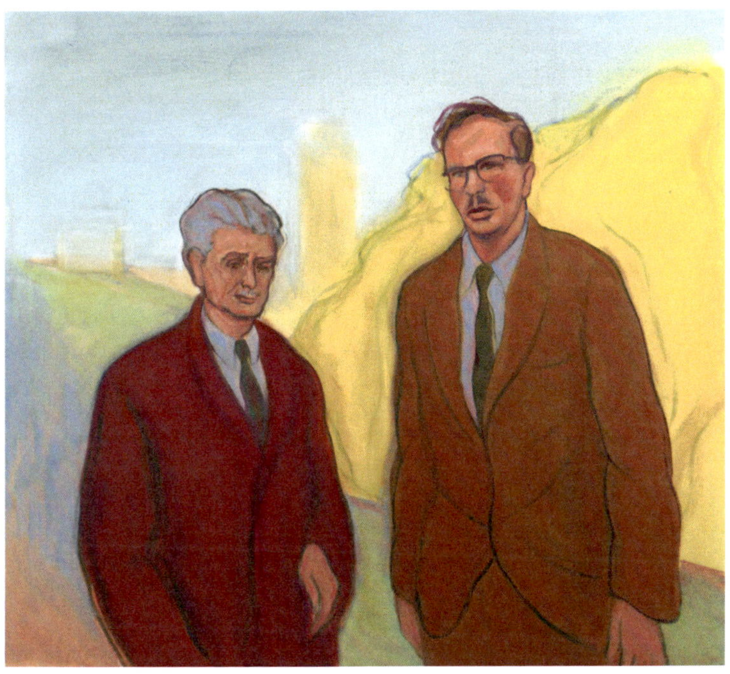

141 *Hugh MacDiarmid and Hamish Henderson* 2018 oil on canvas 122 x 152.5 cm

me to offer a way forward for painting today.

It's true that in my younger days my favourite painters and paintings, writers, composers, etc, all came from the first half of the 20th century. In terms of portraiture, the works of Picasso and Matisse were readily available in books and exhibitions when I was a student, but the German artists associated with the Weimar Republic were mostly under the radar. Grosz, Dix and Beckmann only became visible after a visit to Berlin, Dresden and Leipzig in 1967. What really appealed to me in their portraits was their ability to place the individual within a social context and an unflinching mission to reveal the truth, no matter how ugly or awful it was.

I've already referred to the impact of Kokoschka; moving further north, there's the incomparable figure of Edvard Munch. His portraits were painted very rapidly... there was no overpainting or correcting and their fierce spontaneity has an immediate impact. Munch is an artist who has been more and more in my thoughts in recent years.

The stylistic properties all of these artists seem to have in common is the emphasis they placed on drawing, creating new idioms for the expression of modern life. As a result drawing, especially in relation to the portrait, has always been crucial for me. I consider my portrait drawings to be just as important as my paintings.

Other later discoveries were the portraits of the Polish painters SI Witkiewicz, who committed suicide in 1939, and Olga Boznanska, who died in 1940. Witkiewicz, also known as Witkacy, was a painter, philosopher, novelist, photographer and dramatist and was a great influence on Tadeusz Kantor. Many of his thousands of portraits were made while he experimented with alcohol and drugs.

On a visit to Helsinki in 1996, I came across the remarkable series of self-portraits from the '20s and '30s by the Swedish/ Finnish artist Helene Schjerfbeck and successive visits to Mexico City from 2000 onwards enabled me to see at first hand the portraits of Diego Rivera and Frida Kahlo. All of those artists, though very different in style and from diverse cultural backgrounds, made works that contribute towards what might be

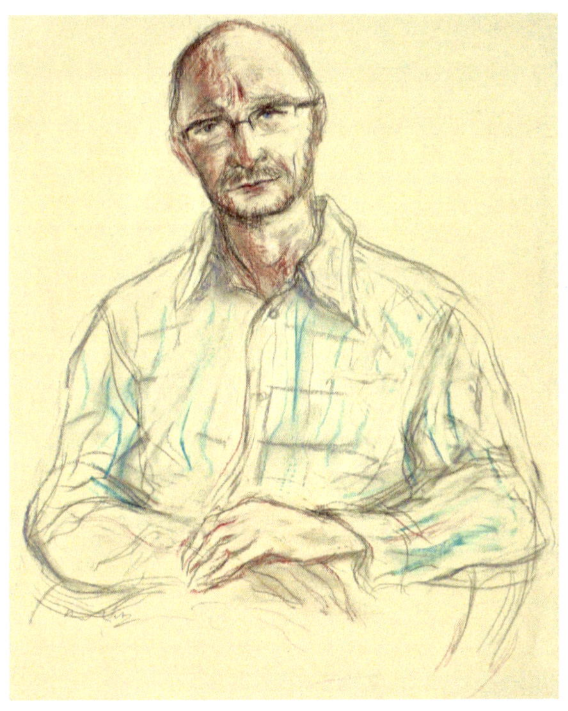

142 *James Robertson* 2013 conte on paper 39 x 33.5 cm

described as a modern portrait tradition.

The Scottish moderns too, have been influential. That's the tradition I hope to have contributed to, after all. James Cowie, Edward Baird and William McCance all made significant contributions with their portraits. The double portrait *Robert Colquhoun and Robert MacBryde* (1937–38) by Ian Fleming that hung on a wall in the east corridor of the Mackintosh Building was a painting I would look at it every day during my Glasgow years. Perhaps it's not a truly great painting, but it has a special resonance in terms of the story of Modernism in Scotland.

There are, however, two remarkable portraits by one of my predecessors as Head of the Painting Department in Glasgow – David Forrester Wilson's *The Young Shepherd* (1929) and *An Islay Woman* (1931) – that stand apart from anything else in Scotland at the time,; and there's a self-portrait by Gillies from 1941 I greatly admire. It's a pity he didn't paint more portraits or self-portraits.

One of the criticisms of Scottish Modernism was that we didn't produce any female artists of the calibre of Frida Kahlo or Paula Modersohn-Becker, but new light has recently been shed on a number of outstanding women artists – who all painted portraits – such as Bessie MacNicol, Agnes Miller Parker and Dorothy Carleton Smyth, who, had she not been struck down with a brain haemorrhage would have become the first female Director of Glasgow School of Art in 1933. Think about that…

BH   In your answer you touch on the subject of Scottish portrait painting. Do you feel that Scottish portraiture has a distinctive character? If so, what are the features of that distinction, and who in your opinion most exemplifies the 'Scottish' approach to portraiture?

AM   Without doubt. There are of course, many who deny there are national differences and distinctiveness with regard to the arts. They claim that art is 'universal' and there's no need for any further explanation. That's fine, but it conveniently side-steps the complexities that surround cultural identity and fails to address

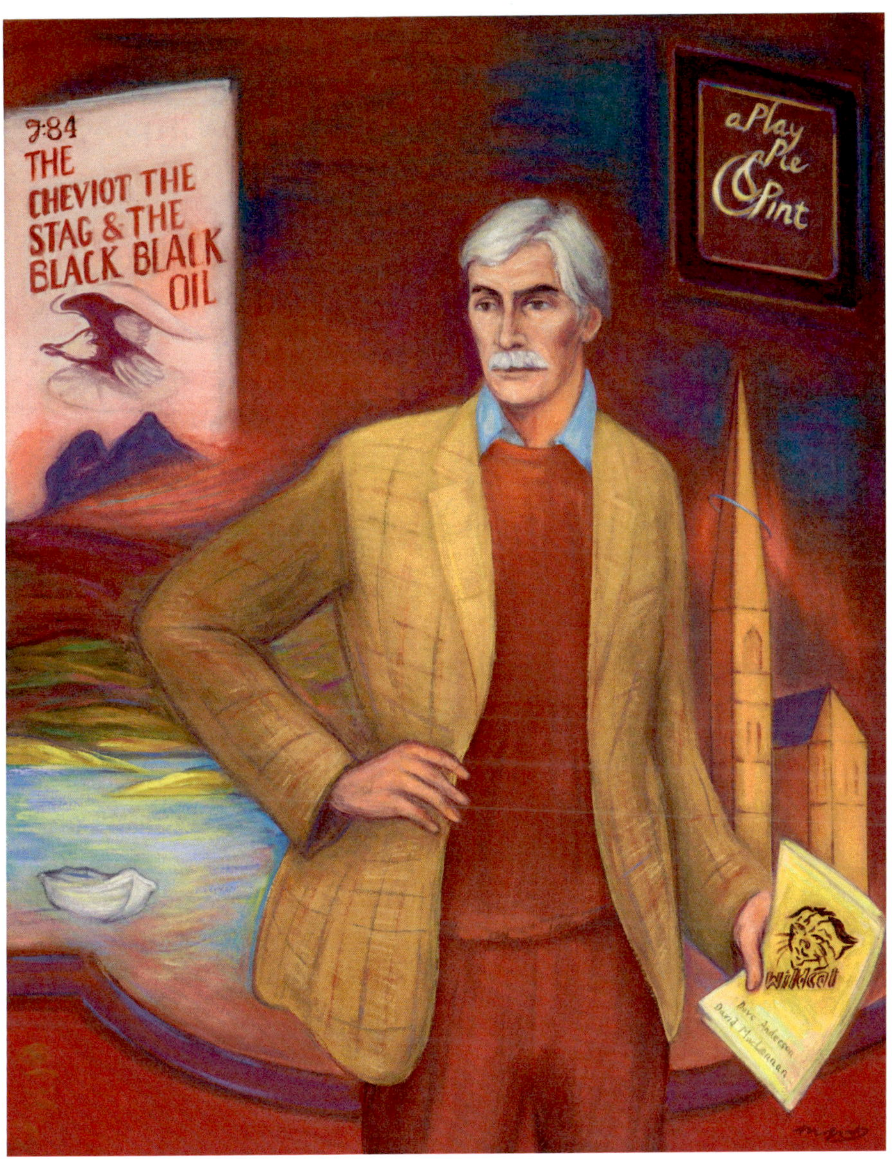

143 *David MacLennan* 2015 oil on canvas 152.4 x 121.9 cm (Òran Mór, Glasgow)

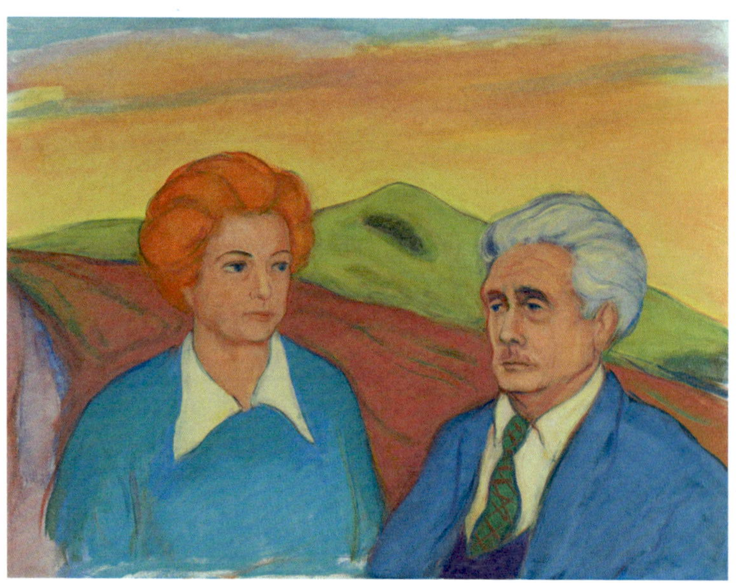

144 *Valda and Chris* 2019 oil on canvas 77 x 102 cm

essentials like the profoundly Russian nature of Stravinsky's music. *The Rite of Spring* may be a high-culture text, the paradigm of Modernism in music, internationally significant way beyond any concerns of 'narrow nationalism'. And yet Stravinsky chose to give it a subtitle, emphatically present in its universal interpretation: *Pictures of Pagan Russia*. Artists and composers cannot simply be described as 'international' modernists who came from nowhere in particular. There's no need to apologise or deny that one is a Scottish artist.

The prevailing view is that Scottish painting is mainly French influenced and to a great extent that is true, and like French

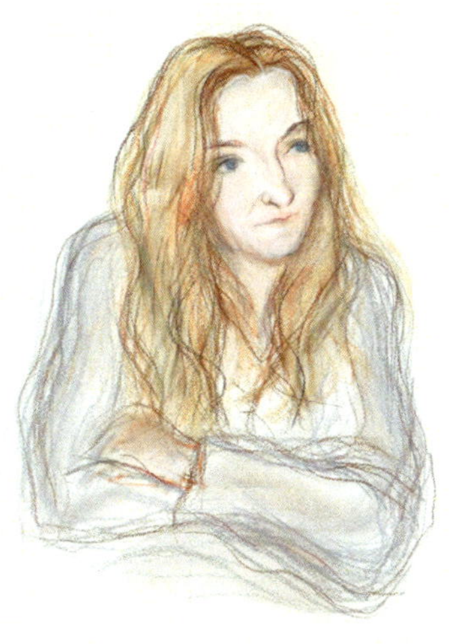

145 *Gerda Stevenson* 2014 pastel on paper
48 x 32 cm

or German painting, there is no one defining style – there are
only individual artists working at different times across the
centuries. I've just talked about some of the moderns who
eschewed what we might call the 'French' influence – Baird
and Cowie for example – and I should name a few more, such
as Steven Campbell, Adrian Wiszniewski and Ken Currie,
bringing the story right up to date. But there is this division
between the classical and the romantic. This merges somewhat
in Enlightenment painters such as Ramsay and Raeburn, but
in the 19th century we have the clarity of Dyce as opposed to
McTaggart's freely painted masterpieces, and the bravura of Wilkie

set against the well crafted decorations of Hornel and Henry, and
in the 20th century we had all sorts of wonderful things going on.

JD Fergusson wrote at great length about the distinctive
character of Scottish painting. Talking about the Glasgow School
he had this to say: 'The whole school at their best had the Scots
characteristic of independence, and vigour, colour and particularly
quality of paint, which means paint that is living and not merely a
coat of paint placed between containing lines like a map.' That's
quite a statement and could certainly be applied to those artists
– Ramsay, Raeburn and Wilkie and onwards via McTaggart to
Fergusson and Bellany, who for me exemplify a Scottish approach
to portraiture.

BH   What do you feel you have learnt for your own practice from
studying the great portrait painters of the past?

AM   In my second year at Edinburgh College of Art there was a weekly
class in the National Gallery taken by the then Director, Colin
Thompson. We studied and analysed the techniques of the old
masters and I actually copied paintings by Titian and Goya – a
very good way of learning how to paint. There was no better
introduction to the old masters and I slowly began to understand
and appreciate how the great artists of the past could suggest
a course of action for the future. What interests me is the way
works of art intervene in time and have permanent value, both in
terms of what they're saying and continue to say, and also in the
way they change the possibilities for what comes later. Elizabeth

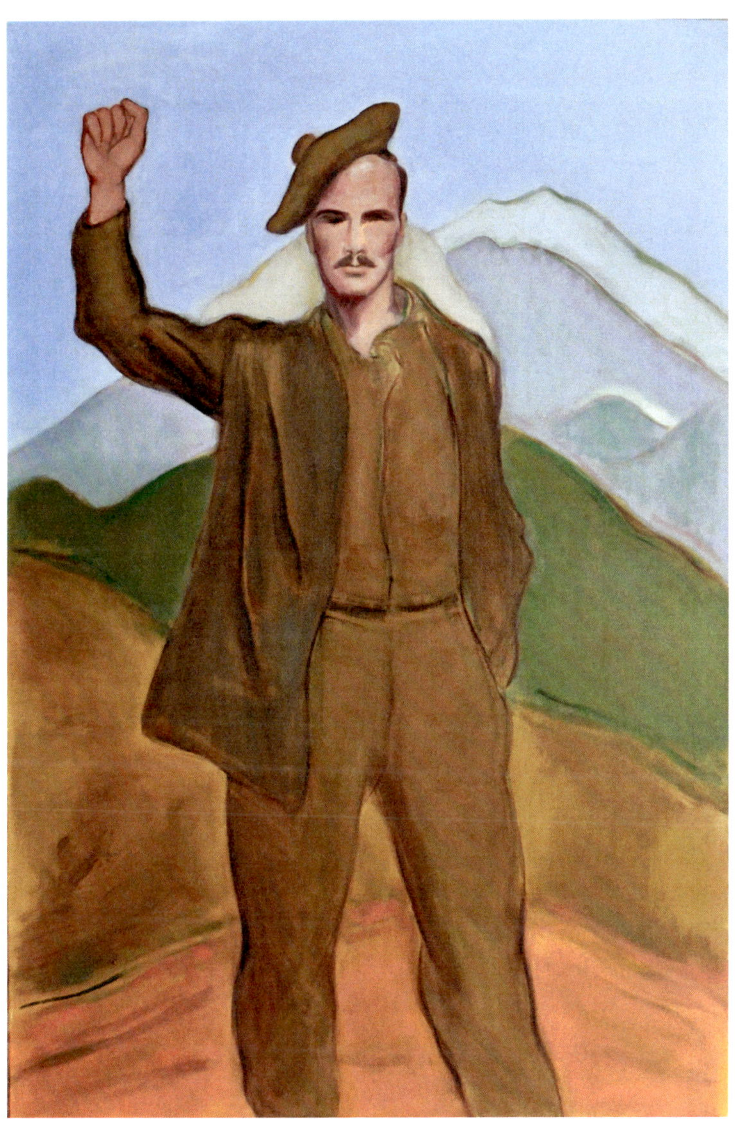

146 *Hamish Henderson: Italy 1944* 2019 oil on canvas 122 x 91 cm

Cowling has pointed out how for Picasso, the old masters were his companions: 'he spoke of being accompanied by other artists as he entered his studio. *I have a feeling that Delacroix, Giotto, Tintoretto, El Greco and the rest… are all standing behind me, watching me at work*'. For Picasso, all these dead artists from different eras and generations were alive, and indeed would never die, and were driven by much the same imperatives as he was. Nearly all of the painters I've been closest to – John Bellany, RB Kitaj, Peter de Francia and Tim Hyman felt the same about the great artists of the past, as do I. Only a few weeks ago I saw exhibitions of both Otto Dix and Lucas Cranach in Düsseldorf. The way Dix used Cranach as a model was instructive. Although deploying tempera as well as oil paint, Dix never resorted to imitation or pastiche. Without any trace of the academic, his portraits retain their own worth as modern classics.

In terms of learning from the great portrait painters we could go on for hours, but let's make a start with Ramsay and Raeburn – you don't get any better than those two. Raeburn is often linked with Velázquez and for obvious reasons. We're indeed fortunate to have Velázquez's youthful masterwork in Edinburgh – his *Old Woman Cooking Eggs* which was for RB Kitaj the greatest painting of all time. There are several portraits of the young Infanta Margarita in Vienna which I think are unsurpassed. Then, there's El Greco who offers something grittier, pointing towards the expressionism of the 20th century.

Speaking of these 17th century Spanish artists, I was in Málaga 15 years ago and witnessed the Good Friday processions which took all night to slowly wind its way through the crowded streets. The lifelike painted sculptures of Christ were austere and realistic in the style of Velázquez and Zurbarán, and it struck me that any other kind of sculpture would be inappropriate in the context of such a sacred event. That in turn begged questions about certain aspects of the art of our own time, questions about what Modernism can do and cannot do in comparison with the great painters of the past. Once again it seems, when considering all of the various aspects that surround portraiture we are continually confronted with key issues regarding form and function, content and style. The notion that we need to make a special case for the validity of portrait painting appears absurd.

BH You have acknowledged the influence of other portrait painters on your own work, but nevertheless, you quickly managed to formulate a very distinctive style which makes your portraits readily recognisable. Looking over your career as a portrait painter – which goes way back to the '60s – do you see your portraits as a coherent and consistent body of work? What do you feel holds them all together?

AM All I can say is that after 50 years of painting portraits I do recognise a certain consistency of approach. There are probably distinct periods – early, middle and later but overall I agree that there is a coherent body of work. Sometimes, however, I've wished that this wasn't the case, that there could have been a few minor eruptions. That might have been useful, perhaps leading to more

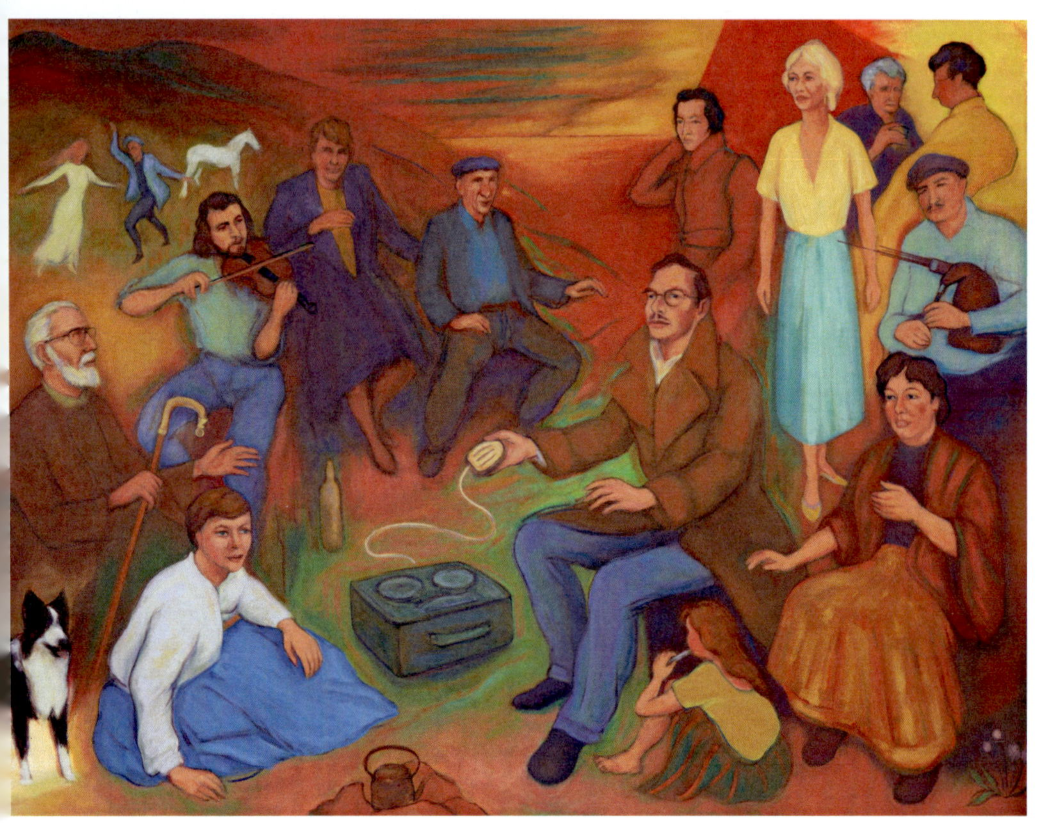

147 *Scotland's Voices* 2016/17 oil on canvas 170 x 230 cm (Saltire Society)
Left to right: Willie Scott, Jean Redpath (seated in foreground), Aly Bain,
Belle Stewart, Jimmy MacBeath, Hamish Henderson, Heinrich Heine, Dolina
MacLennan, Hugh MacDiarmid, Antonio Gramsci, Allan MacDonald and
Jeannie Robertson

experimental pictures or simply taking me in a different direction. There was a period too, during my 50s, when I didn't paint many portraits. I thought I had nothing new to say, that I was simply repeating things I'd done before. I believe a lot of artists experience similar feelings, but eventually we all get going again and find there are new discoveries to be made, new territory to explore. There were failed portraits, of course; some of them, on considering the photographic evidence, should have been retained and not abandoned. I certainly regret my haste in throwing several of them into the bin!

What holds them together? It may well be that my belief in humanity still holds, despite the dark times we have lived through.

BH   Finally, what ambitions and future plans do you have for your portrait painting? Are there still plenty of subjects you would like to tackle?

AM   There are still a few old pals on my list I've yet to portray, so I'll have to sort that out. I've been fortunate in the last few years in having had the opportunity to paint some special people thanks to Democratic Left Scotland commissions – Tom Nairn, who has illuminated the democratic necessity of nationalism in the modern world, TC Smout, the distinguished economic historian, James Robertson, the wonderful novelist and Jim Swire, a man of extraordinary courage who I greatly admire. Long may it continue.

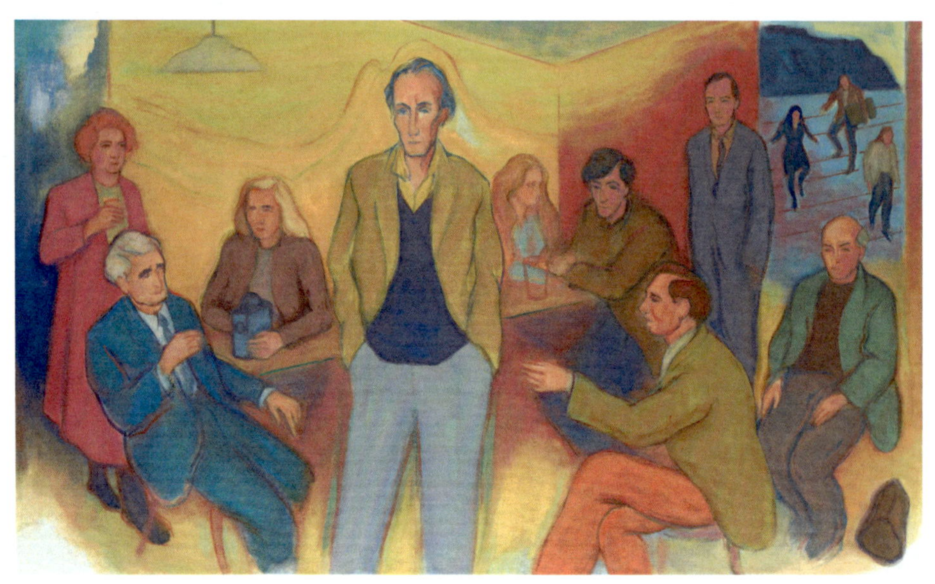

148 *Milne's Bar* 1922 oil on canvas 91 x 152 cm

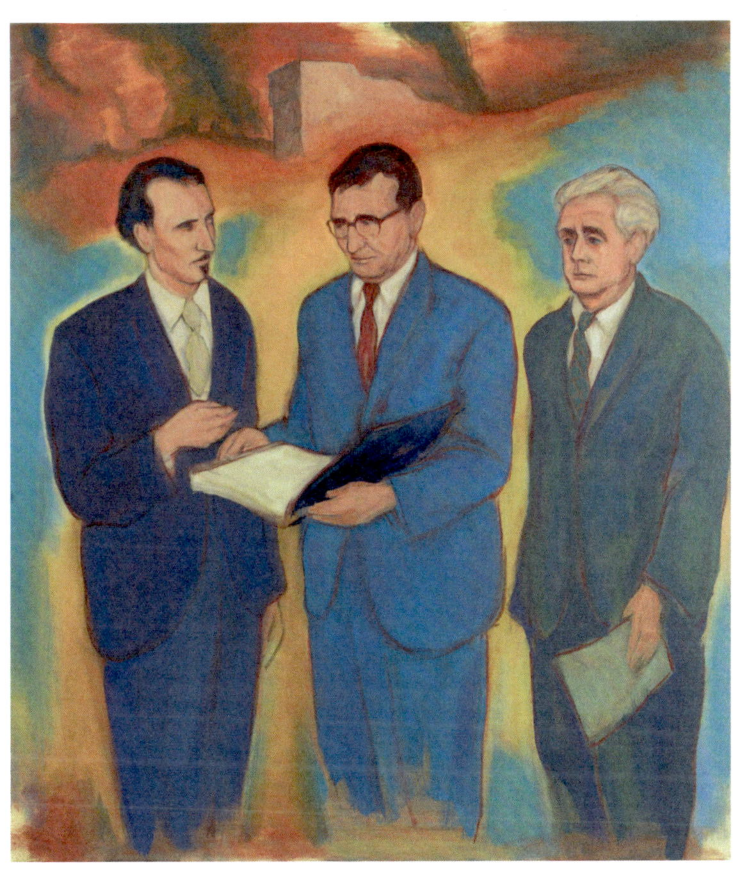

149 *Passacaglia on DSCH (Ronald Stevenson, Dimitri Shostakovich and Hugh MacDiarmid)* 2020 oil on
   canvas 138 x 122 cm

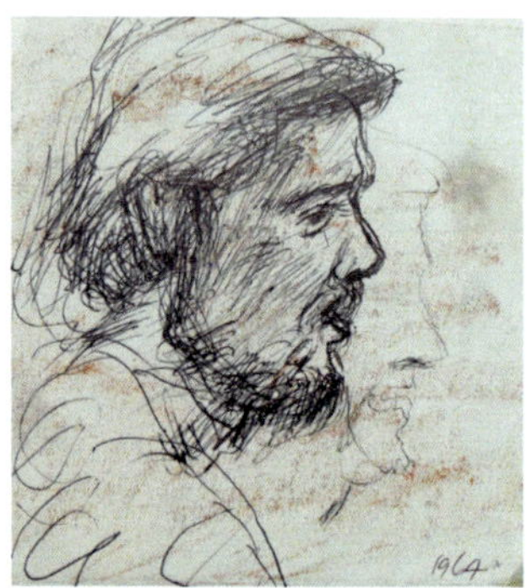

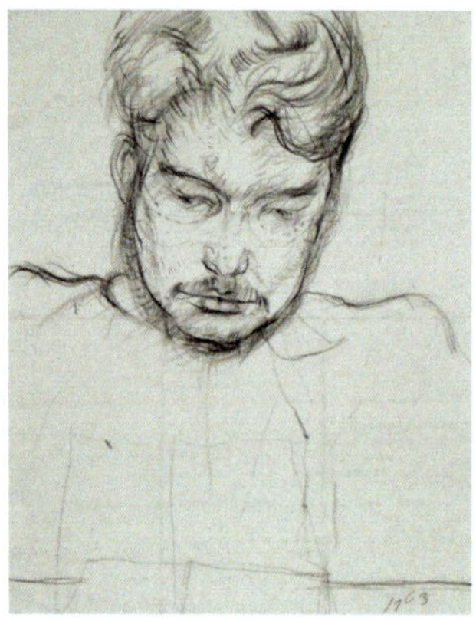

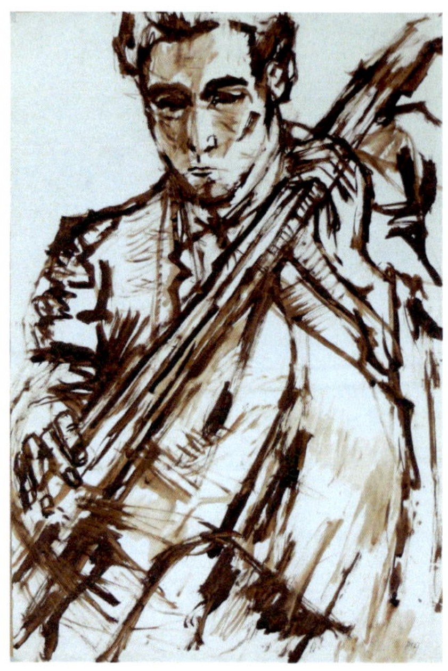

152 *Ian Croal* 1961 brown ink on paper 55.5 x 37.5 cm

150 *Donald Gorrie* 1964 (top) biro on
    paper
    14 x 12.5 cm

151 *Alan Bold* 1963 (bottom) conte on
    paper 25.5 x 20.5 cm

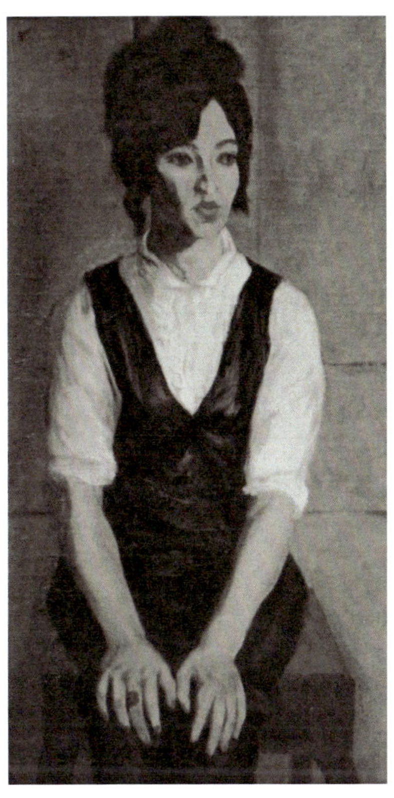

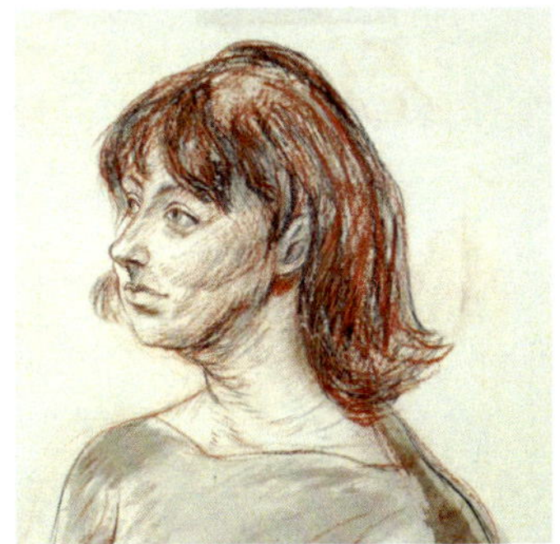

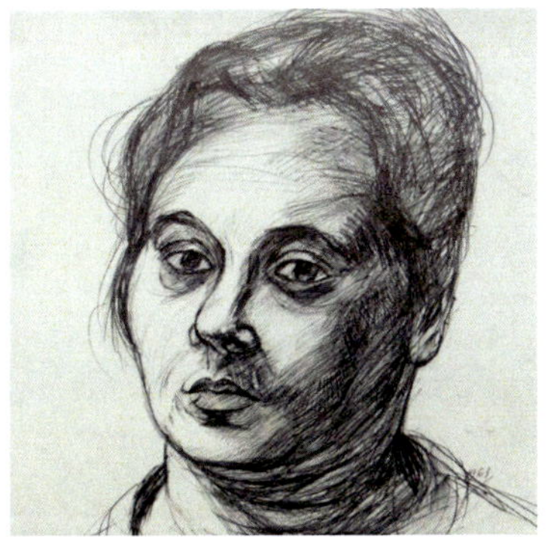

153 *Betty* 1964 oil on canvas 107 x 56 cm

154 *Jean Fayrer* 1963 (top) conte and ink on
     paper 29 x 30 cm

155 *Carol (ECA model)* 1963 (bottom) biro on
     paper 9 x 9.5 cm

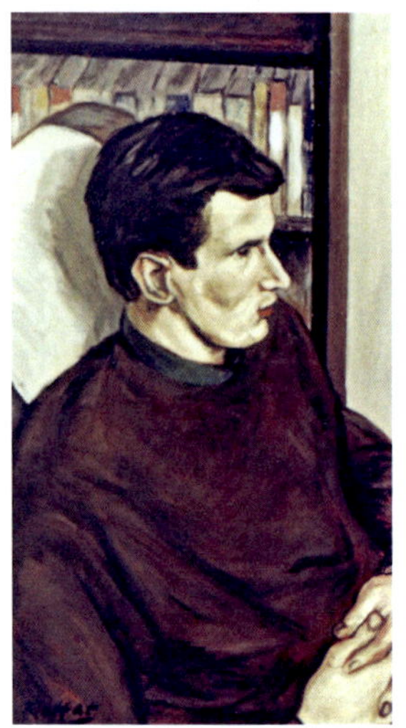

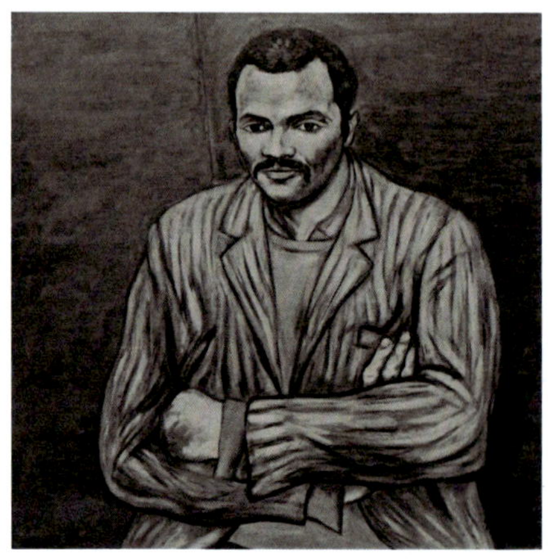

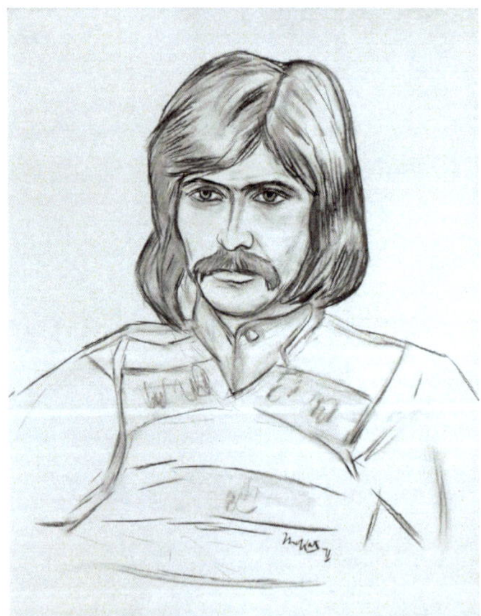

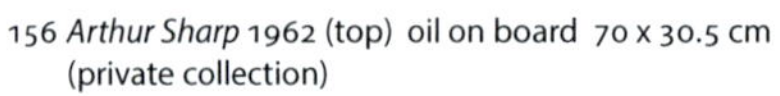

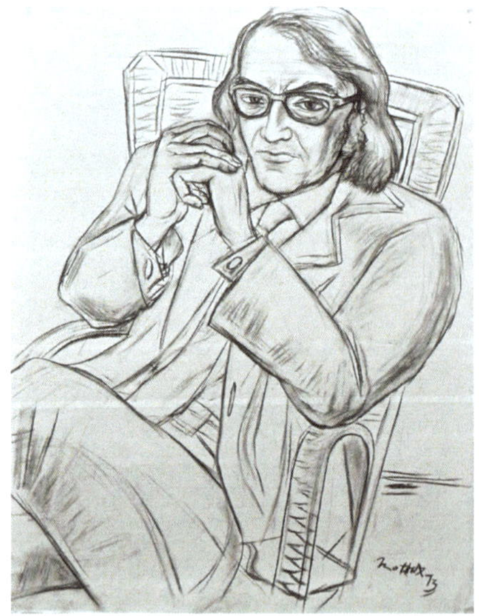

156 *Arthur Sharp* 1962 (top) oil on board 70 x 30.5 cm
   (private collection)

157 *Alan Johnston* 1970 (bottom) charcoal on paper
   58 x 46 cm

158 *Eric Cameron* 1969 (top) oil on board
   91.5 x 91.5 cm (private collection)

159 *W Gordon Smith* 1973 (bottom) charcoal on paper
   56 x 44 cm (private collection)

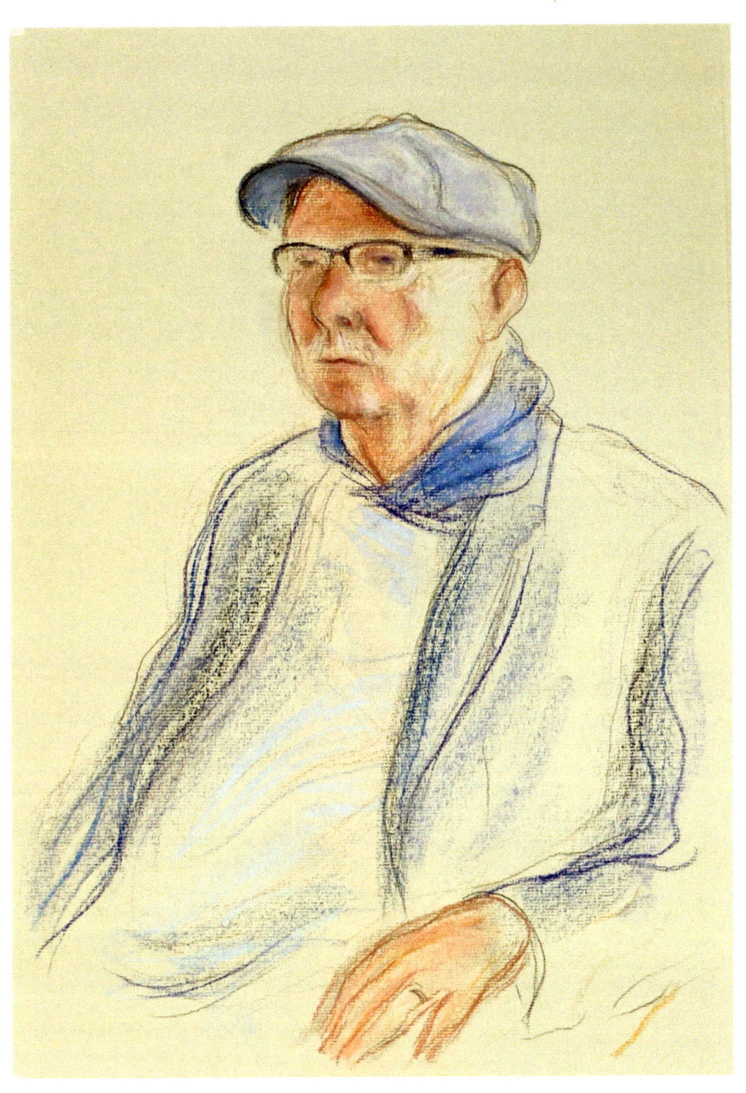

160 *Bill Hare* 2017 pastel on paper 50 x 35 cm

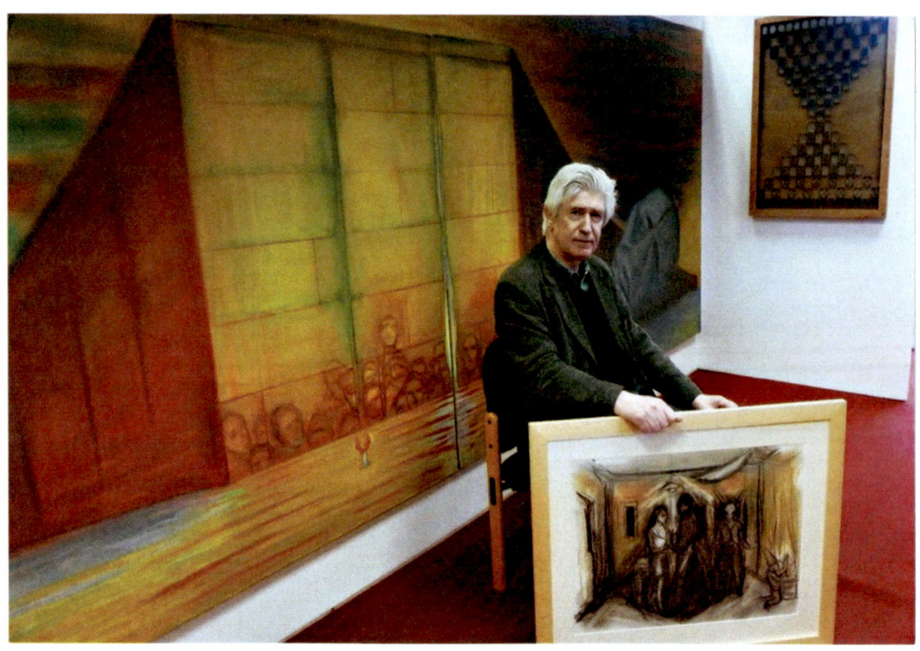

161 Alexander Moffat, event photograph by Richard Demarco, 2012

Alexander Moffat Chronology

1943   Born in Dunfermline where his grandfather has a painting
and decorating business. Grows up in the small Fife villages
of West Wemyss and Lumphinnans. Both his parents are
schoolteachers and his father and elder brother are talented
musicians

1956   Moves to Edinburgh after the death of his father

1960   Enrols as a painting student at Edinburgh College of Art where
William Gillies is Principal and Robin Philipson is Head of
Painting. Fellow students include John Bellany, Bill Gillon,
Kirkland Main, Peter Pretsel, Gordon Bryce, George Garson, Alan
and Merilyn Smith, Barbara Rae and Helen Bellany

1961   Visits Paris for the first time with with Alan Bold and John
Bellany. The Bold/Moffat Quartet is formed, playing in various
jazz clubs in Edinburgh

1963   Bellany/Moffat Edinburgh Festival exhibition at Castle Terrace

Travels to Paris and the south of France. Visits the Picasso
Museum, Antibes, and the Léger Museum, Biot

Meets Hugh MacDiarmid, Norman MacCaig, George Mackay
Brown and John Tonge in Milne's Bar

1964   Bellany/Moffat Edinburgh Festival exhibition at The Mound

Works in an engineering factory, Abbeyhill, Edinburgh (Miller &
Co)

1965   Bellany/Moffat Edinburgh Festival exhibition at The Mound

Drawings published in *Rocket*, edited by Alan Bold

1966   Visits Amsterdam, Rotterdam and Brussels

First meeting with John Berger and Peter de Francia in London

Works as a photographer for the Scottish Central Library

1967   First meeting with the composer, Ronald Stevenson who arranges
a cultural visit to the German Democratic Republic. Travels to
Berlin, Dresden, Leipzig, Halle, and Weimar with John Bellany
and Alan Bold. Meets the artists Willi Sitte and Werner Tubke

and the English composer, Alan Bush. Visits the former Nazi concentration camp at Buchenwald

1968   Paints his first 'literary' portraits of Archie Hind and Norman MacCaig

Chairman of the New 57 Gallery, Edinburgh

1969   Part time teaching post at Winchester School of Art where William Crozier is Head of Painting

1970   Solo exhibition, New 57 Gallery, Edinburgh

Curates *Max Beckmann: Graphic Works*, New 57 Gallery, Edinburgh Festival exhibition

1971   Exhibits in *Scottish Realism,* a Scottish Arts Council touring exhibition curated by Alan Bold

Film: *Alexander Moffat* by W Gordon Smith for *Scope,* BBC Scotland

Invited to take part in the Glasgow Group exhibition

Visits Peter de Francia in Provence

1972   Visits Germany for first time since 1967 and travels to Hanover, Kassel, Wuppertal, and Düsseldorf

Curates *Robert MacBryde 1913–1966,* New 57 Gallery, Edinburgh Festival exhibition

1973   Solo exhibition, *A View of the Portrait,* Scottish National Portrait Gallery

Completes two murals for the Edinburgh Office of the AUEW

W Gordon Smith makes a film about the murals for *Scope,* BBC Scotland

The New 57 Gallery vacates its Rose Street premises

1974   The New 57 Gallery re-opens in the Fruitmarket building

Paints sets for a Lyceum Theatre production of W Gordon Smith's *Vincent* with Tom Fleming in title role

1975   Solo exhibition in Warsaw at the Gallery of the Press Club

Curates *RB Kitaj: Pictures,* New 57 Gallery, Edinburgh Festival exhibition

Founder member and Chairman of the Federation of Artists in Scotland

Exhibits in *Bellany, Dallas Brown, Gillon, Moffat* at the Fruitmarket Gallery, Edinburgh curated by Alan Bold

Part time teaching post at Croydon College of Art where John Bellany is Head of Painting

Meets Neal Ascherson and Tom Nairn

1976   Exhibits in *The Human Clay,* selected by RB Kitaj, Hayward Gallery, London

1977   Curates the Peter de Francia retrospective exhibition for Camden Arts Centre, London

1978   First visit to New York. Stays in Percy Grainger's House in White Plains with Ronald Stevenson. Meets with RB Kitaj and Sandra Fisher

Begins work on the *Seven Poets* commission (Scottish Arts Council)

Paints a portrait of the actor Bertie Scott in the role of William Soutar for the film *The Garden Beyond* by Brian Crumlish and Douglas Eadie

Berliners 3 shown in the Midland Group Gallery, Nottingham

Death of Hugh MacDiarmid

1979   Invited to join staff of Glasgow School of Art

Exhibits in *Narrative Paintings: Figurative Art of Two Generations,* selected by Timothy Hyman, Arnolfini, Bristol, Institute of Contemporary Arts London and Fruitmarket Gallery, Edinburgh

Travels to Skye to paint Sorley MacLean

1980   Travels to Stromness, Orkney to paint George Mackay Brown

Begins work on *Poets' Pub*, a large group portrait of the poets of the Scottish Literary Renaissance

1981   Solo exhibition *Seven Poets* opens at the Third Eye Centre, Glasgow

1982   *Seven Poets* is shown at the Scottish National Portrait Gallery

1983   Visits New York and meets with Steven Campbell

Co-selector with Jon Thomson and Marjorie Allthorpe-Guyton of *the British Art Show 2* (Arts Council of Great Britain)

1984   Portrait of Muriel Spark

1985   Visits the Soviet Union and travels to Moscow and Leningrad

Curates *New Image Glasgow,* Third Eye Centre, Glasgow, and AIR Gallery, London

The Two Musicians (Graeme Durward and Brian Gibb) included in the exhibition *In Their Circumstances,* Usher Gallery, Lincoln, and Ferens Art Gallery, Hull

1986   Visiting lecturer Royal College of Art, London

1988   Solo exhibition, *Portraits of Painters,* Scottish National Gallery of Modern Art

Appointed Senior Lecturer in Painting, Glasgow School of Art

Travels to Venice with Richard Demarco

1989   Visits the Surikov Academy in Moscow and the Repin Academy in Leningrad. Meets Alexander Lavrentiev, grandson of Rodchenko and Varvara Stephanova

1990   Fall of the Berlin Wall. Travels to Berlin with Ken Currie

Solo exhibition, *Historical Landscapes,* Glasgow Art Gallery and Museum

Exhibits in *Scottish Art since 1900,* Barbican Art Gallery, London

1991   Solo exhibition, *Images of People, Places and Country,* at the Pitttencrieff House Museum, Dunfermline

Visits Peter de Francia in Provence

1992   Appointed Head of the Painting Department at Glasgow School of Art

1993   Meets Perry Rathbone the former Director of Museum of Fine Arts, Boston and his wife Euretta, close friends of Max and Quappi Beckmann.

1995   Visits Warsaw, Krakow and Auschwitz with Ken Currie

Attends symposium in the Hochschule der Kunste, Berlin, entitled 'May '45 – Remembrance and the Future – On the Representation of the Non-Representable in the Arts'

Curates *The Continuing Tradition: 75 Years of Painting at Glasgow School of Art,* Glasgow School of Art

1996   Exhibits in the group exhibition *The Scottish Renaissance,* curated by Bill Hare, Rotunda Gallery, Hong Kong

1997   Travels to Oslo and Bergen and sees the works of Edvard Munch

Attends the opening of the *Charles Rennie Mackintosh* exhibition in the County Museum, Los Angeles

1998   Death of Alan Bold

1999   Portrait of George Elder Davie (the Saltire Society)

Selector of *Iontas* with Campbell Bruce, Sligo Art Gallery, Ireland

2000   Portrait of Tom Fleming (the Saltire Society)

Visits Madrid with Ken Currie to see Picasso's *Guernica* newly installed in the Museo Reina Sofia

2001   Portrait of Robin Jenkins (the Saltire Society)

Visits Mexico City with Sam Ainsley and David Harding and sees the work of the great muralists – Rivera, Siqueiros and Orozco.

2003   First visit to China as a guest of the Central Academy of Fine Arts, Beijing. Travels to Xi'an and joins John and Helen Bellany in Beijing

2004   Elected to the Royal Scottish Academy

Second visit to Mexico City

Second visit to China to take part in the Li River project with Alan Riach

2005   Travels to Cuba as a guest of the Ministry of Culture

Travels to Australia and visits Sydney and Melbourne

Retires from the Glasgow School of Art

2006   Spends the summer months in Berlin

Delivers the laudation at the opening of *John Bellany: Eine Schottische Odyssee*, Kunsthalle, Jesuitenkirche, Aschaffenburg

Awarded OBE for services to the arts

2008   AHM formed (Sam Ainsley, David Harding, Alexander Moffat)

AHM begin a residency at the Glasgow Sculpture Studios

Travels in Cuba with Ross Birrell, David Harding and Hugh Watt

Curates *New Scots* exhibition, Royal Scottish Academy

Travels to Gdansk, Warsaw, Krakow and Zakopane to see the work of Witkacy

Solo exhibition in the Open Eye Gallery, Edinburgh

Arts of Resistance, Alexander Moffat and Alan Riach (Luath Press)

2010   Portrait of Alasdair Gray installed in Òran Mór, Glasgow

Takes part in the Norman MacCaig centenary events in Lochinver

First AHM Symposium (Gilmore Centre, University of Glasgow)

2011   Curates the exhibition *Richard Demarco: Scotland in Europe/ Europe in Scotland*, Scotland House, Brussels

AHM's Symposia 2 & 3 take place in Hawthorden Lecture Theatre Edinburgh and Dundee Contemporary Arts

2012   Solo exhibition *MacDiarmid* in the Town Hall Gallery, Langholm

AHM organise *Changin Scotland* conference, Ullapool

Portrait of Tom Nairn

2013   Begins a series of drawings of TC Smout in his Anstruther home

Essay on the RB Kitaj retrospective at the Jewish Museum in Berlin published in *Perspectives* (Democratic Left Scotland)

Death of John Bellany

2014   Travels to Basel and Zurich. Visits the James Joyce Foundation

Arts of Independence, Alexander Moffat and Alan Riach (Luath Press)

Solo exhibition, *Paintings as Arguments*, Peacock Visual Arts, Aberdeen

Paintings as Arguments, Alexander Moffat with Alan Riach (Peacock Visual Arts, Aberdeen)

Poets' Pub included in the exhibition *Montrose & The Scottish Renaissance* (Montrose Art Gallery and Museum)

Exhibits in the exhibition *Where Three Rivers Meet* with Ruth Nicol in Duff House, Aberdeenshire

2015   *Modern Scottish Painting by JD Fergusson*. Edited, introduced and annotated by Alexander Moffat and Alan Riach (Luath Press)

2016   Begins work on *Scotland's Voices,* a large group portrait of Hamish Henderson and the folk singers and musicians he championed

Portrait of David MacLennan installed in Òran Mór, Glasgow

2017   AHM curate INK, an exhibition selected from the Archive of the
Glasgow Print Studio

Scotland's Voices exhibited at the Saltire Society, Edinburgh

2018   Awarded Honorary Doctorate University of Glasgow

Landmarks: Poets, Portraits and Landscapes of Modern Scotland
with Ruth Nicol and Alan Riach Lillie Art Gallery Milngavie

2019   *Scotland's Voices* Scottish Storytelling Centre Edinburgh

2019   *Glasgow Life* Gaelic Arts commission (Aird an Dochais/
Compass of Hope)

2021   *Landmarks: The Brownsbank Years* with Ruth Nicol and Alan
Riach Biggar and Upper Clydesdale Museum

2023   *Artists and their Work* Alexander Moffat at 80

Interview with Beth Junor The Junior Gallery St Andrews

2024   *Alexander Moffat at Eighty* Fire Station Creative Dunfermline

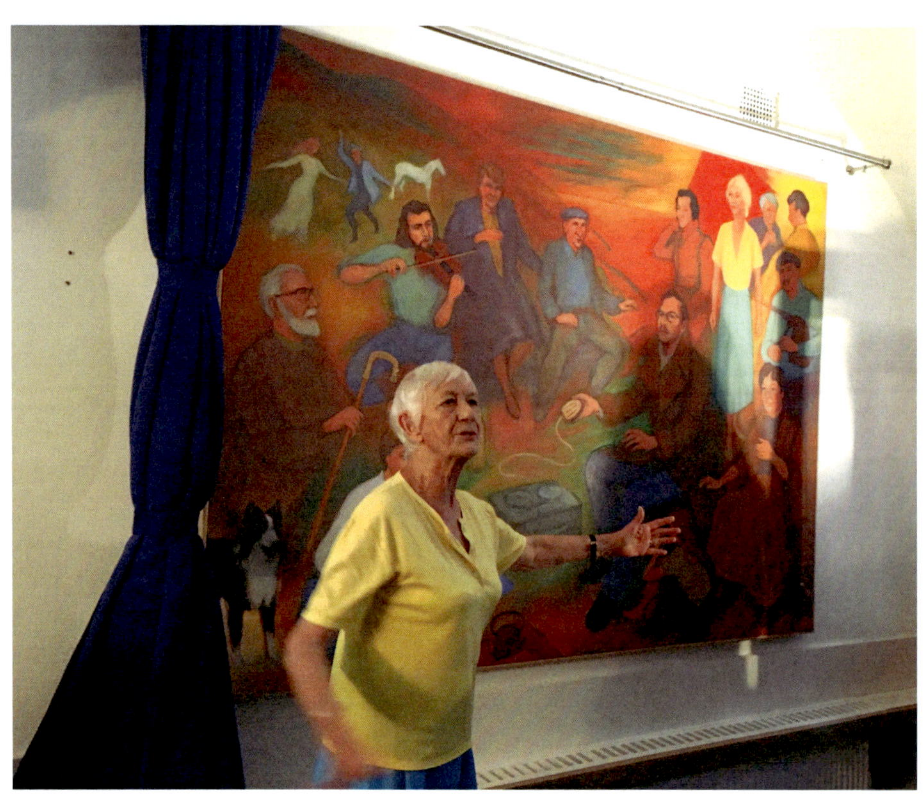

162 Dolina MacLennan unveiling *Scotland's Voices* at the Saltire Society, August 2017

List of Images

Unless otherwise stated, all the works illustrated in this book are by
Alexander Moffat and belong to the artist

1   *Self-Portrait* 1963 oil on board 55 x 44.5 cm

2   *Edinburgh College of Art model* 1962 pencil on paper 24 x 22.5 cm

3   *Edinburgh College of Art model (head study)* 1962 oil on board
    30 x 30.5 cm

4   *My Grandfather* 1962 oil on board 48.5 x 33.5 cm

5   *Ken Harrold (The Young Workman)* 1963 oil on board 81 x 61 cm
    (private collection)

6   *Robert Callender* 1969 charcoal on paper 57 x 45.5 cm

7   *Ronald Stevenson* 1969 charcoal on paper 58 x 42.5 cm

8   *John Bellany* 1968 oil on board 160 x 84 cm (private collection)

9   *Ronald Stevenson* 1969 oil on board 174 x 91.5 cm

10 *Archie Hind* 1968 oil on board 122 x 91.5 cm (Scottish National
    Portrait Gallery)

11 *Tam White* 1967 oil on board 40.5 x 30.5 cm (private collection)

12 Norman MacCaig 1968 oil on board 122 x 91.5 cm (Scottish
    National Portrait Gallery)

13 *Ken and Fiona Harrold* 1968 oil on board 81 x 61 cm (private
    collection)

14 *Ian and Patsy Croal* 1968 oil on board 91.5 x 117 cm (private
    collection)

15 *Claire Murray* 1969 oil on board 183 x 76 cm

16 *Joseph Bonnar* 1968 oil on board 122 x 61 cm (private collection)

17 *Harro Rösing* 1969 oil on board 107 x 84 cm (private collection)

18 *Anna Rösing* 1969 oil on board 107 x 91.5 cm (private collection)

19   *Alan Bold* 1969 charcoal on paper 49 x 46 cm

20   *Alan Bold* 1971 oil on board 91.5 x 61 cm (private collection)

21   *Alice Bold* 1969 oil on board 122 x 76 cm (private collection)

22   *Valentina Bold* 1968 oil on board 91.5 x 61 cm (private collection)

23   *Susan Moffat* 1970 oil on canvas 91.5 x 86.5 cm (private collection)

24   *Iain Patterson* 1970 oil on board 137 x 76 cm (private collection)

25   *Graham Martin* 1970 charcoal on paper 51 x 38 cm

26   *Margot Duffy* 1971 charcoal on paper 64 x 51 cm

27   *Ken and Margo Duffy* 1971 oil on canvas 61 x 74 cm (private collection)

28   *Graham and Eileen Martin* 1970 oil on board 91.5 x 122 cm (private collection)

29   *David Morrison* 1971 oil on canvas 85 x 76 cm (Scottish National Portrait Gallery)

30   *Alan Bold and David Morrison outside Milne's Bar (The Hammer and the Thistle)* 1971 ink and watercolour on paper 21 x 29 cm (Edinburgh Libraries)

31   *Pete Morgan* 1971 charcoal on paper 51 x 44 cm

32   *Pete Morgan* 1971 oil on canvas 144.5 x 91.5 cm (private collection)

33   *Helen Grant* 1972 oil on canvas 106.5 x 85 cm (private collection)

34   *Alan Jackson* 1971 oil on canvas 137 x 76 cm (private collection)

35   *Margaret Jackson* 1971 oil on canvas 137 x 75 cm (private collection)

36   *W Gordon Smith* 1973 oil on canvas 112 x 91.5 cm (private collection)

37   *Alan Bush* 1973 charcoal on paper 57 x 40 cm

38   *John Moffat* 1973 charcoal on paper 52 x 39 cm

39   *Sir Michael Swann* 1974 acrylic on canvas 152 x 122 cm (University of Edinburgh)

40   *Vincent and Camille Butler* 1975 charcoal on paper 38 x 56 cm

41   *Vincent and Camille Butler* 1975 acrylic on canvas 86 x 122 cm (private collection)

42   *Ian Hamilton Finlay* 1975 pastel on coloured paper 54 x 40 cm (Scottish National Gallery of Modern Art)

43   *Isabel Hilton* 1975 oil on canvas 157.5 x 76 cm (private collection)

44   *Lynda Myles* 1976 pastel on coloured paper 79 x 57 cm

45   *Helen Bellany* 1976 pencil and pastel on coloured paper 70 x 45.5 cm
(private collection)

46   *Philip Wright* 1976 coloured pencil on grey paper 68 x 52 cm

47   *Russell Hunter as 'Jock'* 1976 coloured pencil on paper 69 x 49 cm

48   *Susan Johnston* 1976 pastel on coloured paper 59 x 47 cm

49   *Berliners 3* 1978 oil on canvas 119.5 x 188 cm (private collection)

50   Neal Ascherson, Tom Nairn and Isabel Hilton in Alexander Moffat's
studio, 1977

51   *Neal Ascherson (Polish Army Cap)* 1976 charcoal on paper
57 x 39 cm

52   *Neal Ascherson* 1977 oil on canvas 126.5 x 76 cm (private collection)

53   *Maggie Mitchell* 1979 pastel on cream paper 75 x 55 cm

54   *Susie Raeburn (The Ringmistress 2)* 1977 oil on canvas 152.5 x 61 cm
(private collection)

55   *Susie Raeburn (The Ringmistress 1)* 1977 oil on canvas 152.5 x 61 cm
(Russell-Cotes Art Gallery & Museum, Bournemouth)

56   *Hugh MacDiarmid: Hymn to Lenin* 1980 oil on canvas 113 x 190 cm
(Scottish National Portrait Gallery)

57   *Hugh MacDiarmid* 1978 charcoal and pastel on paper 36 x 47.5 cm
(Scottish National Portrait Gallery)

58   *Hugh MacDiarmid* 1978 charcoal and pastel on paper 36 x 47.5 cm
(Scottish National Portrait Gallery)

59   *Hugh MacDiarmid: Brownsbank* 1978 oil on canvas 91.5 x 56 cm
(private collection)

60   *Robert Garioch* 1978 oil on canvas 175 x 113 cm (Scottish National
Portrait Gallery)

61   *Norman MacCaig* 1979 oil on canvas 198 x 106.5 cm (City Art
Centre, Edinburgh)

62   *Robert Garioch* 1978 oil on canvas 59 x 42 cm

63   *Norman MacCaig* 1979 pastel on paper 63.5 x 45 cm

64   *Sorley MacLean* 1979 oil on canvas 152.5 x 91.5 cm (Museum of the
Isle of Skye)

65   *Sorley MacLean* 1979 pencil on paper 59 x 40 cm (private collection)

66   *Sorley MacLean* 1984 lithograph 78 x 57 cm (paper size)

67   *Edwin Morgan* 1980 pencil on paper 27 x 21 cm (private collection)

68   *Edwin Morgan* 1980 pencil on paper 27 x 21 cm (private collection)

69   *Edwin Morgan* 1980 oil on canvas 153 x 101 cm (Scottish National Portrait Gallery)

70   *George Mackay Brown* 1980 oil on canvas 152.5 x 152.5 cm (Stromness Academy, Orkney)

71   *George Mackay Brown* 1980 oil on canvas 37.5 x 30.5cm

72   *George Mackay Brown* 1980 charcoal and pastel on paper 55 x 37.5 cm (private collection)

73   *Poets' Pub* 1980/82 oil on canvas 183 x 244 cm (Scottish National Portrait Gallery)

74   *Iain Crichton Smith* 1980 charcoal on paper 38 x 53 cm

75   *Iain Crichton Smith* 1980 oil on canvas 91.5 x 152.5 cm (Scottish National Portrait Gallery)

76   *Muriel Spark* (study) 1984 oil on canvas 76.2 x 106.5 cm

77   *Muriel Spark* 1984 charcoal on paper 53 x 60.5 cm

78   *Muriel Spark* 1984 oil on canvas 183 x 91.4 cm (Scottish National Portrait Gallery)

79   Muriel Spark sitting for her portrait (photograph: *Scotsman*)

80   *Duncan Thomson* 1981 pencil on paper 46 x 32 cm

81   *Duncan Thomson* 1981 charcoal on paper 50 x 32 cm

82   *Duncan Thomson* 1981 oil on canvas 183 x 123 cm (private collection)

83   *Susanne Dunbar* 1980 pastel on coloured paper 49 x 34.5 cm

84   *Graham Durward and Brian Gibb (The Two Musicians)* 1985 pastel on paper 49.5 x 66 cm

85   Graham Durward and Brian Gibb with Alexander Moffat (photograph: Sean Hudson)

86   *Stephen Barclay* 1987 oil on canvas 122 x 152.5 cm

87   *Peter Howson* 1987 oil on canvas 183 x 91.5 cm (private collection)

88   *Fiona McLeod* 1987 oil on canvas 57 x 52 cm

89   *Jim Birrell* 1987 oil on canvas 122 x 122 cm

90   Adrian Wiszniewski 1987 drypoint 22 x 14.5 cm (plate size)

91   *Ken Currie* 1987 etching 32 x 24.5 cm (plate size)

92   *Alfons Bytautas* 1987 etching 45 x 33 cm (plate size)

93   *Arthur Watson* 1987 oil on canvas 137 x 137 cm

94   Gwen Hardie sitting for her portrait (photograph)

95   *Gwen Hardie* 1987 oil on canvas 152.5 x 122 cm (Scottish National Gallery of Modern Art)

96   *Stuart MacKenzie* 1987 oil on canvas 61 x 71 cm (cut down version)

97   *Stuart MacKenzie* 1987 oil on canvas 152.4 x 152.4 cm (original portrait)

98   *Peter Hill* 1989 oil on canvas 91.5 x 61 cm (private collection)

99   *Emilio Coia* 1989 oil on canvas 91.5 x 61 cm (private collection)

100 *David Hosie* 1988 oil on canvas 175 x 122 cm

101 *Henry Kondracki* 1987 oil on canvas 152 x 106.5 cm

102 *Richard Demarco in Venice* 1988 oil on canvas 137 x 137 cm

103 *Richard Demarco* 1987 etching 33 x 25 cm (plate size)

104 *Richard Demarco* 1988 oil on canvas 122 x 122 cm

105 *Mary MacIver* 1988 oil on canvas 76 x 152 cm (Richard Demarco Archive)

106 *Sandra Fisher* 1991 pastel on coloured paper 48 x 34 cm (private collection)

107 *Albert Irvin* 1989 oil on canvas 106 x 152.4 cm

108 *Albert and Betty Irvin* 1989 oil on canvas 91.5 x 122 cm (private collection)

109 *Timothy Hyman* 1987 oil on canvas 122 x 122 cm (Kirkcaldy Galleries, Fife)

110 *The Munro Family* 1994 oil on canvas 107 x 152.5 cm (private collection)

111 *Self-Portrait in Studio 40* 1987 etching 28 x 20 cm (plate size)

112 *George Davie* 1999 oil and pastel on paper 46 x 61 cm

113 *George Davie* 1999 charcoal on paper 34 x 24 cm

114 *George Davie* 1999 charcoal on paper 34 x 24 cm

115 *George Davie* 1999 pencil on paper 24 x 28 cm

116 *Paul Henderson Scott* 2000 pastel on paper 30.5 x 45 cm

117 Detail: head of a woman from *Concerning the Arrest of Poor EK 1967* (City Art Centre, Edinburgh)

118　Detail: head of a woman from *Concerning the Arrest of Poor EK* 1967 (City Art Centre, Edinburgh)

119　*Tom Fleming* 2000　charcoal and pastel on paper　44 x 30 cm

120　*Tom Fleming* 2000　charcoal on paper　30 x 44 cm

121　*Ian McLeod* 1971　charcoal on paper　53 x 50 cm

122　*Mary McLeod* 1971　charcoal on paper　58 x 45.5 cm

123　*Jimmy Jones* 1965　ink on paper　7.2 x 9 cm

124　*Albert Renwick* 1965　ink on paper　29 x 20 cm　(private collection)

125　*Lynda Myles in fur jacket* 1976　coloured pencil on paper　70 x 50 cm

126　*Eileen Lawrence* 1973　charcoal on paper　58 x 46 cm

127　*Susan Moffat* 1979　pastel on paper　57 x 39 cm

128　*Robin Jenkins* 2002　pastel on paper　50 x 35 cm　(private collection)

129　*Peter Howson* 1987　etching　32.5 x 25 cm　(plate size)

130　*Steven Campbell and Adrian Wiszniewski* 1987　pencil on paper 20 x 27.5 cm

131　*Steven Campbell and Adrian Wiszniewski in Nico's* 1987　etching 24.5 x 32 cm　(plate size)

132　*Alasdair Gray* 2010　pastel on paper　35 x 56 cm

133　*Alasdair Gray* 2010　oil on canvas　137 x 107 cm　(Òran Mór, Glasgow)

134　*Alasdair Gray* 2010　oil on canvas　42 x 46 cm

135　*Alan Bissett* 2013　pastel on cream paper　50 x 32 cm　(private collection)

136　*Alan Bissett* 2013　pastel on cream paper　50 x 32 cm

137　*Mary MacIver* 1988　pastel on coloured paper　54 x 47 cm

138　*Tom Nairn* 2012/14　oil on canvas 107 x 122 cm　(Dundee Art Galleries and Museums Collection, Dundee City Council)

139　*Port Seton Man (John Bellany)* 2023　oil on canvas 91 x 122 cm

140　*TC Smout* 2012　conte on cream paper　53 x 34 cm　(Democratic Left Scotland)

141　*Hugh MacDiarmid and Hamish Henderson* 2018　oil on canvas 122 x 152.5 cm

142　*James Robertson* 2013　conte on paper　39 x 33.5 cm

143　*David MacLennan* 2015　oil on canvas　152.4 x 121.9 cm　(Òran Mór, Glasgow)

144   *Valda and Chris* 2019 oil on canvas 77 x 102 cm

145   *Gerda Stevenson* 2014 pastel on paper 48 x 32 cm

146   *Hamish Henderson: Italy 1944* 2019 oil on canvas 122 x 91 cm

147   *Scotland's Voices* 2016/17 oil on canvas 170 x 230 cm (Saltire Society)

148   *Milne's Bar* 1922 oil on canvas 91 x 152 cm

149   *Passacaglia on DSCH (Ronald Stevenson, Dimitri Shostakovich and Hugh MacDiarmid)* 2020 oil on canvas 138 x 122 cm

150   *Donald Gorrie* 1964 biro on paper 14 x 12.5 cm

151   *Alan Bold* 1963 conte on paper 25.5 x 20.5 cm

152   *Ian Croal* 1961 brown ink on paper 55.5 x 37.5 cm

153   *Betty* 1964 oil on canvas 107 x 56 cm

154   *Jean Fayrer* 1963 conte and ink on paper 29 x 30 cm

155   *Carol (Edinburgh College of Art model)* 1963 biro on paper 9 x 9.5 cm

156   *Arthur Sharp* 1962 oil on board 70 x 30.5 cm (private collection)

157   *Alan Johnston* 1970 charcoal on paper 58 x 46 cm

158   *Eric Cameron* 1969 oil on board 91.5 x 91.5 cm (private collection)

159   *W Gordon Smith* 1973 charcoal on paper 56 x 44 cm (private collection)

160   *Bill Hare* 2017 pastel on paper 50 x 35 cm

161   Sandy Moffat, event photograph by Richard Demarco 2012

162   Dolina MacLennan unveiling *Scotland's Voices* at the Saltire Society, August 2017

Acknowledgements

Alexander Moffat and Bill Hare wish to thank Gavin MacDougall of Luath Press for his whole-hearted belief in this book and for his unstinting support for Scottish culture in all its aspects. We are also greatly indebted to Jennie Renton who worked with great care and understanding on the editing, design and typesetting of the book.

The artist is most grateful to the Royal Scottish Academy (Gillies Bequest) for financial support towards the publication. In addition he thanks Duncan Thomson for his Foreword and both Bill Hare and Duncan Thomson for their contributions as advisers on the content of the publication, and the following photographers for providing the images: Tom and Jim Scott, Antonia Reeve, Chris D'Souza and Jed Gordon.

Luath Press Limited

committed to publishing well written books worth reading

LUATH PRESS takes its name from Robert Burns, whose little collie Luath (*Gael.*, swift or nimble) tripped up Jean Armour at a wedding and gave him the chance to speak to the woman who was to be his wife and the abiding love of his life. Burns called one of the 'Twa Dogs' Luath after Cuchullin's hunting dog in Ossian's *Fingal*. Luath Press was established in 1981 in the heart of Burns country, and is now based a few steps up the road from Burns' first lodgings on Edinburgh's Royal Mile. Luath offers you distinctive writing with a hint of unexpected pleasures.

Most bookshops in the UK, the US, Canada, Australia, New Zealand and parts of Europe, either carry our books in stock or can order them for you. To order direct from us, please send a £sterling cheque, postal order, international money order or your credit card details (number, address of cardholder and expiry date) to us at the address below. Please add post and packing as follows: UK – £1.00 per delivery address; overseas surface mail – £2.50 per delivery address; overseas airmail – £3.50 for the first book to each delivery address, plus £1.00 for each additional book by airmail to the same address. If your order is a gift, we will happily enclose your card or message at no extra charge.

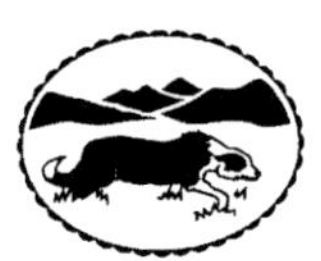

Luath Press Limited
543/2 Castlehill
The Royal Mile
Edinburgh EH1 2ND
Scotland
Telephone: 0131 225 4326 (24 hours)
Email: sales@luath.co.uk
Website: www.luath.co.uk